The STL <Primer>

The STL <Primer>

Graham Glass and Brett L. Schuchert

For book and bookstore information

http://www.prenhall.com

Prentice Hall PTR, Upper Saddle River, New Jersey 07458

Library of Congress Cataloging-in-Publication Data

Glass, Graham.
    The STL <Primer> / Graham Glass and Brett L. Schuchert.
        p.   cm.
    Includes index.
    ISBN 0-13-454976-7 (pbk. : alk. paper)
    1. Electronic digital computers — Programming. I. Schuchert.
Brett L. II. Title.
QA76.6.G5585 1995   95-47483
005.13'3–dc20   CIP

Cover Design Director: *Jerry Votta*
Cover Design: *Design Source*
Manufacturing: *Alexis R. Heydt*
Acquisitions Editor: *Paul W. Becker*
Production Management: *Digital Communications Services, Inc.*

© 1996 Prentice Hall PTR
Prentice-Hall, Inc.
A Simon & Schuster Company
Upper Saddle River, New Jersey 07458

The publisher offers discounts on this book when ordered in bulk
quantities. For more information, contact Corporate Sales Department,
Prentice Hall PTR, One Lake Street, Upper Saddle River, New Jersey 07458.
Phone: 800-382-3419; Fax: 201-236-7141; e-mail: corpsales@prenhall.com

Printed in the United States of America

10 9 8 7 6 5 4 3 2 1

ISBN 0-13-454976-7

Prentice-Hall International (UK) Limited, *London*
Prentice-Hall of Australia Pty. Limited, *Sydney*
Prentice-Hall Canada Inc., *Toronto*
Prentice-Hall Hispanoamericana, S.A., *Mexico*
Prentice-Hall of India Private Limited, *New Delhi*
Prentice-Hall of Japan, Inc., *Tokyo*
Simon & Schuster Asia Pte. Ltd., *Singapore*
Editora Prentice-Hall do Brasil, Ltda., *Rio de Janeiro*

To Alex Stepanov and Meng Lee, the creators of STL

— Graham

To Mom and Dad

— Brett

Contents

List of Tables and Diagrams

Tables

Diagrams

Preface

About this Book

STL is a challenging topic to write about. If the order of presentation is not carefully thought out, it can be confusing and frustrating. This book is the distillation of many public presentations of STL and associated topics, and has been carefully designed to introduce readers to STL in a natural and concise fashion. This book has been used in the ObjectSpace "Mastering STL" training classes with great success. We hope that you enjoy reading this book as much as we enjoyed writing it!

The Book Layout

This book is divided into six main sections:

"Preface", which contains a road map of the rest of this book.

"Overview", which highlights the features of STL using a mix of examples and text.

"Using STL", which describes every STL topic using a mix of examples and text.

"Class Catalog", which contains a concise description of every STL class in alphabetical order. Every entry includes a synopsis, a description of the class' public functions, and some examples when appropriate.

"Algorithm Catalog", which contains a description of every STL algorithm in alphabetical order. Every entry contains a synopsis, the algorithm's declaration, a description of the algorithm, and some examples.

"Appendix", which is a collection of useful information including notes on how STL was implemented, some other sources of information about STL, and several troubleshooting tips.

The Chapter Layout

Every chapter in this book has a standard prologue, as follows:

Motivation
Why it's useful to learn the material that follows.

Objectives
   A list of the topics that are presented.

In addition, every chapter ends with a review section which contains the following:

Checklist
   A recap of the topics.

Quiz
   A quick self-test.

Exercises
   A list of exercises, rated easy, medium, or hard.

Examples

The examples in this book are available from the world wide web site of ObjectSpace, Inc., whose URL is www.objectspace.com. This site also contains the source code of the STL helper algorithms that are described in this book.

STL Implementations

There are several implementations of STL that are currently available:

   • STL<ToolKit> from ObjectSpace, Inc.
   • STL++ from Modena.
   • The public domain implementation of STL from Hewlett Packard.

Acknowledgements

Thanks to the following people for their feedback and encouragement during the creation of this book: Mike Klobe, Chris Thomas, Paul Becker, and Alex Stepanov.

Conventions

The following conventions were used in this document:

```
Example code is in 9 point mono spaced courier.
```

Runtime output is in bold 9 point mono spaced courier.

Regular text is in 10 point New Century Schoolbook

All examples are preceded by the path that describes their location in the public domain examples directory structure at the ObjectSpace world wide web site. For example:

Example <vec1.cpp>

About the Authors, by the Authors

Graham

My name is Graham Glass. I graduated from the University of Southampton, England, with a Bachelor's degree in Computer Science in 1983. I then emigrated to the United States and obtained by Master's Degree in Computer Science from the University of Texas at Dallas in 1985. After that, I worked in industry as a UNIX/C systems analyst, and became heavily involved with research in neural networks and parallel distributed processing. Interested in becoming a professor, I then began teaching at the University of Texas at Dallas, covering a wide area of courses, including UNIX, C, assembly language, programming languages, C++, and Smalltalk. I then branched out into industry and cofounded a company called ObjectSpace. ObjectSpace is now a recognized leader in object technology that provides object-oriented products, consulting, and training. One of our products, STL<ToolKit>, is the best-selling implementation of STL. In my spare time I sleep.

Brett

My name is Brett L. Schuchert. I graduated from the University of Iowa with a Bachelor's degree in Computer Science in 1992. Throughout working on my degree, I taught computer literacy courses at Kirkwood Community College. Near the middle of my college career, I started using C++ as a research assistant for the Center for Computer Aided Design and at the same time took my first seminar in Object Oriented Programming using Smalltalk. I later took a teaching assistant position teaching C programming in an embedded environment. When I graduated, I felt fairly comfortable with object oriented programming and C++. I moved to Dallas, TX, and worked as a developer using C++ in Unix and had my hand in some GUI development using Motif. In addition to my day job, I taught at the University of Texas at Arlington's Continuing Education Department, teaching courses like C Programming in a Unix Environment, C++ Programming, and Advanced C Programming in a Unix Environment. I joined ObjectSpace as a developer, but as the demand for training increased, I started training and developing course material on topics such as Object Oriented Programming Using C++, Advanced C++ Programming, Object Oriented Analysis and Design, and Object Oriented Programming Using Smalltalk. I've recently switched over to consulting for ObjectSpace and may be working in Smalltalk or C++ during any given period. In my copious free time, I enjoy rock climbing (mostly indoor), reading, Tae Kwon Do, Volleyball and Video Games.

Overview

An Overview of STL

Motivation

It is important to learn the standard template library (STL) for two main reasons. First, it's an ANSI standard and therefore will become a necessary part of every C++ programmer's skill set. Secondly, it embodies several new design philosophies that can be used to create superior class libraries.

Objectives

This chapter describes the events that led up to the creation of STL and provides a brief overview of its primary features.

Overview

Almost all programmers who write C++ programs have to write or purchase a set of data structure classes such as vectors, lists, and sets. Up until now, every commercial offering has had one or more of the following drawbacks:

- Since there was no ANSI standard for collection classes, every vendor's collection classes were incompatible. It was therefore very difficult to decide how to return a collection of results from an object, since one user of an object might be using collections from vendor A, and another user might be using collections from vendor B.

- Many collection hierarchies made use of inheritance and virtual functions, which tended to reduce their performance. Although in many cases this is not a problem, many programmers will not use libraries unless they perform within a few percentage points of hand-coded C equivalents. Use of virtual functions also makes objects difficult to instantiate in shared memory, which is a useful thing to be able to do.

- Every vendor's collection classes placed the code for algorithms that worked on the collections within the collection classes themselves. For example, code for sorting often ended up in a collection called "SortedCollection," and code for applying a function to every element in a collection often ended up in an abstract base class called "Collection." This approach made it hard to add new algorithms without editing and recompiling the vendor's source code, which for maintenance reasons is usually best to avoid.

- Several of the original collection classes were not type-safe. Use of these collections required heavy use of casting, which goes against one of the main spirits of C++ - static type checking.

- All of the commercially available collection classes had their memory allocation policies woven deeply into the code of the containers. This meant that if you wanted to allocate space for a collection from shared memory instead of from the heap, you couldn't.

In response to this situation, the ANSI standards committee decided to search for a standard set of collection classes that would overcome these difficulties. Alex Stepanov and Meng Lee of the Hewlett Packard Laboratories proposed STL as the standard, based on their successful work in the area of generic programming. In July of 1994, STL was chosen as the ANSI/ISO standard because of the following reasons:

- STL is very efficient. The implementations of STL container classes are lean and mean, using no inheritance and no virtual functions. STL is type-safe throughout due to its extensive use of C++ template features. STL includes a wide variety of container classes, including vectors, lists, deques, sets, multisets, maps, multimaps, stacks, queues, and priority queues. Here's an example that illustrates the use of a simple vector.

```
#include <vector.h>
#include <iostream.h>

int main ()
{
  vector<int> v; // Create empty vector of ints.
  v.push_back (42); // Append an int.
  v.push_back (1); // Append another int.
  cout << "v.size () = " << v.size () << endl; // Display size.
  return 0; // Done.
}
```

v.size () = 2

- STL makes heavy use of iterators, which are a kind of generalized pointer. STL iterators allow you to access the contents of any STL container in the same way that you can access and iterate through regular "C" arrays. STL includes many kinds of iterators, including random access iterators, reverse iterators, and iostream iterators. Here's an example that illustrates the similarity between STL iterators and regular "C" pointers:

```
#include <vector.h>
#include <iostream.h>

int array [] = { 1, 42, 3 }; // Regular "C" array.
vector<int> v; // STL vector of integers.
```

```
int main ()
{
   int* p1; // Use pointer as iterator.
   // Iterate through regular "C" array.
   for (p1 = array; p1 != array + 3; p1++)
     cout << "array has " << *p1 << endl;
   v.push_back (1);
   v.push_back (42);
   v.push_back (3);
   vector<int>::iterator p2; // Declare iterator.
   // Iterate through STL container.
   for (p2 = v.begin (); p2 != v.end (); p2++)
     cout << "vector has " << *p2 << endl;;
   return 0;
}
```

array has 1
array has 42
array has 3
vector has 1
vector has 42
vector has 3

- STL algorithms are not member functions of its container classes, and do not access STL containers directly. Instead, they are stand-alone functions that operate upon data via the use of iterators. This indirect approach allows algorithms to work with regular "C" arrays as well as the STL containers. In addition, it allows the library to be extended without modifying the source code of the containers. STL contains over 70 algorithms. Here's an example that uses the sort() algorithm to sort both a regular "C" array and an STL vector:

```
#include <vector.h>
#include <iostream.h>

int array [] = { 1, 42, 3 };
vector<int> v;

int main ()
{
   sort (array, array + 3); // Supply start & "past-the-end" ptrs.
   int* p1; // Use pointer as iterator.
   for (p1 = array; p1 != array + 3; p1++) // Display result.
     cout << "array has " << *p1 << endl;
   v.push_back (1); // Add some items to the STL vector.
   v.push_back (42);
   v.push_back (3);
   // Supply start & "past-the-end" ptrs
   sort (v.begin (), v.end ());
   vector<int>::iterator p2; // Declare iterator.
   for (p2 = v.begin (); p2 != v.end (); p2++) // Display result.
     cout << "vector has " << *p2 << endl;
   return 0;
```

```
}
```

```
array has 1
array has 3
array has 42
vector has 1
vector has 3
vector has 42
```

- STL function objects allow functions to be encapsulated and associated with data. They also allow functions to be created, stored, and destroyed just like any other kind of object. Many STL containers and algorithms use function objects to perform their duties. STL contains over 30 function objects. Here's an example that uses a less function object to order an STL set:

```
#include <set.h>
#include <iostream.h>

int main ()
{
    // Order set using "less" function object.
    set<int, less<int> > s;
    s.insert (1);
    s.insert (42);
    s.insert (3);
    set<int, less<int> >::iterator p;
    for (p = s.begin (); p != s.end (); p++) // Display contents.
        cout << *p << endl;
    return 0;
}
```

```
1
3
42
```

- In order to accommodate varying mechanisms for memory allocation, STL does not explicitly use the standard new() and delete() operators any-where in the library. Instead, all STL containers use special objects called *allocators* to allocate and deallocate storage. Programmers can replace the standard allocator objects with their own, thus modifying the container's memory allocation policies. For example, you could add a custom allocator that grabs storage from an object-oriented database instead of from the heap.

Now that STL has become an accepted standard, it is very likely that class libraries of the future will adopt STL as the preferred way to represent collections of objects. The rest of this book describes the STL components in detail and includes two extensive catalogs for locating information about specific classes or algorithms.

Checklist

The main points made by this chapter were:

- STL is the first ANSI standard for templatized containers and algorithms.
- STL is very efficient and its containers do not use inheritance.
- STL makes heavy use of iterators, a kind of generalized pointer.
- STL algorithms use iterators to access data.
- STL algorithms work with many kinds of data structure.
- Function objects allow functions to be encapsulated and associated with data.
- Memory allocation and deallocation is performed by *allocator* objects.

Quiz

1. When was STL accepted as an ANSI standard?
2. What are the names of the two original proponents of STL?
3. Name two types of STL container.
4. Name an STL algorithm.
5. Why might you want to use a custom allocator?

Exercises

1. What are the pros and cons of avoiding inheritance? [*medium*]
2. How might you integrate a library that uses STL with a library that uses another vendor's proprietary container library? [*medium*]
3. Investigate how other class libraries perform memory allocation and deallocation and contrast this with the STL allocator approach. What are the pros and cons? [*medium*]

Using STL

Containers, Part 1

Motivation

If STL is approached in the right manner, it is fairly straightforward to learn. The quickest way to learn STL is to study a single STL container and some of its most basic operations. Once these are mastered, it's relatively painless to add more container types and operations to your repertoire.

Objectives

This chapter briefly describes the similarities and differences between the ten STL containers. It then uses the simplest data structure — a vector — to illustrate the ten operations that are common to all STL containers.

Introduction

STL includes three categories of containers:

1. *Sequential*, which maintain items in a linear fashion.
2. *Associative*, which maintain items in a structure suited for fast associative lookup.
3. *Adapters*, which provide a different interface to another kind of collection.

This chapter provides an overview of each category of container and describes the operations that are common to all containers. Subsequent chapters provide a more detailed description of each particular class of container.

Hierarchy of Containers

The following hierarchy shows how the categories of container are related, together with a list of their associated concrete STL containers:

Collection
    First Class Collection
       Sequential
          vector...................linear, contiguous storage, fast inserts at end only
          deque ....linear, non-contiguous storage, fast inserts at
                         extremities
          list........................doubly-linked list, fast inserts anywhere
       Associative
          multiset ....set of items, fast associative lookup, duplicates
                         allowed
          set ....like multiset except that no duplicates are
                         allowed
          multimap.............collection of 1-to-many mappings
          map.....................collection of 1-1 mappings
    Adapter
          stack ....strict first-in, last-out data structure
          queue ....strict first-in, first-out data structure
          priority_queue......maintains items in a sorted order

An efficient way to learn about all ten containers is to first study the characteristics shared by all containers. This chapter describes these common characteristics using the simplest STL collection — a vector. Specifics of each kind of collection are described in the chapter called "Containers, Part 2."

Preparing a class for use with STL

All classes whose instances are to be stored into an STL container must have a minimal set of characteristics:

- a copy constructor
- operator=

If you wish to sort or compare containers using any of the relational operators such as operator==, the class must include the following operators[1]:

- operator==
- operator<

Some compilers have problems with calling template destructors. If this is true for your compiler, the class must also include the following:

- a default constructor[2]

---

[1] Even if you don't actually use the relational operators, some compilers try to compile them anyway, so you might have no choice but to add these operators.
[2] Required by the implementations of STL that work around the template destructor problem.

Typedefs

STL was designed to operate on a variety of memory architectures, from the old segmented 16-bit models to the more modern 32- and 64-bit architectures. STL therefore hides the types that vary with the memory architecture behind a layer of typedefs. Each collection defines several typedefs, including the following:

Table 1: Typedefs

Typedef	Meaning
size_type	the type that can hold the maximum number of elements
pointer	the type of a pointer to an element of the collection
const_pointer	the type of a pointer to a constant element of the collection
reference	the type of a reference to an element of the collection
const_reference	the type of a reference to a constant element of the collection

The default memory model is a 32-bit flat memory address space. The actual type associated with every typedef is set based on the memory model that STL is compiled for. For example, here are the types that would be defined for a vector of T objects in a 16-bit and 32-bit memory model, respectively:

Table 2: More Typedefs

Typedef	16-bit	32-bit
size_type	int	long
pointer	near T*	T*
const_pointer	near const T*	const T*
reference	near T&	T&
const_reference	near const T&	const T&

The interface to all STL containers is defined using these typedefs. Examples of such an interface appear in the next section.

Allocators

The introduction mentioned that all memory allocation for STL containers is done by special objects called *allocators*. The last template parameter of each container class is the kind of allocator that the container should use. By default, an allocator of type `allocator` is used, which allocates storage space from the heap. For example, here's the declaration of the `vector` class:

```
template <class T, class Allocator = allocator>
class vector
  {
  ....
  };
```

A detailed discussion of allocators is deferred to the chapter called "Allocators." In the meantime, all of the examples use default allocators.

Common Functions

Although every kind of STL collection has a different set of characteristics, they all support ten common functions. This section describes each of these functions, using a vector of T objects as a concrete example.

The first five common functions allow you to construct, destroy, and perform size-related functions:

Constructor   *vector ()*
                    Construct myself to be empty.

Destructor   *~vector ()*
                    Destroy myself, erasing all of my items.

empty   *bool empty () const*
                    Return true if I contain no entries.

max_size   *size_type max_size () const*
                    Return the maximum number of entries that I can contain.

size   *size_type size () const*
                    Return the number of entries that I contain.

The following example illustrates each of these functions using a vector of integers. It makes use of a vector-specific function called `push_back()`, which appends a copy of its argument to the end of the vector.

Example <vec1.cpp>

```
#include <vector.h>
#include <iostream.h>

int main ()
{
    vector<int> v1; // Empty vector of integers.
    cout << "empty = " << v1.empty () << endl;
    cout << "size = " << v1.size () << endl;
    cout << "max_size = " << v1.max_size () << endl;
    v1.push_back (42); // Add an integer to the vector.
    cout << "size = " << v1.size () << endl;
    cout << "v1[0] = " << v1[0] << endl;
    return 0;
}
```

```
empty = 1
size = 0
max_size = 1073741823
size = 1
v1[0] = 42
```

The next two common functions allow you to assign one collection to another, and to swap the contents of two collections:

=   *vector<T>& operator = (const vector<T>& vector_)*
                                Replace my contents by a copy of vector_'s.

swap   *void swap (vector<T>& vector_)*
                                Swap my contents with vector_'s.

Here's an example that illustrates these two functions using a vector of doubles:

Example <vec2.cpp>

```cpp
#include <iostream.h>
#include <vector.h>

void print (vector<double>& vector_)
{
   for (int i = 0; i < vector_.size (); i++)
     cout << vector_[i] << " ";
   cout << endl;
}

int main ()
{
   vector<double> v1; // Empty vector of doubles.
   v1.push_back (32.1);
   v1.push_back (40.5);
   vector<double> v2; // Another empty vector of doubles.
   v2.push_back (3.56);
   cout << "v1 = ";
   print (v1);
   cout << "v2 = ";
   print (v2);
   v1.swap (v2); // Swap the vector's contents.
   cout << "v1 = ";
   print (v1);
   cout << "v2 = ";
   print (v2);
   v2 = v1; // Assign one vector to another.
   cout << "v2 = ";
   print (v2);
   return 0;
}
```

```
v1 = 32.1 40.5
v2 = 3.56
v1 = 3.56
v2 = 32.1 40.5
v2 = 3.56
```

The remaining functions allow you to copy and compare collections:

Constructor   *vector (const vector<T>& vector_)*
                       Construct myself to be a copy of vector_.

==   *bool operator == (const vector<T>& vector_) const*
                       Return true if I contain the same items in the same order as
                       vector_.

<   *bool operator < (const vector<T>& vector_) const*
                       Return true if I'm lexicographically less than vector_.

Since the comparison operators !=, >, <=, and >= can be defined in terms of ==
and <, STL provides template functions in <utility.h> that define the last four
operators in terms of the first two. Therefore, as long as you provide operator==
and operator< for an object, the other four are provided automatically. This is
true for all objects that you create, not just containers. Here's an example that
uses these operators to compare two vectors of characters:

Example <vec3.cpp>

```cpp
#include <vector.h>
#include <iostream.h>

int main ()
{
  vector<char> v1; // Empty vector of characters.
  v1.push_back ('h');
  v1.push_back ('i');
  cout << "v1 = " << v1[0] << v1[1] << endl;
  vector<char> v2 (v1); // v2 gets a copy of v1's contents.
  v2[1] = 'o'; // Replace second character.
  cout << "v2 = " << v2[0] << v2[1] << endl;
  cout << "(v1 == v2) = " << (v1 == v2) << endl;
  cout << "(v1 < v2) = " << (v1 < v2) << endl;
  return 0;
}
```

```
v1 = hi
v2 = ho
(v1 == v2) = 0
(v1 < v2) = 1
```

Checklist

The main points made by this chapter were:

- There are three main categories of container: sequential, associative, and adapter.
- Each container defines useful several typedefs.
- Every STL container supports ten common operations.
- STL defines template functions for !=, >, <=, and >=.

Quiz

1. Name each STL container and the category that it belongs to. [*easy*]
2. Name three typedefs that a container defines. [*easy*]
3. Name the operations common to all STL containers. [*easy*]
4. Describe the main characteristics of a vector. [*easy*]

Exercises

1. How would you implement the template function for >=? [*medium*]
2. Would `add()` have been a better name than `push_back()`? [*medium*]
3. What is the type of `vector<int>::size_type`? [*easy*]

Error Handling

Standard Exceptions

The ANSI standard specifies that an STL error should cause a standard C++ exception to be thrown. The exceptions that STL can throw are a subset of the exception classes defined in `<stdexcept.h>`. Here is a hierarchy of the exceptions that STL can throw, together with a brief description of when the exception is thrown. Abstract exception classes are indicated by italics:

exception ....the root of all exceptions
  bad_alloc...................memory allocation error
  logic_error ....the root of exceptions caused by a violation of preconditions
    invalid_argument ..attempt to create a container with an invalid size such as -1
    length_error ....attempt to create a string with an illegal length
    out_of_range ....attempt to reference a container using an illegal index

The following example illustrates the use of exception handling to trap an illegal vector index error:

```cpp
#include <vector.h>
#include <iostream.h>

int main ()
  {
  vector<int> v;
  for (int j = 0; j < 10; j++) // Add some values to the vector.
    v.push_back (j);
  bool loop = true;
  while (loop)
  {
    try
    {
      int index;
      cout << "Please enter an index: ";
      cin >> index;
      int i = v [index];
      cout << "v [" << index << "] = " << v[index] << endl;
    }
    catch (out_of_range& error)
    {
```

```
        cout << "An out of range exception was caught" << endl;
        loop = false;
    }
}
cout << "Terminating program" << endl;
return 0;
}
```

```
Please enter an index: 5
v [5] = 5
Please enter an index: -4
An out of range exception was caught
Terminating program
```

Some commerical implementations of STL have the ability to call a user-supplied error handler instead of throwing an exception.

Iterators

Motivation

One of the novel features of STL that distinguishes it from other libraries is its heavy use of iterators, which are a kind of generalized pointer. A solid understanding of iterators is necessary to realize the full power of STL.

Objectives

This chapter describes the characteristics of the main iterator classes and shows how an iterator may be used to traverse every element of an STL container.

Introduction

Before delving into the details of each STL container, it's important to examine the topic of *iterators*. An iterator is a generalized pointer that may be used to traverse the elements of a collection, whether they are contained in an STL container, a regular "C" array, or a C++ iostream. At any point in time, an iterator is positioned at exactly one place in a collection, and will remain positioned at that location until instructed to move.

Categories of Iterator

STL defines five main categories of iterator:

Table 3: Iterator Types

Iterator Type	Characteristic
input	can read one item at a time, in a forward direction only
output	can write one item at a time, in a forward direction only
forward	combines characteristics of input and output iterators
bidirectional	like forward, plus the ability to move backwards
random access	like bidirectional, plus the ability to jump by an arbitrary distance

These iterator categories and their interfaces may be arranged in a hierarchical fashion, as shown by the following diagram:

Figure 1: Hierarchy of Iterators

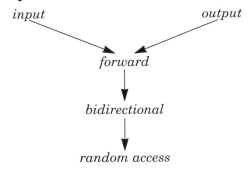

In addition to these basic types of iterators, there are more exotic iterators that have special characteristics such as the ability to move in a reverse fashion through a collection, as well as `const` versions of the iterators that allow you to iterate through read-only collections.

Iterator Behaviors

The interfaces provided by the various categories of iterator are fairly simple. Assuming that i and j are both iterators, and n is an integer, here is a list of all the iterator functions, arranged in order from the most general to the most specific.

Common to all iterator types.

++i	Advance one element and return a reference to i.
i++	Advance one element and return i's previous value.

Input

***i**	Return a read-only reference to the element at i's current position.
i == j	Return true if i and j are both positioned at the same element.
i != j	Return true if i and j are positioned at different elements.

Output

***i**	Return a writeable reference to the element at i's current position.
i = j	Set i's position to the same as j's.

Bidirectional

--i	Retreat one element and return i's new value.
i --	Retreat one element and return i's previous value.

Random access

i += n	Advance by n locations and return a reference to i.
i -= n	Retreat by n locations and return a reference to i.

i + n   Return an iterator that is positioned n elements ahead of i's current position.

i - n   Return an iterator that is positioned n elements behind i's current position.

i[n]   Return a reference to the nth element from i's current position.

Note that according to this hierarchy of interfaces, a regular "C" pointer is considered to be a random access iterator. Indeed, many STL algorithms (described in the next chapter) can accept regular C pointers as well as custom STL iterators. In addition, many proprietary class libraries define iterator objects that have the characteristics that were just described. The STL algorithms can therefore also accept these iterators as arguments.

Iterating through Collections

The type of iterator associated with a particular entity depends on how easily an iterator can move through the entity, and whether the entity is readable and/or writeable. For example, C++ input streams (such as `cin`) are associated with input iterators. Vectors and deques have random access iterators, and all other first-class collections have bidirectional iterators. Here's a table that shows the mapping between the STL container types and their associated iterator types:

Table 4: Containers and their Iterator Types

Container	Iterator type
vector	random access
deque	random access
list	bidirectional
multiset	bidirectional
set	bidirectional
multimap	bidirectional
map	bidirectional
stack	none
queue	none
priority_queue	none

Most of the time, you don't have to remember this information, as each collection defines the following useful typedefs:

Table 5: Iterator Types and their Meaning

Typedef	Meaning
iterator	type that can iterate forwards through a writeable collection
const_iterator	type that can iterate forwards through a read-only collection
reverse_iterator	type that can iterate backwards through a writeable collection
const_reverse_iterator	type that can iterate backwards through a read-only collection

For example, to declare an iterator `iter1` that can iterate through a vector of integers, you can write:

```
vector<int>::iterator iter1;
```

Similarly, to declare an iterator `iter2` that can iterate backwards through a list of integers, you can write:

```
list<int>::reverse_iterator iter2;
```

Every first-class collection provides the following set of functions for obtaining an iterator positioned at an extremity:

begin   *iterator begin ()*
                   Return an iterator positioned at my first item.

begin   *const_iterator begin () const*
                   Return a const iterator positioned at my first read-only item.

end   *iterator end ()*
                   Return an iterator positioned immediately after my last item.

end   *const_iterator end () const*
                   Return a const iterator positioned immediately after my last read-only item.

When an iterator is positioned inside its collection, it may be safely dereferenced. However, when it goes beyond the last element of its collection, it is set to a *past-the-end* value equal to `end()`, and any attempt to dereference it may cause a run-time error.

The following example shows how an iterator may be used to display every element of a collection. It uses the `++` operator to advance the iterator, the `*` operator to access the iterator's associated element, and the `!=` operator to compare the position of the iterator against its past-the-end value.

Example <iter1.cpp>

```
#include <vector.h>
#include <iostream.h>

int main ()
{
  vector<char*> v; // Vector of character strings.
  v.push_back ("zippy"); // First element.
  v.push_back ("motorboy"); // Second element.
  vector<char*>::iterator i;
  for (i = v.begin (); i != v.end (); i++)
    cout << *i << endl; // Display item.
  return 0;
}
```

zippy
motorboy

A standard range notation is often used to describe the range of items that is visited by an operation. When an item is included in a range, it is bounded by a bracket ([), and when the item is not included, a parentheses is used instead. For example, the print loop in the example shown above visits the items [v.begin..v.end).

Note that since all first-class containers support iterator access, you can use the same technique for iterating through any kind of container, including sets and maps. Note also that although the following code segment *could* have been used in the last example for performing the loop, it would only work with containers that have random access iterators. This is because random access iterators are the only kinds of iterators that supply a < operator. The preferred method for iteration through a container is therefore to always use the != operator for past-the-end checking.

```
// OK for collections that have random access iterators,
// but not recommended.
for (i = v.begin (); i < v.end (); i++)
  cout << *i << endl; // Display item.
```

Const Iterators

The only way to iterate through a const collection is to use a const iterator. The * operator of const iterators returns a const reference to its associated item, thus preventing you from accidentally modifying the underlying collection. The following example illustrates the use of a const iterator:

Example <iter2.cpp>

```
#include <vector.h>
#include <iostream.h>

void print (const vector<char*>& v_)
{
  vector<char*>::const_iterator i;
  for (i = v_.begin (); i != v_.end (); i++)
    cout << *i << endl;
}

int main ()
{
  vector<char*> v; // Vector of character strings.
  v.push_back ("zippy");
  v.push_back ("motorboy");
  print (v); // Pass const reference to vector.
  return 0;
}
```

zippy
motorboy

Reverse Iterators

Reverse iterators are just like regular iterators except that they traverse a collection backwards instead of forwards. Every first-class container supports the following functions for obtaining a reverse iterator positioned at an extremity:

rbegin   *reverse_iterator rbegin ()*
                     Return a reverse iterator positioned at my last item.

rbegin   *const_reverse_iterator rbegin () const*
                     Return a const reverse iterator positioned at my last read-only item.

rend   *reverse_iterator rend ()*
                     Return a reverse_iterator positioned immediately *before* my first item.

rend   *const_reverse_iterator rend () const*
                     Return a const reverse_iterator positioned immediately *before* my first read-only item.

The following example uses a reverse iterator for iterating backwards through a vector of strings:

Example <iter3.cpp>

```cpp
#include <vector.h>
#include <iostream.h>

int main ()
{
  vector<char*> v; // Vector of character strings.
  v.push_back ("zippy"); // First element.
  v.push_back ("motorboy"); // Second element.
  vector<char*>::reverse_iterator i;
  for (i = v.rbegin (); i != v.rend (); i++)
    cout << *i << endl; // Display item.
  return 0;
}
```

motorboy
zippy

Random Access Iterators

In addition to moving forwards and backwards by one position, random access iterators can jump. Here's an example that illustrates this point:

Example <iter4.cpp>

```cpp
#include <vector.h>
#include <iostream.h>

int main ()
{
  vector<int> v; // Empty vector of integers.
  v.push_back (1);
  v.push_back (2);
  v.push_back (3);
  // Position immediately after last item.
  vector<int>::iterator i = v.end ();
  // Move back one and then access.
  cout << "last element is " << *--i << endl;
  i -= 2; // Jump back two items.
  cout << "first element is " << *i << endl;
  return 0;
}
```

last element is 3
first element is 1

Hierarchy of Iterators

In addition to the iterator classes defined for containers, STL includes several other useful iterator classes. In the following hierarchy, abstract classes are shown in italics:

input_iterator
    istream_iterator............................iterates over a C++ input stream (like `cin`)

output_iterator
    ostream_iterator..........................iterates over a C++ output stream (like `cout`)
    back_insert_iterator ....always inserts at the end of a container
    front_insert_iterator..................always inserts at the front of a container
    insert_iterator............................inserts at its current position
    raw_storage_iterator ....iterates over raw memory

bidirectional_iterator
    reverse_bidirectional_iterator....iterates backwards

random_access_iterator
    reverse_iterator ....iterates backwards

A detailed description of each of these iterators is included in the class catalog at the end of this book.

Checklist

The main points made by this chapter were:

- Iterators are a kind of generalized pointer.
- The main iterator types are input, output, forward, bidirectional, and random access.
- The iterator operators are similar to those of a regular "C" pointer.
- Each STL container has a set of typedefs that describe its associated iterator types.
- There are four functions for getting an iterator positioned at a container extremity.
- `end()` always yields a past-the-end value.
- Const iterators allow you to iterate through read-only data structures.
- Reverse iterators allow you to move backwards through a data structure.
- Random access iterators may jump about the elements of a data structure.

Quiz

1. What are the operations associated with a bidirectional iterator? [*medium*]
2. Name the four operations for getting an iterator positioned at a container extremity? [*easy*]
3. Draw the hierarchical relationship between the main five types of iterator. [*easy*]

Exercises

1. What kind of iterator is a regular "C" pointer? [*easy*]
2. Write the code for a function called `palindrome` that takes a const vector as its parameter and returns a bool that is equal to true only if the vector is equal to the reverse of itself. Use iterators to perform the comparison. [*medium*]
3. Why didn't the designers of STL define `end()` to return an iterator positioned at the last element of a data structure rather than its past-the-end value? [*medium*]

Algorithms

Motivation

Alex Stepanov, the inventor of STL, specializes in the field of generic algorithms. His interests are manifest in the design of STL, which treats algorithms as first-class entities that can be applied to a variety of different data structures. Knowledge of STL algorithms is useful for two reasons. First, they can help you to perform common chores that often occur in the creation of software. Second, understanding the STL approach to separating algorithms from data structures will allow you to create generic algorithms of your own.

Objectives

This chapter introduces STL algorithms by describing a couple of algorithms in detail. It then describes the relationship between algorithms and iterators, and concludes with a complete list of STL algorithms, grouped by category.

Introduction

Interestingly enough, the bulk of STL implementation code is not dedicated to its containers, but to its algorithms. This mirrors the goal of STL's inventors, which was to produce a set of library protocols and code that would allow the creation of reusable algorithms. STL comes complete with over 70 reusable algorithms, ranging from simple to complex. As a simple example, STL includes the algorithms `min()` and `max()`:

Example <alg1.cpp>

```
#include <algorithm.h>
#include <iostream.h>

int main ()
{
  int i = min (4, 7);
  cout << "min (4, 7) = " << i << endl;
  char c = max ('a', 'z');
  cout << "max ('a', 'z') = " << c << endl;
  return 0;
}


min (4, 7) = 4
max ('a', 'z') = z
```

In addition to supplying many pre-prepared algorithms, STL allows you to add new algorithms without modifying any of the existing STL implementation code. This was another of the key goals of STL's creators — to create a library that was extensible.

Algorithms and Iterators

Although `min()` operates on pairs of values, most STL algorithms operate on sequences of elements. For example, `count()` counts the number of items in a sequence that match a particular value. To allow the algorithms to operate on a wide range of sequences, including regular "C" arrays, STL containers, and other vendors' collections, STL algorithms only access data via the use of *iterators*. Before an example of `count()` is shown, here is how it is described in the algorithm catalog at the back of this book:

Synopsis
Count items in a range that match a value.

Signature
```
template<class InputIterator, class T, class Size>
void count
(
    InputIterator first_,
    InputIterator last_,
    const T& value_,
    Size& n_
)
```

Description
`count()` counts the number of elements in the range [first_, last_) that match value_ using operator== and adds this count to n_. Note that n_ is not automatically initialized to zero prior to the counting procedure. `count()` assumes that operator== performs only constant operations upon the elements.

Complexity
Time complexity is linear, as (last_ - first_) comparisons are performed. Space complexity is constant.

Since a regular "C" pointer is upwards compatible with an input iterator, `count()` may be used to count values in a regular "C" array. Note that `last_` is set to be positioned immediately beyond the end of the array:

Example <alg2.cpp>

```
#include <algorithm.h>
#include <iostream.h>

int i [] = { 1, 4, 2, 8, 2, 2 }; // Six elements.

int main ()
{
  int n = 0; // Must be initialized, as count increments n.
  count (i, i + 6, 2, n);
  cout << "count of 2s = " << n << endl;
  return 0;
}
```

count of 2s = 3

Since the iterators associated with all first-class STL containers are upwards
compatible with input iterators, count() may also be used to count elements in
any STL container. The following example uses count() to count matching elements in a vector:

Example <alg3.cpp>

```
#include <vector.h>
#include <algorithm.h>
#include <iostream.h>

int main ()
{
  vector<int> i;
  i.push_back (1);
  i.push_back (4);
  i.push_back (2);
  i.push_back (8);
  i.push_back (2);
  i.push_back (2);
  int n = 0; // Must be initialized, as count increments n.
  count (i.begin (), i.end (), 2, n);
  cout << "count of 2s = " << n << endl;
  return 0;
}
```

count of 2s = 3

Algorithm Interfaces

Some algorithms require more "powerful" iterators that others. For example, `sort()` will only work with random access iterators. Since vectors have random access iterators, the following example compiles and works fine:

Example <alg4.cpp>

```
#include <vector.h>
#include <algorithm.h>
#include <iostream.h>

int main ()
{
  vector<int> years;
  years.push_back (1962);
  years.push_back (1992);
  years.push_back (2001);
  years.push_back (1999);
  sort (years.begin (), years.end ()); // Sort using < operator.
  vector<int>::iterator i;
  for (i = years.begin (); i != years.end (); i++)
    cout << *i << endl;
  return 0;
}

1962
1992
1999
2001
```

However, if you try to use `sort()` with a less "powerful" iterator, either a compiler error or a linker error will occur. The following example causes a compiler error because `sort()` is attempted on a list, which only provides bidirectional iterators.

Example <alg5.cpp>

```
#include <vector.h>
#include <algorithm.h>
#include <iostream.h>

int main ()
{
  list<int> years;
  years.push_back (1962);
  years.push_back (1992);
  years.push_back (2001);
  years.push_back (1999);
  sort (years.begin (), years.end ());
  list<int>::iterator i;
  for (i = years.begin (); i != years.end (); i++)
    cout << *i << endl;
```

```
    return 0;
}
```

Many STL algorithms require a predicate, function, or function object as a parameter. For example, there is an algorithm called `for_each()` that applies a supplied function to every item in a sequence. Similarly, there is an algorithm called `count_if()` that counts all of the elements in a sequence that satisfy a particular predicate. For examples and further information about predicates and function objects, consult the next chapter.

List of Algorithms by Category

This section lists all of the standard STL algorithms by category, together with an encoded description of their input parameters and a brief synopsis. For detailed information about a particular algorithm, consult the algorithm catalog at the end of this book.

Table 6: Algorithm Interface Key

Key	Meaning
b	bidirectional iterator
f	forward iterator
g	function object
i	input iterator
o	output iterator
p	predicate
r	random access iterator
v	value
&	reference to a value

Applying
    for_each ....iig......apply a function to every item in a range

Bounding
    equal_range...........................ffv......return the lower and upper bounds within a range
    lower_bound..........................ffv......return the lower bound within a range
    upper_bound ....ffv......return the upper bound within a range

Comparing
    equal.....................................iii.......check that two sequences match
    lexicographical_compare ......iii.......lexicographically compare two sequences
    mismatch...............................iii.......search two sequences for a mismatched item

Copying
  copy..iio......copy a range of items to another area
  copy_backward......................bbb....copy a range of items backwards to
                                                         another area

Counting
  count......................................iiv......count items in a range that match a value
  count_if..................................iip......count items in a range that satisfy a
                                                         predicate

Filling
  fill ....ff........set every item in a range to a particular
                                                         value
  fill_n ....o ....set n items to a particular value

Filtering
  unique ....ff........collapse all consecutive values in a
                                                         sequence
  unique_copy ....iio......copy a sequence, collapsing consecutive
                                                         values

Generating
  generate ....ffg......fill a sequence using a generator function
  generate_n ....og ......generate a specified number of items

Heap
  make_heap............................rr.......make a sequence into a heap
  pop_heap ....rr.......pop the top value from a heap
  push_heap..............................rr.......place the last element into a heap
  sort_heap...............................rr.......sort a heap

Math Operations
  accumulate............................iiv......sum the values in a range
  adjacent_difference...............iio......calculate the difference between adjacent
                                                         pairs of values
  inner_product.......................iiiv.....calculate the inner product of two
                                                         sequences
  iota...ffv......fill a range with ascending values
  partial_sum...........................iio......fill a range with a running total
  median...................................vvv ....calculate the median of three values

Merging
  inplace_merge.......................bbb....merge two sorted lists in place into a
                                                         single sorted list
  merge......................................iiiio....merge two sorted lists into a single sorted
                                                         list

Min / Max

min ....&& ....return the minimum of two items
max......................................&& ....return the maximum of two items
min_element ....ii........return the minimum item within a range
max_element.........................ii........return the maximum item within a range

Partitioning

nth_element ....rrr .....partition a range by its nth element
partition ....bbp ....partition a range using a predicate
stable_partition ....bbp ....partition a range using a predicate

Permuting

next_permutation ....bb ......change sequence to next lexicographic
    permutation
prev_permutation ....bb ......change sequence to last lexicographic
    permutation

Removing

remove..................................ffv......remove all matching items from a
    sequence
remove_copy..........................iiov ....copy a sequence, removing all matching
    items
remove_copy_if.....................iiop ....copy sequence, removing all that satisfy
    predicate
remove_if..............................ffp .....remove items that satisfy predicate from
    sequence

Replacing

replace..................................ffvv ....replace specified value in a sequence with
    another
replace_copy..........................iiovv ..copy sequence, replacing matching values
replace_copy_if.....................iiopv ..copy sequence, replacing values that
    satisfy predicate
replace_if..............................ffpv ....replace specified values that satisfy a
    predicate

Reversing

reverse..................................bb ......reverse the items in a sequence
reverse_copy..........................bbo ....create a reversed copy of a sequence

Rotating

rotate ....fff ......rotate a sequence by n positions
rotate_copy...........................fffo.....copy a sequence, rotating it by n positions

Searching

adjacent_find ....ii........locate consecutive sequence in a range

binary_search ....ffv......locate an item in a sorted sequence

find ....iiv......locate an item in a sequence

find_if..................................iip......locate an item that satisfies a predicate in
                                                            a range

search ....ffff.....locate one sequence within another

Set Operations

includes ....iiii .....search for one sequence in another
                                                            sequence

set_difference.......................iiiio....create set of elements in 1st sequence that
                                                            are not in 2nd

set_intersection....................iiiio....create set of elements that are in both
                                                            sequences

set_symmetric_difference.....iiiio....create set of elements that are not in both
                                                            sequences

set_union..............................iiiio....create set of elements that are in either
                                                            sequence

Shuffling

random_shuffle....................rr.......randomize sequence using random shuffles

Sorting

partial_sort ....rrr .....sort the smallest n elements of a sequence

partial_sort_copy ....iirr ....sort the smallest n elements of a sequence

sort.......................................rr.......sort a sequence

stable_sort............................rr.......sort a sequence

Swapping

iter_swap..............................ff........swap the values indicated by two iterators

swap ....&& ....swap two values

swap_ranges ....fff ......swap two ranges of items

Transforming

transform ....iiog....transform one sequence into another

Multiple Implementations of Algorithms

There are some algorithms whose implementation can be optimized for a particular kind of iterator. For example, it is slightly faster to reverse a sequence using a random access iterator than using a bidirectional iterator. In these cases, STL supplies both forms of the algorithm and uses a compile-time technique for automatically selecting the best version based on the types of the iterator arguments. For information about how STL does this, consult the Appendix section of this book.

Checklist

The main points made by this chapter were:

- STL includes about 70 algorithms.
- STL algorithms operate on data structures indirectly via iterators.
- STL algorithms can operate on STL containers and regular "C" arrays.
- Some algorithms have several implementations, optimized for each iterator type.

Quiz

1. What is meant by the syntax [begin, end)? [*easy*]

Exercises

1. Examine the source code for `sort()`, and describe why `sort()` can only accept random access iterators? [*medium*]
2. How likely is it that a market will be created for reusable algorithms? [*hard*]
3. Select five algorithms at random that work on a vector, consult the algorithm catalog at the end of this book to learn more about them, and then write a piece of code that demonstrates their use. [*medium*]
4. Use the `remove()` algorithm to remove some items from a vector. Notice that the vector's size does not decrease. Explain the reason and write some code that does actually *remove* the elements. Do you think that `remove()` was a good name for this algorithm? [*medium*]
5. Use `accumulate()` to subtract instead of add. Supply a complete example. [*easy*]
6. What is the result of using one compare function when sorting a container and then other compare function when searching the container using `binary_search()`? [*medium*]

Making STL Easier to Use

Motivation

Feedback from the C++ community regarding the ease of use of STL has been very encouraging. After a brief period of adjustment to the new philosophy, users seem to enjoy their new-found power. Some areas of STL can be simplified via a variety of different mechanisms. An understanding of these approaches will allow you to reduce your STL learning curve and make your source code easier to debug.

Objectives

This chapter starts by describing some of the problem areas of STL. It then discusses and compares some proposed solutions.

The main concern about STL usability centers around the possible misuse of algorithms. For example, although the count() algorithm expects iterators that reference the same container, there is nothing to stop a programmer from messing up like this:

```
vector<int> v1 (10);
vector<int> v2 (10);
// ... fill v1 and v2 with values.
int n; // Oops, n should be initialized to zero!
count (v1.begin (), v2.end (), 42, n); // Oops!
```

One possible way to help programmers to avoid this is to add a new derived class to each STL container that contains "user-friendly" versions of the most common algorithms. For example:

```
template <class T>
class non_standard_vector : public vector<T>
{
  public:
    int count (const T& value_) const
    {
      int n = 0;
      count( begin(), end(), value_, n ); // Call standard.
      return n;
    }

    // ... rest of easier interface goes here ...
};
```

would allow you to write:

```
non_standard_vector<int> v1 (10); // NON-STANDARD VECTOR!
int n = v1.count (42); // Easier.
```

An alternative approach is to encapsulate every STL container in a non-standard and "easier-to-use" version:

```
template< class T > class non_standard_vector
{
  public:
    int count (const T& value_) const
    {
      int n = 0;
      count( v.begin(), v.end(), value_, n ); // Call standard.
      return n;
    }

    // ... rest of easier interface goes here ...

    vector<T>& standard(); // Return encapsulated vector.

  private:
    vector<T> v; // Encapsulated standard version.
};
```

Although these approaches seem reasonable at first glance, there are several problems:

- They *double* the number of classes.

- They require the user-friendly version of the algorithm to be *declared* in every extra non-standard class.

- They require programs to be *littered with non-standard types*, like non_standard_vector, which defeats the purpose of having a standard in the first place.

- The first approach reduces efficiency by introducing *unnecessary inheritance* and *virtual destructors*.

- Both approaches only provide user-friendly versions of the algorithm for the non-standard derived classes, and *cannot be extended* to provide user-friendly algorithms that work with other vendor's containers.

In other words, both approaches are contrary to the original aims of the STL design. An alternative *helper algorithm* solution does not have any of these problems and is in perfect harmony with the STL philosophy.

A helper algorithm is a templatized non-member function that does some of the error-prone work that a programmer would otherwise have to do manually, but is just as efficient as the original. For example, here's the source code of a helper function called os_count[3] () that makes the standard count() algorithm easier to use.

```
template <class Container, class T>
inline int // Inline for efficiency.
os_count (const Container& c, const T& value)
{
   int n = 0;
   // Call standard algorithm.
   count (c.begin (), c.end (), value, n);
   return n;
}
```

Here is an example that uses this helper algorithm:

```
vector<int> v1 (10); // Standard vector!
int n = os_count (v1, 42); // Easiest!
```

The significance of the helper algorithms becomes more apparent when you consider an operation such as removing items from a container. Without the helper algorithms, the following code is required to remove all of the 42s from the vector v:

```
v.erase( remove( v.begin (), v.end (), 42 ), v.end () );
```

The os_erase() helper algorithm allows you to write the following code instead:

```
os_erase (v, 42);
```

Here is an implementation of the os_erase() helper algorithm:

```
template <class Container, class T>
inline void
os_erase (Container& c, const T& t)
{
   // Call standard.
}
   c.erase (remove (c.begin (), c.end (), t), c.end ());
```

Another candidate helper function is os_release() , which assumes that every element of its container argument is a pointer to some heap and deletes each item:

---

[3] The os_prefix is due to ObjectSpace, who published these helper algorithms to the public domain.

```
template <class Container>
inline void

os_release (Container& c)
{
  Container::iterator i;
  for (i = c.begin (); i != c.end (); i++)
    delete *i;
}
```

Helper versions can be written for many of the STL algorithms, and at least one vendor has made these helper algorithms available in the public domain[4].

Checklist

The main points made by this chapter were:

- There are some aspects of STL that are error-prone, especially for beginners.
- There are at least three different ways to make STL easier to use.
- The "helper algorithm" approach is the most in-tune with the STL philosophy.
- Helpers are generally very simple and may be written for many algorithms.

Quiz

1. Describe the three main approaches that can make STL easier to use. [*medium*]
2. What are the disadvantages of subclassing from the standard STL containers? [*medium*]

Exercises

1. Write a helper algorithm for sort() that takes a single argument which is a container to sort. [*easy*]
2. Write a helper algorithm for_each() that takes two arguments — a container and a function — and applies the function to every element of the container. [*easy*]
3. Invent a fourth approach that makes STL easier to use. [*hard*]
4. Locate the public domain set of helper algorithms and examine their implementation. [*easy*]

---

[4] See the appendix section for more details.

Functions and Function Objects

Motivation
One well-known feature of STL is that it treats algorithms as first class entities. A lesser-known fact is that is also defines *function objects* that allow functions to be encapsulated as objects. This design technique is used by STL to allow for user-programmable algorithms as well as a convenient way to specify predicates to algorithms such as count_if(). An understanding of function objects increases your access to the full power of STL as well as improving your knowledge of useful design concepts.

Objectives
This chapter introduces the three main kinds of function objects using a mix of text and examples. It then describes *adapter* functions, which are functions for conveniently creating function objects. It ends by providing a complete list to every function object in STL together with a brief description.

Introduction

Many of the STL algorithms and containers require you to specify a function to perform their operation. A function that takes one parameter is called a *unary* function, whereas a function that takes two parameters is called a *binary* function. STL categorizes functions as follows:

- *Predicates* always return true or false, and are used for triggering actions.
- *Comparitors* always return true or false, and are used for ordering elements.
- *General functions* often return a numeric value, and perform an arbitrary operation on one or more arguments.

These functions can generally be supplied as either pointers to regular "C" functions, or as function objects. The STL function objects are declared in <functional.h>[5]. A function object may be created, stored, and destroyed just like any other kind of object. However, unlike regular "C" functions, a function object can have associated data. Every function object supplies a () operator so that it can be executed using the regular function call syntax. In addition, most function objects are templatized for typesafety. For example, here's a description of the binary function object called greater, taken from the class catalog at the end of this book:

---

[5] Called <function.h> in some 8.3 implementations.

Description

`greater` is a binary function object that returns true if its first operand is greater than its second operand.

Declaration

```
template<class T>
struct greater : binary_function<T, T, bool>
```

Interface

()   *bool operator () (const T& x_, const T& y_) const*
                      Return x_ > y_.

The following example uses a `greater` object to compare two numbers:

```
#include <functional.h>
#include <iostream.h>

int main ()
{
   // Create instance of "greater" function object.
   greater<int> f;
   // Compare operands.
   cout << "(4 > 32) = " << f (4, 32) << endl;
   return 0; // Done.
}
```

(4 > 32) = 0

The rest of this chapter describes the various kinds of function objects in detail.

Predicates

Predicates are used to trigger actions, and always return true or false. For example, the `count_if()` algorithm allows you to count all of the values in a sequence that satisfy a user-supplied predicate. The following example passes the address of the regular "C" function `bigger()` to `count_if()`, which in turn uses it to count the numbers in a sequence that are greater than three.

Example <func1.cpp>

```
#include <vector.h>
#include <algorithm.h>
#include <iostream.h>

bool bigger (int i_)
{
   return i_ > 3;
}
```

```
int main ()
{
  vector<int>v;
  v.push_back (4);
  v.push_back (1);
  v.push_back (5);
  int n = 0;
  count_if (v.begin (), v.end (), bigger, n);
  cout << "number greater than 3 = " << n << endl;
  return 0;
}
```

number greater than 3 = 2

STL includes a unary function object called logical_not that returns true if its single operand is false. The following example uses an instance of this class to count all of the false elements in an array:

Example <logicnot.cpp>

```
#include <iostream.h>
#include <algorithm.h>
#include <functional.h>

int input [7] = { 1, 0, 0, 1, 1, 1, 1 };

int main ()
{
  int n = 0;
  count_if (input, input + 7, logical_not<int> (), n);
  cout << "count = " << n << endl;
  return 0;
}
```

count = 2

For reference, here's a list of the algorithms that can accept unary predicates:

- count_if
- find_if
- partition
- replace_copy_if
- remove_if
- remove_copy_if
- replace_if
- stable_partition

Similarly, here's a list of the algorithms that can accept binary predicates:

- adjacent_find
- search

- unique_copy
- unique

Comparitors

Comparitors are binary functions that are used to order elements, and always return true or false. When a comparitor returns true, it generally means that the first parameter should be ordered before the second parameter. For example, one variation of sort() allows you to specify a function that is used to control the order of sorting. In the following example, bigger_than() tells sort() to place x_ to the left of y_ if x_ is greater than y_.

Example <func2.cpp>

```
#include <vector.h>
#include <algorithm.h>
#include <iostream.h>

bool bigger_than (int x_, int y_)
{
   return x_ > y_;
}

int main ()
{
   vector<int>v;
   v.push_back (4);
   v.push_back (1);
   v.push_back (5);
   sort (v.begin (), v.end (), bigger_than);
   vector<int>::iterator i = v.begin ();
   while (i != v.end ())
      cout << *i++ << endl;
   return 0;
}

5
4
1
```

The next example uses a greater function object to sort a collection of items in descending order.

Example <func3.cpp>

```
#include <vector.h>
#include <algorithm.h>
#include <functional.h>
#include <iostream.h>

int main ()
```

```
{
  vector<int> v;
  v.push_back (4);
  v.push_back (1);
  v.push_back (5);
  sort (v.begin (), v.end (), greater<int> ());
  vector<int>::iterator i = v.begin ();
  while (i != v.end ())
    cout << *i++ << endl;
  return 0;
}


5
4
1
```

The last example uses inline construction of a greater function object for convenience. Note that the following code achieves the same effect:

```
greater<int> g; // Construct a greater function object.
sort (v.begin (), v.end (), g); // Call with function object.
```

For reference, here's a list of the algorithms that can accept a comparitor:

- binary_search
- equal_range
- includes
- inplace_merge
- lower_bound
- make_heap
- median
- merge
- next_permutation
- nth_element
- partial_sort
- partial_sort_copy
- pop_heap
- prev_permutation
- push_heap
- set_difference
- set_intersection
- set_symmetric_difference
- set_union
- sort
- sort_heap
- stable_sort
- upper_bound

STL containers often contain pointers to objects or strings. The ANSI standard STL does not contain function objects for comparing these two kinds of items properly, but they are fairly easy to add. For example, here's the source code for a function object called less_p(x_, y_) that returns true if the object pointed to by x_ is less than the object pointed to by y_:

```
template <class T>
struct less_p : public binary_function<T, T, bool>
{
   bool operator () (const T& x_, const T& y_) const
   {
      return (*x_) < (*y_);
   }
};
```

Similarly, here's a function object called less_s(x_,y_) that returns true if the regular "C" string x_ is less than the regular "C" string y_:

```
class less_s :
   public binary_function<const char*, const char*, bool>
{
   bool operator () (const char* x_, const char* y_) const
   {
      return (strcmp (x_, y_) < 0);
   }
};
```

General Functions

Many algorithms use a general function to apply a mathematical operation to every element in a collection. For example, transform() applies a function to every item in a collection and stores the result into another collection. The following example uses a negate object to negate every element in a collection:

```
#include <functional.h>
#include <iostream.h>
#include <algorithm.h>

int array [] = { 1, 5, 2, 3 };
int result [4];

int main ()
{
   transform (array, array + 4, result, negate<int> ());
   for (int i = 0; i < 4; i++)
      cout << array[i] << "   ";
   cout << endl;
   return 0;
}

-1  -5  -2  -3
```

For reference, here's a list of the algorithms that use a unary operation:

- transform

Similarly, here's a list of the algorithms that use a binary operation:

- transform
- accumulate
- inner_product
- partial_sum
- adjacent_difference

Adapters

Several function objects have an associated *adapter* function that allows you to create an instance of the function more easily. For example, without adapter functions, you'd have to write the following code to perform negation on an odd object:

Example <unegate1.cpp>

```
#include <iostream.h>
#include <algorithm.h>
#include <functional.h>

struct odd : unary_function<int, bool>
{
  bool operator () (int n_) const { return (n_ % 2) == 1; }
};

int array [3] = { 1, 2, 3 };

int main ()
{
  int* p = find_if (array, array + 3, unary_negate<odd> (odd
  ())));
  if (p != array + 3)
    cout << *p << endl;
  return 0;
}
```

However, unary_negate has an adapter function called not1 that automatically returns a correctly parameterized instance of unary_negate:

Example <unegate2.cpp>

```
#include <iostream.h>
#include <algorithm.h>
#include <functional.h>
```

```
struct odd : unary_function<int, bool>
{
  bool operator () (int n_) const { return (n_ % 2) == 1; }
};

int array [3] = { 1, 2, 3 };

int main ()
{
  int* p = find_if (array, array + 3, not1 (odd ()));
  if (p != array + 3)
    cout << *p << endl;
  return 0;
}
```

If a function object has an adapter, it is described in that function object's entry in the class catalog at the end of this book.

List of Function Objects

Opposite is a complete list of all the standard STL function objects, together with their argument count and a description of their operation. For a detailed description of a particular function object, consult the class catalog. Function objects with an asterisk could also have non-standard _p and _s variations for comparing objects via pointers and for comparing strings.

Checklist

The main points made by this chapter were:

- Function objects allow functions to be associated with data and treated as first-class objects.
- There are at three main kinds of STL function objects: predicates, comparitors, and general functions.
- Adapter functions allow function objects to be created more easily.
- STL includes at least 25 different function objects.
- Helpers are generally very simple and may be written for many algorithms.

Quiz

1. Define the difference between predicates, comparitors, and general functions, and supply an example of each. [*easy*]

Exercises

1. Write a function object called `choose()` that takes two arguments and randomly returns one of them each time it is called. [*medium*]

Table 7: Standard Functions

Function	# args	Operation	Adaptor
binary_compose	1	P(Q(x), R(x))	compose 1
binary_negate	2	!P(x,y)	not2
binder1st	1	P(V,x)	bind1st
binder2nd	1	P(x, V)	bind2nd
divides	2	x / y	
equal_to*	2	x == y	
greater*	2	x > y	
greater_equal*	2	x >= y	
indent	1	x	
less*	2	x < y	
less_equal*	2	x <= y	
logical_and	2	x && y	
logical_not	1	!x	not1
logical_or	2	x || y	
minus	2	x - y	
modulus	2	x % y	
negate	1	-x	
not_equal_to*	2	x != y	
plus	2	x + y	
pointer_to_binary_function	2	P(x, y)	ptr_fun
pointer_to_unary_function	1	P(x)	ptr_fun
select1st	1	x.first	
times	2	x * x	
unary_compose	1	P(Q(x))	
unary_negate	1	!P(x)	

Pairs

Motivation
Several of the STL containers and algorithms use an object called a *pair* to either contain or return pairs of objects.

Objectives
This chapter describes pairs by illustrating their use in conjunction with algorithms and containers.

Introduction

In order that pairs of objects can be conveniently stored and passed around as parameters, STL defines a templatized pair[6] object in <utility.h> that simply contains two objects. Once constructed, a pair's items can be accessed using first and second. Several algorithms use pair objects to return a pair of items. For example, mismatch() returns a pair of iterators that point to the items that mismatched:

Example <pair0.cpp>

```
#include <utility.h>
#include <algorithm.h>
#include <iostream.h>

int array1 [] = { 1, 4, 8, 3, 2 };
int array2 [] = { 1, 4, 7, 2, 3 };

int main ()
{
  pair<int*, int*> p = mismatch (array1, array1 + 5, array2);
  cout << "mismatch @ " << *(p.first) << ", " << *(p.second) <<
  endl;
  return 0;
}
```

mismatch @ 8, 7

Several of the STL containers use pair objects to return pairs of items. For example, equal_range() causes a multiset (described in the next chapter) to return

---

[6] Attention Smalltalkers: equivalent to an Association.

a pair of iterators that indicate the first and last locations that a value could be positioned without violating the ordering criteria:

Example \<mset4.cpp>

```
#include <set.h>
#include <iostream.h>

int array [] = { 3, 6, 1, 2, 3, 2, 6, 7, 9 };

int main ()
{
  typedef multiset<int, less<int> > mset;
  mset s (array, array + 9);
  pair<mset::const_iterator, mset::const_iterator> p =
    s.equal_range (3);
  cout << "lower bound = " << *(p.first) << endl;
  cout << "upper bound = " << *(p.second) << endl;
  return 0;
}
```

```
lower bound = 3
upper bound = 6
```

The make_pair() function allows you to conveniently create a pair from two items:

Example \<pair2.cpp>

```
#include <utility.h>
#include <iostream.h>

int main ()
{
  pair<int, int> p = make_pair (1, 10);
  cout << "p.first = " << p.first << endl;
  cout << "p.second = " << p.second << endl;
  return 0;
}
```

```
p.first = 1
p.second = 10
```

Checklist

The main points made by this chapter were:

- Pair objects are used to bind two items.
- make_pair() is the easiest way to create a pair.

Quiz

1. What are the names of the data members for accessing the elements of a pair? [*easy*]

Exercises

1. Does the pair class define a public constructor? If not, why not? [*medium*]

Containers, Part 2

Motivation

One of the most useful portions of STL is its rich set of sequential and associative containers. Understanding their use can save you large amounts of time that would otherwise be spent on creating your own custom collections.

Objectives

This chapter begins by describing the similarities and differences between the various STL containers. It then uses the simplest container — a vector — to illustrate the functions that are common to all containers. Additional containers are only introduced when they are required to describe new functionality. This approach minimizes the amount of information overlap as well as emphasizing the important differences between the container types.

Introduction

This chapter describes each kind of STL container in detail. The best way to start learning the various STL containers is by studying their public interfaces, which are related in a hierarchical fashion as illustrated by the diagram on the following page (Figure 2).

Thankfully, every function with a particular name performs the same conceptual task for every collection in which it appears. Therefore, to minimize the amount of replication in this book, this chapter only describes each function in the context of the first collection in which it appears. For example, `push_back()` is described in the context of a vector, even though it also appears in list and deque. To begin, let's examine the vector class.

vector

Overview

A vector is a sequential container that is very similar to a regular "C" array except that it can expand to accomodate new elements.

Iterator Type

In most STL implementations, a vector's iterator is a regular "C" pointer. For example, `begin()` returns a pointer to the first element in a vector. Since a pointer may be incremented and decremented by an arbitrary amount, a vector's iterator is therefore a random access iterator.

Figure 2: Container Interface Hierarchy

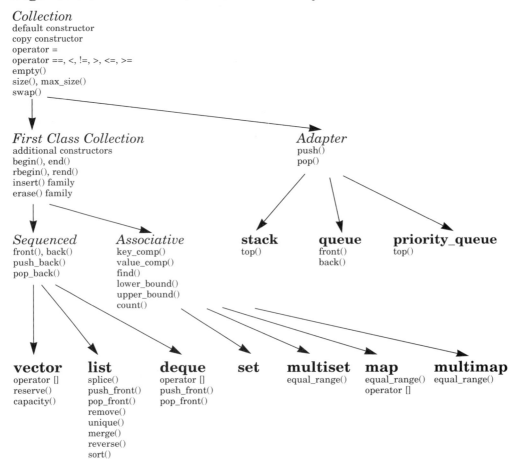

Collection
default constructor
copy constructor
operator =
operator ==, <, !=, >, <=, >=
empty()
size(), max_size()
swap()

First Class Collection
additional constructors
begin(), end()
rbegin(), rend()
insert() family
erase() family

Adapter
push()
pop()

Sequenced
front(), back()
push_back()
pop_back()

Associative
key_comp()
value_comp()
find()
lower_bound()
upper_bound()
count()

stack
top()

queue
front()
back()

priority_queue
top()

vector
operator []
reserve()
capacity()

list
splice()
push_front()
pop_front()
remove()
unique()
merge()
reverse()
sort()

deque
operator []
push_front()
pop_front()

set

multiset
equal_range()

map
equal_range()
operator []

multimap
equal_range()

Implementation

Most vector implementations store elements in a contiguous linear memory
space so that index-based access is very quick. When a vector's originally allocated memory space is exceeded, its elements are copied into a new memory
space that is larger than the old space and then the old space is deallocated. For
efficiency, memory is typically allocated in units of the machine's page size. For
compilers that don't automatically optimize the storage that is used by a vector
of `bool`, many STL implementations supply a class called `bit_vector` that
emulates a `vector<bool>`.

Insertion Notes

If an insertion causes reallocation, all iterators and references are invalidated;
otherwise, only the iterators and references after the insertion point are invalidated. Inserting a single element into a vector is linear in the distance from the
insertion point to the end of the vector. The amortized complexity over the life-

time of a vector of inserting a single element at its end is constant. Insertion of multiple elements into a vector with a single call of the insert member is linear in the sum of the number of elements plus the distance to the end of the vector. In other words, it is much faster to insert many elements into the middle of a vector at once than to do the insertion one at a time.

Erasure Notes

An erasure invalidates all of the iterators and references after the point of the erase. The destructor is called the number of times equal to the number of elements erased, but the assignment operator is called the number of times equal to the number of elements in the vector after the erased elements.

Common Uses

The underlying architecture of vectors makes them ideal for storing elements whose order is significant and where fast numeric indexing is important. Inserting elements anywhere except at the end of a vector is slow, so they should not be used where this kind of operation is common. If inserting is common, consider using a list or a deque instead.

Description

A vector is the simplest kind of STL container. In addition to the common container functions described earlier in this book, a vector includes functions for accessing its extremities, appending, inserting, erasing, and adjusting its capacity. The next few sections describe each of these functions in detail.

The default constructor for a vector creates an empty vector with no associated memory storage. If you wish, you may supply an initial size during construction which causes the vector to contain the specified number of elements set to their default value. Here is a summary of some of the most basic vector facilities:

Constructor   *vector (size_type n_)*
Construct me to contain n_ elements set to their default value.

back   *T& back ()*
Return a reference to my last element.

front   *T& front ()*
Return a reference to my first element.

push_back   *void push_back (const T& value_)*
Add value_ at my end, expanding my storage to accomodate the new element if necessary.

pop_back   *void pop_back ()*
Erase my last element.

[]   *T& operator [] (int index_)*
                            Return a reference to my index_th element.

There are also `const` versions of `front()`, `back()`, and `operator []`. The following example illustrates these functions:

Example <vec4.cpp>

```
#include <vector.h>
#include <iostream.h>

int main ()
{
  vector<int> v (4);
  v[0] = 1;
  v[1] = 4;
  v[2] = 9;
  v[3] = 16;
  cout << "front = " << v.front () << endl;
  cout << "back = " << v.back () << ", size = " << v.size () <<
  endl;
  v.push_back (25);
  cout << "back = " << v.back () << ", size = " << v.size () <<
  endl;
  v.pop_back (); // Note that this does not return a value.
  cout << "back = " << v.back () << ", size = " << v.size () <<
  endl;
  return 0;
}

front = 1
back = 16, size = 4
back = 25, size = 5
back = 16, size = 4
```

`vector` has additional constructors for creating a vector with a specified number of initialized elements, or with a copy of elements within a specified range.

Constructor   *vector (size_type n_, const T& value_)*
                       Construct me to contain n_ copies of value_.

Constructor   *vector (const T* first_, const T* last_)*
                       Construct me to contain copies of all of the elements in the
                       range [first_, last_).

The following example uses the second form of constructor to build a vector initialized from a regular "C" array. Note that the second parameter must point to the element immediately *after* the last element of the data source.

Example <vec5.cpp>

```
#include <vector.h>
#include <iostream.h>

int array [] = { 1, 4, 9, 16 };

int main ()
{
   // array+4 points immediately after last element of array.
   vector<int> v (array, array+4);
   for (int i = 0; i < v.size (); i++)
     cout << "v[" << i << "] = " << v[i] << endl;
   return 0;
}

v[0] = 1
v[1] = 4
v[2] = 9
v[3] = 16
```

An STL container always stores copies of the items that are added to it. When an STL container is destroyed, it invokes the destructor of each item. If the items are *pointers* to objects that are stored on the heap, the heap-based objects are not automatically destroyed. To do this, use the os_release ()[7] helper algorithm prior to destroying the container, as shown in the following example.

Example <release1.cpp>

```
#include <vector.h>
#include <iostream.h>

class X
{
   public:
      X (int i_) : i (i_) {}
      ~X () { cout << "Delete X(" << i << ")" << endl; }
      int i;
};

ostream& operator << (ostream& stream_, const X& x_)
{
   return stream_ << "X(" << x_.i << ")";
}

int main ()
{
   vector<X*> v; // Vector of pointers to X objects.
   v.push_back (new X (2));
   v.push_back (new X (1));
   v.push_back (new X (4));
   vector<X*>::iterator i;
```

---

[7] Non-standard, described earlier in this book.

```
      for (i = v.begin (); i != v.end (); i++)
        cout << *(*i) << endl;
      os_release (v); // Delete heap-based objects.
      return 0;
    }

    X(2)
    X(1)
    X(4)
    Delete X(2)
    Delete X(1)
    Delete X(4)
```

For more information about os_release(), consult the algorithm catalog at the end of this book.

STL provides a comprehensive set of functions for erasing an element from a container:

erase   *void erase (iterator pos_)*
                             Erase the element at pos_.

erase   *void erase (iterator first_, iterator last_)*
                             Erase the elements in range [first_, last_).

When an element is erased, it is removed from the container and then its destructor is called. When an element is erased from a vector, the remaining elements shift one position to the left to fill the "vacuum", and its size decrements by one.

Care must be taken when supplying the iterator arguments to erase(). For example, a common mistake is to think that v.erase (v.end ()) will erase the last element of v. The correct way to do this is to write v.erase (v.end () - 1), since v.end () is positioned immediately *after* the last element. Here are some examples of the erase() family in action:

Example <vec6.cpp>

```
    #include <vector.h>
    #include <iostream.h>

    int array [] = { 1, 4, 9, 16, 25, 36 };

    int main ()
    {
      vector<int> v (array, array + 6);
      for (int i = 0; i < v.size (); i++)
        cout << "v[" << i << "] = " << v[i] << endl;
      cout << endl;
      v.erase (v.begin ()); // Erase first element.
      for (i = 0; i < v.size (); i++)
```

```
          cout << "v[" << i << "] = " << v[i] << endl;
        cout << endl;
        v.erase (v.end () - 1); // Erase last element.
        for (i = 0; i < v.size (); i++)
          cout << "v[" << i << "] = " << v[i] << endl;
        cout << endl;
        // Erase all but first and last elements.
        v.erase (v.begin () + 1, v.end () - 1);
        for (i = 0; i < v.size (); i++)
          cout << "v[" << i << "] = " << v[i] << endl;
        cout << endl;
        v.erase (v.begin (), v.end ()); // Erase all elements.
        return 0;
      }

v[0] = 1
v[1] = 4
v[2] = 9
v[3] = 16
v[4] = 25
v[5] = 36

v[0] = 4
v[1] = 9
v[2] = 16
v[3] = 25
v[4] = 36

v[0] = 4
v[1] = 9
v[2] = 16
v[3] = 25

v[0] = 4
v[2] = 25
```

Note that most STL containers do not provide member functions for erasing elements with a particular value. Instead, this functionality is provided by the remove() family of STL algorithms. Note also that if an STL container contains pointers to heap-based objects, erase() will not delete the objects when the pointers are erased. If you wish to do this, you should use the os_release() algorithm prior to erasing the pointers.

Example <release2.cpp>

```
#include <vector.h>
#include <iostream.h>

class X
{
  public:
    X (int i_) : i (i_) {}
    ~X () { cout << "Delete X(" << i << ")" << endl; }
    int i;
```

```
  };

  ostream& operator << (ostream& stream_, const X& x_)
  {
    return stream_ << "X(" << x_.i << ")";
  }

  int main ()
  {
    vector<X*> v;
    v.push_back (new X (2));
    v.push_back (new X (1));
    v.push_back (new X (4));
    vector<X*>::iterator i;
    cout << "Initial contents:" << endl;
    for (i = v.begin (); i != v.end (); i++)
      cout << "   " << *(*i) << endl;
    delete v.begin (); // Delete the first heap-based object.
    v.erase (v.begin ()); // Erase the first element.
    cout << "Remaining contents:" << endl;
    for (i = v.begin (); i != v.end (); i++)
      cout << "   " << *(*i) << endl;
    os_release (v); // Delete remaining heap objects.
    v.erase (v.begin (), v.end ()); // Erase remaining elements.
    return 0;
  }

Initial contents:
  X(2)
  X(1)
  X(4)
Delete X(2)
Remaining contents:
  X(1)
  X(4)
Delete X(1)
Delete X(4)
```

STL provides the following functions for inserting an item into a container:

insert   *iterator insert (iterator pos_, const T& value_)*
                        Insert a copy of value_ at pos_ and return an iterator
                        pointing to the new element's position.

insert   *void insert (iterator pos_, size_type n_, const T& value_)*
                        Insert n_ copies of value_ at pos_.

insert   *void insert (iterator pos_, const T* first_, const T* last_)*
                        Insert copies of the elements in the range [first_, last_) at
                        pos_.

Inserting an item into a vector causes all of the items to the right of the insertion
point to be shifted one place to the right, and for more storage to be allocated if

necessary. An item may be inserted after the last item by specifing `end()` as the insertion point, and before the first item by specifying `begin()` as the insertion point. Here's an example of some insertions:

Example <vec7.cpp>

```
#include <vector.h>
#include <iostream.h>

int array1 [] = { 1, 4, 25 };
int array2 [] = { 9, 16 };

int main ()
{
  vector<int> v (array1, array1 + 3);
  v.insert (v.begin (), 0); // Insert before first element.
  v.insert (v.end (), 36); // Insert after last element.
  for (int i = 0; i < v.size (); i++)
    cout << "v[" << i << "] = " << v[i] << endl;
  cout << endl;
  // Insert contents of array2 before fourth element.
  v.insert (v.begin () + 3, array2, array2 + 2);
  for (i = 0; i < v.size (); i++)
    cout << "v[" << i << "] = " << v[i] << endl;
  return 0;
}
```

```
v[0] = 0
v[1] = 1
v[2] = 4
v[3] = 25
v[4] = 36

v[0] = 0
v[1] = 1
v[2] = 4
v[3] = 9
v[4] = 16
v[5] = 25
v[6] = 36
```

None of the preceding functions are unique to vectors. However, the last two functions in this section apply only to vectors, and allow you to directly access and modify the amount of a vector's underlying storage.

capacity	*size_type capacity () const* Return the number of elements that I can contain without allocating more memory.
reserve	*void reserve (size_type n_)* Pre-allocate enough space to hold up to n_ elements. This operation does not change the value returned by size().

reserve () is particulary useful if you know how big a vector will grow to and you want to avoid the overhead of unnecessary memory reallocations. The following example uses reserve () to boost a vector's underlying capacity to 5000 elements. Note how the vector's memory allocation scheme causes 4K of memory (1K x 4 bytes) to be allocated when the first element is added.

Example <vec8.cpp>

```
#include <vector.h>
#include <iostream.h>

int main ()
{
  vector<int> v;
  cout << "capacity = " << v.capacity () << endl;
  v.push_back (42);
  cout << "capacity = " << v.capacity () << endl;
  v.reserve (5000);
  cout << "capacity = " << v.capacity () << endl;
  return 0;
}

capacity = 0
capacity = 1024
capacity = 5000
```

deque

Overview
A deque is a sequential container that is optimized for fast indexed-based access and efficient insertion at either of its extremities.

Iterator Type
A deque has a random access iterator.

Implementation
Most STL implementations allocate storage for a deque's elements in 4K blocks (a usual page size) of contiguous memory, and use an array to keep track of a deque's blocks. When a deque is constructed, it has no associated storage. As elements are added, blocks of storage are added to the beginning or the end of the deque as necessary. A result of this architecture is that items may be inserted very efficiently near either extremity. Once a block has been allocated to a deque, it is not deallocated until the deque is destroyed. Insertions are careful to expand the deque in the direction that involves the least amount of copying. Erasures take similar precautions.

Insertion Notes
If an insertion causes reallocation, all iterators and references are invalidated; otherwise, iterators and references are only invalidated if an item is not insert-

ed at an extremity. In the worst cast, inserting a single element into a deque takes linear time in the minimum of the distance from the insertion point to the beginning of the deque and the distance from the insertion point to the end of the deque. Inserting a single element either at the beginning or end of a deque always takes constant time and causes a single call to the element's copy constructor.

Erasure Notes

If the first or last item is erased, all iterators and references remain valid; if any other item is erased, all iterators and references are invalidated. The number of calls to the destructor is the same as the number of elements erased, but the number of calls to the assignment operator is equal to the minimum of the number of elements before the erased element and the number of elements after the erased elements.

Common Uses

Deques are useful in circumstances where order, compact storage, and fast insertion at extremities is important. A deque is ideal for implementing any kind of FIFO structure. If a strict FIFO structure is required that does not allow index-based access, then you should consider using a queue adapter with a deque as the underlying container. If you require very fast insertion near the middle of a sequential structure, then consider using a list instead of a deque.

Description

Since a deque has almost the same interface as a vector, there are only a few additional functions to describe:

insert   *void insert (iterator pos_, const_iterator first_, const_iterator last_)*
                    Insert copies of the elements in the range [first_, last_) at pos_.

pop_front   *void pop_front ()*
                    Erase my first element.

push_front   *void push_front (const T& value_)*
                    Insert a copy of value_ in front of my first element.

The additional `insert()` function is required because a deque's iterator is not simply a "C" pointer. `pop_front()` and `push_front()` allow you to take advantage of a deque's ability to perform O(1) insertion and deletion of its first element. Here's an example of these functions:

Example <deque1.cpp>

```
#include <deque.h>
#include <iostream.h>
```

```
int main ()
{
  deque<int> d;
  d.push_back (4);  // Add after end.
  d.push_back (9);
  d.push_back (16);
  d.push_front (1);  // Insert at beginning.
  for (int i = 0; i < d.size (); i++)
    cout << "d[" << i << "] = " << d[i] << endl;
  cout << endl;
  d.pop_front ();  // Erase first element.
  d[2] = 25;  // Replace last element.
  for (i = 0; i < d.size (); i++)
    cout << "d[" << i << "] = " << d[i] << endl;
  return 0;
}
```

```
d[0] = 1
d[1] = 4
d[2] = 9
d[3] = 16

d[0] = 4
d[1] = 9
d[2] = 25
```

list

Overview
A list is a sequential container that is optimized for insertion and erasure at arbitrary points in its structure at the expense of giving up indexed-based access.

Iterator Type
A list has a bidirectional iterator.

Implementation
A list is normally implemented as a doubly linked list in which every node in the list has a pointer to the previous node and a pointer to the next node. To reduce the amount of unnecessary heap access, all lists of a particular type share a common pool of free nodes. When a node is no longer used by a list, it is placed into the pool so that it may be reused. When the number of lists of a particular type drops to zero, the nodes in the associated common pool are finally deallocated.

Insertion Notes
Insertion does not affect iterators or references. Insertion of a single element into a list takes constant time and exactly one call to the copy constructor. Insertion of multiple elements into a list is linear in the number of elements inserted, and the number of calls to the copy constructor is exactly equal to the number of elements inserted.

Erasure Notes
Erasure only invalidates the iterators and references to the erased elements. Erasing a single element is a constant time operation with a single call to the destructor. Erasing a range in a list is linear time in the size of the range, and the number of calls to the destructor is exactly equal to the size of the range.

Common Uses
A list is useful when the order of items and fast arbitrary insertion/erasure are important. Lists are not as efficient as deques when insertion and erasure only take place at the extremities.

Description
Lists have a fuller interface than any of the other sequential containers. They include functions for splicing, removing, filtering, merging, and sorting. The next few sections contain examples of each of these features.

The splicing functions allow you to move a sequence of one or more elements from one list to another. Here is the simplest variation of splice(), followed by an example:

splice   *void splice (iterator pos_, list<T>& list_)*
                    Remove all of the elements in list_ and insert them before position pos_. Assume that list_ != *this.

Example <list1.cpp>

```
#include <list.h>
#include <iostream.h>

int array1 [] = { 9, 16, 36 };
int array2 [] = { 1, 4 };

int main ()
{
  list<int> l1 (array1, array1 + 3);
  list<int> l2 (array2, array2 + 2);
  l1.splice (l1.begin (), l2);
  list<int>::iterator i = l1.begin ();
  while (i != l1.end ())
    cout << *i++ << endl;
  return 0;
}

1
4
9
16
36
```

Here are the remaining variations of splice(), together with an example that illustrates the last variation:

splice   *void splice (iterator to_, list<T>& list_, iterator from_)*
                        Remove the element in list_ at position from_ and insert it at position to_. This form of splice() does not require that list != *this.

splice   *void splice (iterator pos_, list<T>& list_, iterator first_, iterator last_)*
                        Remove the elements from list_ in the range [first_, last_) and insert them at position pos_. This form of splice() does not require that list != *this.

Example <list2.cpp>

```
#include <list.h>
#include <iostream.h>

int array1 [] = { 1, 16 };
int array2 [] = { 4, 9 };

int main ()
{
   list<int> l1 (array1, array1 + 2);
   list<int> l2 (array2, array2 + 2);
   list<int>::iterator i = l1.begin ();
   i++; // Position at second element in l1.
   l1.splice (i, l2, l2.begin (), l2.end ());
   i = l1.begin ();
   while (i != l1.end ())
      cout << *i++ << endl;
   return 0;
}

1
4
9
16
```

List also contains several useful functions that perform the same tasks as the STL algorithms with the same name, except that they are optimized for the internal architecture of a list:

remove   *void remove (const T& value_)*
                        Erase all elements that match value_, using == to perform the comparison.

reverse   *void reverse ()*
                        Reverse the order of my elements. The time complexity is O(N).

unique   *void unique ()*
                    Replace all repeating sequences of a single element by a
                    single occurrence of that element.

sort   *void sort ()*
                    Sort my elements using operator <. The time complexity is
                    O(NlogN).

Here's an example that demonstrates these four functions:

Example \<list3.cpp>

```
#include <list.h>
#include <iostream.h>

char array [] = { 'x', 'l', 'x ', 't', 's', 's' };

int main ()
{
  list<char> str (array, array + 6);
  list<char>::iterator I;
  cout << "original: " << endl;
  for (i = str.begin (); i != str.end (); i++)
    cout << *i;
  cout << endl << "reversed: " ;
  str.reverse ();
  for (i = str.begin (); i != str.end (); i++)
    cout << *i;
  cout << endl << "removed: ";
  str.remove ('x');
  for (i = str.begin (); i != str.end (); i++)
    cout << *i;
  cout << endl << "uniqued: ";
  str.unique ();
  for (i = str.begin (); i != str.end (); i++)
    cout << *i;
  cout << endl << "sorted: ";
  str.sort ();
  for (i = str.begin (); i != str.end (); i++)
    cout << *i;
  cout << endl;
  return 0;
}
```

```
original: xlxtss
reversed: sstxlx
removed: sstl
uniqued: stl
sorted: lst
```

Last of all, list supplies a specialized version of the merge() algorithm that is optimized for merging lists. Here is a description of the function followed by an example:

merge   *void merge (const list<T> list_)*
                       Move the elements of list_ into myself and place them so that
                       all of my elements are sorted using the < operator. This
                       operation assumes that both myself and list_ were already
                       sorted using operator <.

Example <list4.cpp>

```
#include <list.h>
#include <iostream.h>

int array1 [] = { 1, 3, 6, 7 };
int array2 [] = { 2, 4 };

int main ()
{
   list<int> l1 (array1, array1 + 4);
   list<int> l2 (array2, array2 + 2);
   l1.merge (l2);
   list<int>::iterator i = i1.begin ();
   while (i != l1.end ())
      cout << *i++ << " ";
   cout << endl;
   return 0;
}

1 2 3 4 6 7
```

multiset

Overview
A multiset is a container that is optimized for fast associative lookup. Items are
matched using their == operator. When an item is inserted into a multiset, it is
stored in a data structure that allows the item to be found very quickly. Within
the data structure, the items are ordered according to a user-defined comparitor
function object. A typical user-supplied function object is less (), which causes
the items to be ordered in ascending order. Care must be taken to ensure that
items implement the operations that are required by the comparitor. For example, the less function object requires items to be comparable using operator<.
Unlike sets, a multiset can contain multiple copies of the same item.

Iterator Type
A multiset has a bidirectional iterator.

Implementation
There are many different approaches that could be used to implementing an
associative container. For example, most of the older libraries used a hashing
scheme for positioning and retrieving items. Current implementations of STL
use a data structure called a red-black tree. A red-black tree is a binary search

tree that uses an extra field in every node to store the node's color. Red-black trees constrain the way that nodes may be colored in such a way that the tree remains reasonably balanced. This property is important for ensuring a good overall performance — red-black trees guarantee that the worst case performance for the most common dynamic set operations is O(log N). One conseqence of using a binary tree for storage of data is that the items remain in a sorted order. This allows STL users to iterate through an associative container and access its elements in a sequenced manner. For flexibility, an associative container may be instantiated with any kind of comparator function as one of its template arguments.

Insertion Notes
Insertion does not affect iterators or references. Insertion of a single element causes exactly one call to the copy constructor. When inserting multiple elements, the number of calls to the copy constructor is exactly equal to the number of elements inserted.

Erasure Notes
Erasure only invalidates the iterators and references to the erased elements. Erasing a single element causes a single call to the destructor. Erasing a range causes a number of calls to the destructor exactly equal to the size of the range.

Common Uses
Multisets are useful when fast associate lookup is important, when index-based lookup is unnecessary, and when duplicates are allowed.

Description
As the overview indicated, a comparison object must be specified when a multiset is instantiated so that the multiset knows how to order its items. Most of the examples in this section use the less function object to order the elements. For more information about function objects, consult the "Function Objects" chapter.

Here is a list of the most basic multiset operations that allow you to insert, find, count, and erase items:

Constructor	*multiset ()* Construct myself to be an empty multiset that orders elements using the compare function specified when my template was instantiated.
count	*size_type count (const Key& key_) const* Return the number of elements that I contain that match key_.
erase	*size_type erase (const Key& key_)* Erase all elements that match key_ and return the number of elements that were erased.

find   *iterator find (const Key& key_) const*
                       If I contain an element that matches key_, return an iterator
                       positioned at the matching element, otherwise return an
                       iterator positioned at end().

insert   *iterator insert (const Key& key_)*
                       Insert a copy of key_ and return an iterator positioned at the
                       new element.

The following example illustrates all of these operations:

Example <mset1.cpp>

```cpp
#include <set.h>
#include <iostream.h>

int main ()
{
   typedef multiset<int, less<int> > mset;
   mset s; // Construct an empty multiset.
   cout << "count (42) = " << s.count (42) << endl;
   s.insert (42); // Add an item.
   cout << "count (42) = " << s.count (42) << endl;
   s.insert (42); // Add the same item again.
   cout << "count (42) = " << s.count (42) << endl;

   mset::iterator i = s.find (40);
   if (i == s.end ())
     cout << "40 Not found" << endl;
   else
     cout << "Found " << *i << endl;

   i = s.find (42);
   if (i == s.end ())
     cout << "Not found" << endl;
   else
     cout << "Found " << *i << endl;

   // Erase every element that matches 42.
   int count = s.erase (42);
   cout << "Erased " << count << " instances" << endl;
   return 0;
}
```

```
count(42) = 0
count(42) = 1
count(42) = 2
40 not found
Found 42
Erased 2 instances
```

For convenience, a multiset contains a constructor and an insert function that
allow you to operate with a range of elements:

Constructor   *multiset (const Key* first_, const Key* last_)*
Construct myself to contain copies of the elements in the
range [first_, last_), using the comparitor function specified
when my template was instantiated.

insert   *void insert (const Key* first_, const Key* last_)*
Insert copies of the elements in the range [first_, last_).

If you iterate through an associative container, you will traverse the container
according to its sorting criteria. The next example makes use of the variation of
insert() that was just described to fill a multiset with strings, and then dis-
plays those strings to reveal their sorted sequence.

Example <mset2.cpp>

```
#include <set.h>
#include <iostream.h>
#include <string.h>

struct less_s
{
  bool operator () (const char* x_, const char* y_) const
  {
    return strcmp (x_, y_) < 0;
  }
};

char* names[] = {"dave", "alf", "chas", "bob", "ed", "chas"};

int main ()
{
  typedef multiset<char*, less_s> mset;
  mset s;
  s.insert (names, names + 6); // Insert all the names
  // Display each name in turn.
  for (mset::iterator i = s.begin (); i != s.end (); i++)
    cout << *i << endl;
  return 0;
}
```

```
alf
bob
chas
chas
dave
ed
```

To obtain lower and upper bounds information, use the following functions:

lower_bound   *iterator lower_bound (const Key& key_) const*
Return an iterator positioned at the first location that key_
could be inserted without violating the ordering criteria. For

example, if the elements are arranged in ascending order
using operator<, lower_bound() returns an iterator positioned
at the first element that is not less than key_. If no such
location is found, return an iterator positioned at end().

upper_bound   *iterator upper_bound (const Key& key_) const*
Return an iterator positioned at the last location that key_
could be inserted without violating the ordering criteria. For
example, if the elements are arranged in ascending order
using operator<, upper_bound() returns an iterator positioned
at the first element that is greater than key_. If no such
location is found return an iterator positioned at end().

In the following example, a multiset is initialized to contain a collection of integers. lower_bound(3) returns an iterator positioned at the first instance of 3, and upper_bound(3) returns an iterator positioned at the first occurrence of 6.

Example <mset3.cpp>

```
#include <set.h>
#include <iostream.h>

int array [] = { 3, 6, 1, 2, 3, 2, 6, 7, 9 };

int main ()
{
   set<int, less<int> > s (array, array + 9);
   set<int, less<int> >::iterator i;
   // Return location of first element that is not less than 3
   i = s.lower_bound (3);
   cout << "lower bound = " << *i << endl;
   // Return location of first element that is greater than 3
   i = s.upper_bound (3);
   cout << "upper bound = " << *i << endl;
   return 0;
}
```

```
lower bound = 3
upper bound = 6
```

equal_range() allows you to conveniently obtain the lower bound and the upper bound in one fell swoop:

equal_range   *pair <const_iterator, const_iterator>*
equal_range (const Key& value_) const
Return a pair of iterators whose first element is equal to
lower_bound() and whose second element is equal to
upper_bound().

Example <mset4.cpp>

```cpp
#include <set.h>
#include <iostream.h>

int array [] = { 3, 6, 1, 2, 3, 2, 6, 7, 9 };

int main ()
{
   typedef multiset<int, less<int> > mset;
   mset s (array, array + 9);
   pair<mset::const_iterator, mset::const_iterator> p =
      s.equal_range (3);
   cout << "lower bound = " << *(p.first) << endl;
   cout << "upper bound = " << *(p.second) << endl;
   return 0;
}
```

lower bound = 3
upper bound = 6

There may be times that you wish to instantiate many multisets that vary only on their sort criteria. If you supply a different function object type with each instantiation, you will cause the template code to be recompiled for each separate type, potentially creating a large amount of code. An alternative technique is to use a function object that contains a pointer to the actual function to be used and then supply the actual function object to be used via the following constructor:

Constructor   *multiset (const Compare& compare_)*
                     Construct myself to be an empty multiset that orders
                     elements using the compare function compare_.

The following example uses a `pointer_to_binary_function` object to allow a single multiset type to sort integers both in ascending and descending order.

Example <mset5.cpp>

```cpp
#include <set.h>
#include <iostream.h>

bool less_than (int a_, int b_)
{
   return a_ < b_;
}

bool greater_than (int a_, int b_)
{
   return a_ > b_;
}

int array [] = { 3, 6, 1, 9 };
```

```
int main ()
{
   typedef pointer_to_binary_function<int, int, bool> fn_type;
   typedef multiset<int, fn_type> mset;
   fn_type f (less_than); // Use less_than function.
   mset s1 (array, array + 4, f);
   mset::const_iterator i = s1.begin ();
   cout << "Using less_than:" << endl;
   while (i != s1.end ())
      cout << *i++ << endl;
   fn_type g (greater_than); // Use greater_than function.
   mset s2 (array, array + 4, g);
   i = s2.begin ();
   cout << "Using greater_than" << endl;
   while (i != s2.end ())
      cout << *i++ << endl;
   return 0;
}
```

```
Using less_than:
1
3
6
9

Using greater_than:
9
6
3
1
```

To obtain a copy of a multiset's comparitor object, use either of the following functions:

key_comp   *Compare key_comp () const*
                      Return my comparison object.

value_comp   *Compare value_comp () const*
                      Return my comparison object.

set

Overview
A set is identical in behavior to a multiset except that it does not allow an item to be inserted if a matching item is already present.

Iterator Type
A set has a bidirectional iterator.

Implementation
A set is implemented as a red-black tree whose nodes hold the set's items.

Insertion Notes

Insertion does not affect iterators or references. Insertion of a single element causes exactly one call to the copy constructor. When inserting multiple elements, the number of calls to the copy constructor is exactly equal to the number of elements inserted.

Erasure Notes

Erasure only invalidates the iterators and references to the erased elements. Erasing a single element causes a single call to the destructor. Erasing a range causes a number of calls to the destructor exactly equal to the size of the range.

Common Uses

Sets are useful when fast associate lookup is important, when index-based lookup is unnecessary, and when duplicates are not allowed.

Description

The main difference between a set and a multiset is that a set cannot contain matching items; attempts to add a duplicate item are ignored. This is illustrated by the following example, which attempts to add the number 42 twice into a set.

Example <set1.cpp>

```
#include <set.h>
#include <iostream.h>

int main ()
{
  // Construct an empty set.
  // Order its elements in ascending order.
  set<int, less<int> > s;
  cout << "count (42) = " << s.count (42) << endl;
  s.insert (42);
  cout << "count (42) = " << s.count (42) << endl;
  s.insert (42);
  cout << "count (42) = " << s.count (42) << endl;
  count = s.erase (42);
  cout << count << " elements erased" << endl;
  return 0;
}
```

```
count(42) = 0
count(42) = 1
count(42) = 1
1 elements erased
```

A set's insert() function is slightly different from that of a multiset: it returns a pair object which contains the result of the insert operation:

insert   *pair <const_iterator, bool> insert (const Key& key_)*
                          If I don't contain an element that matches key_, insert a copy
                          of key_ and return a pair whose first element is an iterator
                          positioned at the new element and whose second element is
                          true. If I already contain an element that matches key_,
                          return a pair whose first element is an iterator positioned at
                          the existing element and whose second element is false.

In the following example, the first insertion was successful but the second insertion failed:

Example <set2.cpp>

```
#include <set.h>
#include <iostream.h>

int main ()
{
  set<int, less<int> > s;
  pair<set<int, less<int> >::const_iterator, bool> p;

  p = s.insert (42); // Add element for the first time.
  if (p.second)
    cout << "Inserted new element " << *(p.first) << endl;
  else
    cout << "Existing element = " << *(p.first) << endl;

  p = s.insert (42); // Attempt to add duplicate.
  if (p.second)
    cout << "Inserted new element " << *(p.first) << endl;
  else
    cout << "Existing element = " << *(p.first) << endl;
  return 0;
}

Inserted new element 42
Existing element = 42
```

multimap

Overview
A multimap is an associative container that manages a set of ordered key/value pairs. The pairs are ordered by key, based on a user-supplied comparitor function. Care must be taken to ensure that items implement the operations that are required by the comparitor. For example, the `less` function object requires items to be comparable using `operator<`. More than one value may be associated with a particular key. A multimap's underlying data structure allows you to very efficiently find all of the values associated with a particular key.

Iterator Type
A multimap has a bidirectional iterator.

Implementation
A multimap is implemented using a red-black binary search tree where each node holds a `pair<const Key,Value>` object. The comparitor object is used to order the pairs based only on their keys. Note that some compilers do not compile `const` templates correctly; in these cases, a multimap's tree is defined to hold `pair<Key,Value>` objects.

Insertion Notes
Insertion does not affect iterators or references. Insertion of a single element causes exactly one call to the copy constructor. When inserting multiple elements, the number of calls to the copy constructor is exactly equal to the number of elements inserted.

Erasure Notes
Erasure only invalidates the iterators and references to the erased elements. Erasing a single element causes a single call to the destructor. Erasing a range causes a number of calls to the destructor exactly equal to the size of the range.

Common Uses
A multimap is useful for implementing a collection of one-to-many mappings.

Description
Here is a list of the most basic multimap operations that allow you to insert, find, count, and erase key/value pairs:

Constructor	*multimap ()* Construct myself to be an empty multimap that orders its keys using the compare function specified when my template was instantiated.
count	*size_type count (const Key& key_) const* Return the number of key/value pairs whose key matches key_.
erase	*size_type erase (const Key& key_)* Erase all key/value pairs whose key matches key_ and return the number of pairs that were erased.
find	*iterator find (const Key& key_)* If I contain a key/value pair whose key matches key_, return an iterator positioned at the key/value pair, otherwise return an iterator positioned at end().

insert   *iterator insert (const value_type& pair_)*
                        Insert a copy of the key/value pair pair_ and return an
                        iterator positioned at the new key/value pair.

The following example uses a multimap to associate two different values with the
letter 'X'. find() is used to locate the first pair whose key is equal to 'X', and
then all of the pairs are displayed from this point until the end is reached.

Example <mmap1.cpp>

```
#include <map.h>
#include <iostream.h>

int main ()
{
    typedef multimap<char, int, less<char> > mmap;
    mmap m;
    cout << "count ('X') = " << m.count ('X') << endl;
    m.insert (mmap::value_type ('X', 10));
    cout << "count ('X') = " << m.count ('X') << endl;
    m.insert (mmap::value_type ('X', 20));
    cout << "count ('X') = " << m.count ('X') << endl;
    m.insert_pair ('Y', 32);
    mmap::iterator i = m.find ('X'); // Find first match.
    while (i != m.end ()) // Loop until end is reached.
    {
        cout << (*i).first << " -> " << (*i).second << endl;
        i++;
    }
    int count = m.erase ('X');
    cout << "Erased " << count << " items" << endl;
    return 0;
}
```

```
count ('X') = 0
count ('X') = 1
count ('X') = 2
'X' -> 1
'X' -> 2
'Y' -> 32
Erased 2 items.
```

Like all other STL collections, a multimap defines a constructor that allows you
to initialize it with a sequence of values.

Constructor   *multimap (const value_type* first_, const value_type* last_)*
                        Construct myself to contain copies of the key/value pairs in
                        the range [first_, last_), using the compare function specified
                        when my template was instantiated.

Similarly, multimaps support the bounds operators that are common to all STL associative containers:

equal_range   *pair <iterator, iterator> equal_range (const Key& key_)*
Return a pair of iterators whose first element is equal to lower_bound() and whose second element is equal to upper_bound().

lower_bound   *iterator lower_bound (const Key& key_)*
Return an iterator positioned at the first location where a pair with key key_ could be inserted without violating the ordering criteria. If no such location is found, return an iterator positioned at end().

upper_bound   *iterator upper_bound (const Key& key_)*
Return an iterator positioned at the last location where a pair with key key_ could be inserted without violating the ordering criteria. If no such location is found, return an iterator positioned at end().

The following example illustrates the features that were just described, and has an analogous version in the section that describes multisets.

Example <mmap2.cpp>

```
#include <iostream.h>
#include <map.h>

typedef multimap<int, char, less<int> > mmap;
typedef pair<const int, char> value_type;

value_type p1 (3, 'c');
value_type p2 (6, 'f');
value_type p3 (1, 'a');
value_type p4 (2, 'b');
value_type p5 (3, 'x');
value_type p6 (6, 'f');

value_type array [] =
  {
    p1,
    p2,
    p3,
    p4,
    p5,
    p6
  };

int main ()
{
  mmap m (array, array+7);
  mmap::iterator i;
```

```
      // Return location of first element that is not less than 3
      i = m.lower_bound (3);
      cout << "lower bound:" << endl;
      cout << (*i).first << " -> " << (*i).second << endl;
      // Return location of first element that is greater than 3
      i = m.upper_bound (3);
      cout << "upper bound:" << endl;
      cout << (*i).first << " -> " << (*i).second << endl;
        return 0;
  }
```

```
  lower bound:
  3 -> c
  upper bound:
  6 -> f
```

In a manner similar to sets, multimaps allow you to specify an instance of their comparitor object during construction:

Constructor   *multimap (const Compare& compare_)*
                     Construct myself to be an empty multimap that orders its
                     keys using the compare function compare_.

Constructor   *multimap (const value_type* first_, const value_type* last_,*
                     const Compare& compare_)
                     Construct myself to contain copies of the key/value pairs in
                     the range [first_, last_), using compare_ to order my keys.

Likewise, there are a couple of functions for obtaining copies of the container's comparitor objects:

key_comp   *Compare key_comp () const*
                     Return the comparison object used for comparing my keys.

value_comp   *map_compare<Key,Value,Compare> value_comp () const*
                     Return the comparison object using for comparing my
                     key/value pairs.

map

Overview
A map is identical in behavior to a multimap except that it does not allow a pair
to be inserted if a pair with a matching key is already present.

Iterator Type
A map has a bidirectional iterator.

Implementation

A map is implemented using a red-black binary search tree where each node holds a `pair<const Key,Value>` object. The comparitor object is used to order the pairs based only on their keys. Note that some compilers do not compile `const` templates correctly; in these cases, a map's tree is defined to hold `pair<Key,Value>` objects.

Insertion Notes

Insertion does not affect iterators or references. Insertion of a single element causes exactly one call to the copy constructor. When inserting multiple elements, the number of calls to the copy constructor is exactly equal to the number of elements inserted.

Erasure Notes

Erasure only invalidates the iterators and references to the erased elements. Erasing a single element causes a single call to the destructor. Erasing a range causes a number of calls to the destructor exactly equal to the size of the range.

Common Uses

A map is useful for implementing a collection of one-to-one mappings.

Description

From an interface standpoint, there are two main differences between a multimap and a map. First of all, the `insert()` operator returns a paired result rather than a simple iterator:

insert   *pair <iterator, bool> insert (const value_type& pair_)*
                      If I don't contain a key/value pair whose key matches that of
                      pair_, insert a copy of pair_ and return a pair whose first
                      element is an iterator positioned at the new key/value pair
                      and whose second element is true. If I already contain a
                      key/value pair whose key matches that of pair_, return a pair
                      whose first element is an iterator positioned at the existing
                      key/value pair and whose second element is false.

Secondly, a [] operator exists to conveniently access and modify a key's associated value. It's important to note in the following descriptions that the [] operator will add an association to a key if one doesn't already exist.

[]   *Value& operator [] (const Key& key_)*
                      If no value is associated with key_, associate key_ with a
                      default-constructed value and return a reference to this new
                      value, otherwise return a reference to the value already associated with key_.

The following example illustrates both of these functions:

Example <map1.cpp>

```
#include <map.h>
#include <iostream.h>

int main ()
{
   typedef map<char, int, less<char> > maptype;
   maptype m; // Construct an empty map.
   // Store mappings between roman numerals and decimals.
   m['l'] = 50;
   m['x'] = 20; // Deliberate mistake.
   m['v'] = 5;
   m['i'] = 1;
   cout << "m['x'] = " << m['x'] << endl;
   m['x'] = 10; // Correct mistake.
   cout << "m['x'] = " << m['x'] << endl;
   // Note that in the next list, a default value (0) is added.
   cout << "m['z'] = " << m['z'] << endl;
   cout << "m.count ('z') = " << m.count ('z') << endl;
   pair<maptype::iterator, bool> p; // For result of insert().
   p = m.insert (maptype::value_type ('c', 100));
   if (p.second)
      cout << "First insertion successful" << endl;
   p = m.insert (maptype::value_type ('c', 100));
   if (p.second)
      cout << "Second insertion successful" << endl;
   else
      cout << "Existing pair " << (*(p.first)).first
           << " -> " << (*(p.first)).second << endl;
   return 0;
}
```

```
m['x'] = 20
m['x'] = 10
m['z'] = 0
m.count ('z') = 1
First insertion successful
Existing pair c -> 100
```

stack

Overview
A stack is an adapter that allows you to use any container that supports push_back() and pop_back() as a first-in, last-out data structure.

Iterator Type
Since adapters do not support iteration, a stack has no associated iterator.

Implementation
stack is implemented as a class comprised wholly of inline functions that convert

push() and pop() messages into push_back() and pop_back() messages. Although a stack may use any kind of sequential container as its underlying data structure, a deque or vector yields the best performance.

Common Uses
Stacks are useful for implementing strictly first-in, last-out data structures where direct indexed access to the items should not be performed.

Description
In addition to the common set of collection operations, stacks offer the following specialized behaviors:

push   *void push (const T& value_)*
                    Push a copy of value_.

pop   *void pop ()*
                    Erase my top element.

top   *T& top ()*
                    Return a reference to my top element.

Note that pop() does not return a value.

Here's an example of a stack that uses a deque as its underlying data structure:

Example <stack1.cpp>

```
#include <deque.h>
#include <stack.h>
#include <iostream.h>

int main ()
{
  stack<deque<int> > s;
  s.push (42);
  s.push (101);
  s.push (69);
  while (!s.empty ())
  {
    cout << s.top () << endl;
    s.pop ();
  }
  return 0;
}

69
101
42
```

Here's the same program, this time using a list as the underlying data structure:

Example <stack2.cpp>

```
#include <list.h>
#include <stack.h>
#include <iostream.h>

int main ()
{
  stack<list<int> > s;
  s.push (42);
  s.push (101);
  s.push (69);
  while (!s.empty ())
  {
    cout << s.top () << endl;
    s.pop ();
  }
  return 0;
}

69
101
42
```

queue

Overview
A queue is an adapter that allows you to use any container that supports push_back() and pop_front() as a first-in, first-out data structure.

Iterator Type
Since adapters do not support iteration, a queue has no associated iterator.

Implementation
queue is implemented as a class comprised wholly of inline functions that convert push() and pop() messages into push_back() and pop_front() messages. The only STL containers that support these functions are list and deque. Of these two containers, deque yields a much better performance.

Common Uses
queues are useful for implementing strictly first-in, first-out data structures where direct indexed access to the items should not be performed.

Description
queue does not introduce any new functions, but its implementation of pop() operates differently from that of stack. Here's an example that illustrates the first-in, first-out nature of a queue:

Example <queue1.cpp>

```
#include <list.h>
#include <queue.h>
#include <iostream.h>

int main ()
{
  queue<list<int> > q;
  q.push (42);
  q.push (101);
  q.push (69);
  while (!q.empty ())
  {
    cout << q.front () << endl;
    q.pop ();
  }
  return 0;
}

42
101
69
```

priority_queue

Overview
A priority_queue is an adapter that allows you to use any sequential container that has a random access iterator to maintain a sorted collection of items. It allows you to specify a comparator that is used to sort the items.

Iterator Type
Since adapters do not support iteration, a priority_queue has no associated iterator.

Implementation
priority_queue is implemented as a class comprised wholly of inline functions that convert push() and pop() messages into calls to push_back(), pop_back(), and heap algorithms. The only sequential containers that have random access iterators and support these functions are vector and deque. Of these two containers, deque generally yields a better performance.

Common Uses
priority_queues are useful for implementing sorted collections.

Description
priority_queue does not introduce any new functions, but its implementation of pop() operates differently from those of stack and queue. Here's an example that uses a priority_queue to order a set of integers into ascending order:

Example <pqueue1.cpp>

```
#include <deque.h>
#include <queue.h>
#include <functional.h>
#include <iostream.h>

int main ()
{
  priority_queue<deque<int>, less<int> > q;
  q.push (42);
  q.push (101);
  q.push (69);
  while (!q.empty ())
  {
    cout << q.top () << endl;
    q.pop ();
  }
  return 0;
}
```

```
101
69
42
```

Here's another example that uses a priority_queue to order a set of strings in descending order:

Example <pqueue2.cpp>

```
#include <iostream.h>
#include <deque.h>
#include <queue.h>

int main ()
{
  priority_queue<deque<char*>, greater_s> q;
  q.push ("cat");
  q.push ("dog");
  q.push ("ape");
  while (!q.empty ())
  {
    cout << q.top () << endl;
    q.pop ();
  }
  return 0;
}
```

```
ape
cat
dog
```

Checklist

The main points made by this chapter were:

- There are three sequential containers: vector, deque, and list.
- There are four associative containers: multiset, set, multimap, and map.
- There are three adapters: stack, queue, and priority_queue.

Quiz

1. What kind of container is ideal for storing 1:many relationships? [*easy*]
2. Is a vector or a deque better for random index-based access? [*medium*]
3. What kind of container is ideal for FILO (first-in, last-out)? [*easy*]

Exercises

1. List the algorithms and containers that could be used to create a game of Poker. [*easy*]
2. Implement a game of Poker using STL. [*medium*]
3. What container is ideal for maintaining the relationship between a company and its employees? [*easy*]
4. What container is ideal for maintaining the relationship between a car and its tires? [*easy*]

Strings

Motivation

Although it's not part of STL, the ANSI string is an integral and common part of the standard C++ library. An understanding of its operation is therefore a fundamental and necessary part of every C++ programmer's skill set.

Objectives

This chapter contrasts the design of the ANSI string against other string implementations and then describes its most common functions.

Introduction

The ANSI string is called `basic_string` and is unlike most other commercially available strings due to two features:

1. It is templatized. The first template parameter allows you to specify the type of element that the string is comprised of. For example, you may instantiate a `basic_string` of `char` to emulate a traditional "C-like" string, or a `basic_string` of `wchar_t` (wide characters) to emulate an international string.

2. The second template parameter allows you to specify the string's traits. A trait class is an auxiliary "helper" class that tells the `basic_string` class how to assign and compare elements, calculate the length of strings, and what value should be used to denote "end-of-string". This approach allows you to vary specific low-level characteristics of each string type without having to alter the code for `basic_string`.

Although these features allow you to create a wide variety of different strings, most C++ programs only require a couple of common string types. The ANSI standard therefore includes the following typedefs that handle most situations:

```
typedef basic_string< char, string_char_traits_char >
    string; // Regular string of characters.

typedef basic_string< wchar_t, string_char_traits< wchar_t > >
    wstring; // Regular string of wide characters.
```

`string_char_traits` is the standard template class that contains the default behaviors for a string's traits. `string_char_traits_char` is derived from this class and contains specialized behaviors for a string of regular chars .

For simplicity, this chapter uses a string to demonstrate the basic_string interface. Note, however, that since all string variations are created from the same template, the examples apply equally well to other string variations such as wstring. The first example illustrates how a string may be created and how its individual elements may be accessed:

Example <string1.cpp>

```cpp
#include <string.h>
#include <iostream.h>

int
main()
  {
  string str = "Lotus"; // Simple initialization.
  cout << "str = " << str << endl;
  size_t size = str.size(); // Obtain size of string.
  cout << "str.size() = " << size << endl;
  for ( size_t i = 0; i < size; i++ ) // Display characters.
    cout << "str[ " << i << " ] = " << str[ i ] << endl;
  for ( size_t j = 0; j < size; j++ ) // Assignment to elements.
    str[ j ] = 'x';
  cout << "str = " << str << endl;
  return 0;
  }
```

```
str = Lotus
str.size() = 5
str[ 0 ] = L
str[ 1 ] = o
str[ 2 ] = t
str[ 3 ] = u
str[ 4 ] = s
str = xxxxx
```

Strings may be compared using either the familiar relational operators or using the compare() function:

Example <string2.cpp>

```cpp
#include <string.h>
#include <iostream.h>

int
main()
  {
  string str1 = "adam";
  string str2 = "zacharia";
  cout << str1 << " > " << str2 << " = " << (str1 > str2) <<
  endl;
  int compare = str1.compare( str2 ); // Similar to strcmp().
```

```
      cout << "compare = " << compare << endl;
      cout << str2 << " > " << str1 << " = " << (str2 > str1) <<
      endl;
      compare = str2.compare( str1 );
      cout << "compare = " << compare << endl;
      cout << str1 << " > " << str1 << " = " << (str1 > str1) <<
      endl;
      compare = str1.compare( str1 );
      cout << "compare = " << compare << endl;
      cout << "'adam' > " << str2 << " = " << ("adam" > str2) <<
      endl;
      return 0;
      }
```

```
  adam > zacharia = 0
  compare = -1
  zacharia > adam = 1
  compare = 1
  adam > adam = 0
  compare = 0
  'adam' > zacharia = 0
```

Strings may be appended, inserted, located, removed, and replaced. The following example contains a single example of each of these operations.

Example <string3.cpp>

```
  #include <string.h>
  #include <iostream.h>

  int
  main()
    {
    string str = "hello";
    cout << "str = " << str << endl;
    str += " old chap"; // Append a string.
    cout << "str = " << str << endl;
    str.insert( 6, "there " ); // Insert before char at index 6.
    cout << "str = " << str << endl;
    size_t i = str.find( "old chap" ); // Get index of string.
    cout << "Found 'old chap' at index " << i << endl;
    str.remove( i, 8 ); // Remove eight chars starting at index i.
    cout << "str = " << str << endl;
    str.replace( 6, 5, "goodbye" ); // Replace 5 chars at index 6.
    cout << "str = " << str << endl;
    return 0;
    }
```

```
  str = hello
  str = hello old chap
  str = hello there old chap
  Found 'old chap' at index 12
  str = hello there
  str = hello goodbye
```

The string class does not contain an implicit const char* conversion operator. If you wish to use a string where a const char* is expected, use c_str(), which returns a pointer to a null-terminated array of the string's data.

Example <string4.cpp>

```
#include <string.h>
#include <iostream.h>

int
main()
  {
  string str = "hello";
  const char* c_str = str.c_str(); // View as a "C" string.
  // Call "C" function to get its length.
  int len = strlen( c_str ); // Call "C" function to get its
  length.
  for ( size_t i = 0; i < len; i++) // Display all elements.
    cout << "c_str[ " << i << " ] = " << c_str[i] << endl;
  return 0;
  }
```

```
c_str[ 0 ] = h
c_str[ 1 ] = e
c_str[ 2 ] = l
c_str[ 3 ] = l
c_str[ 4 ] = o
```

By default, a string's storage space is increased on demand. If you know how big a string will grow ahead of time, you may use reserve() to pre-allocate storage space for the string. This prevents unnecessary re-allocation of the string's storage as it grows towards its final size. If you wish to simply expand or truncate a string, use resize() instead.

In the following example, note that although the string grows to eight characters and ends with the substring "dog," the string is only printed up to its first null.

Example <string5.cpp>

```
#include <string.h>
#include <iostream.h>

int
main()
  {
  string str = "catty";
  cout << "str = " << str << ", size = " << str.size() << endl;
  str.resize( 3 ); // Truncate to 3 chars.
  cout << "str = " << str << ", size = " << str.size() << endl;
  str.resize( 5 ); // Expand to 5 chars, padding with nulls.
  str += "dog"; // 2 nulls remain between "cat" and "dog".
  cout << "str = " << str << ", size = " << str.size() << endl;
  str.reserve( 100 ); // Reserve 100 chars for future growth.
  cout << "str = " << str << ", size = " << str.size() << endl;
```

```
    return 0;
    }
```

```
str = catty, size = 5
str = cat, size = 3
str = cat, size = 8
str = cat, size = 8
```

For compatibility with the Standard Template Library (STL), a string allows you to obtain an iterator to an extremity using begin() or end(). This interface allows you to apply any of the standard STL algorithms to a string, such as sort() and reverse(). For a complete description of iterators, consult the "Iterators" chapter of this book. The following example illustrates the use of iterators, reverse iterators, and a couple of STL algorithms:

Example <string6.cpp>

```cpp
#include <string.h>
#include <algorithm.h> // For STL algorithms.
#include <iostream.h>

int
main()
  {
  os_string str = "the quick brown fox";
  os_string::iterator i;
  cout << "iterate forwards = ";
  for ( i = str.begin(); i != str.end(); i++ )
    cout << *i;
  cout << endl;
  cout << "reversed = ";
  reverse( str.begin(), str.end() ); // Reverse the string.
  cout << str << endl;
  cout << "sorted = ";
  sort( str.begin(), str.end() ); // Sort the string.
  cout << str << endl;
  return 0;
  }
```

```
iterate forwards = the quick brown fox
reversed = xof nworb kciuq eht
sorted =      bcefhiknooqrtuwx
```

Checklist

The main points made by this chapter were:

- The ANSI string is templatized to accomodate a variety of element types.
- A trait encapsulates special processing associated with a particular element type.
- The ANSI string defines iterators for compatibility with STL algorithms.
- c_str() allows you to obtain a null-terminated version of an ANSI string.

Quiz

1. What is the difference between `reserve()` and `resize()`? [*easy*]

Exercises

1. Would it make sense to create a basic_string of int? [*medium*]
2. What are the differences between traits for `chars` and `wchar_ts`? [*hard*]
3. What is the type of a string's iterator? [*easy*]
4. The ANSI string interface does not support operations such as upper_case(). Why not? [*medium*]
5. How could you add a function like `upper_case()` and stay within the STL philosophy? [*medium*]

STL in a Multi-threaded Environment

Although a multi-threaded environment allows powerful programs to be written that maximize concurrency, it also requires a greater discipline from developers. For example, most objects are not thread-aware — they are not written with multi-threading in mind. If two threads of control enter the same object and the object is not thread-aware, its internal data structures can easily be corrupted. The ANSI STL document does not specify how its containers and algorithms behave in multi-threaded situations. The next few sections describe some of the possible techniques for making STL containers thread-safe.

Let's take a look at a common situation that involves producers and consumers. Each producer has its own thread and adds items to a `vector` using `push_front()`. Each consumer has its own thread and removes items from the `vector` using `pop_back()`. A non-thread aware version of `vector<T>::push_back()` has inherent problems in a multi-threaded environment:

```
void push_back (const_reference value_)
{
   if (finish != end_of_storage) // Is some storage left?
     construct (finish++, value_); // Use existing storage.
   else
     insert_aux (end (), value_); // Insert some more storage.
}
```

If two producers evaluate the first line concurrently when only one item of storage is left, both producers will assume that storage is left. The result will be a memory overrun, which is clearly a problem.

One solution to this problem is to add an object called a *mutex* around the critical section. A mutex can only be locked by one thread at a time, thus ensuring that the critical section is only executed by one thread at any moment in time. Here's a "thread-aware" version of `push_back()`:

```
template <class T>
class vector
{
   public:
     void push_back (const T& value_)
     {
       lock.obtain(); // Lock critical region.
       if (finish != end_of_storage)
          construct (finish++, value_);
       else
```

```
              insert_aux (end (), value_);
          lock.release(); // Unlock critical region.
      }

    private:
      mutex lock; // For locking critical sections.
  };
```

This approach is invasive; it requires that special synchronization code is inserted into the `vector` class. There are at least two disadvantages of this strategy:

1. It's very tedious and error-prone.

2. Even in a multi-threaded environment, there are many situations in which you know that an object will not be entered by more than one thread at a time. If every instance of the object contains the multi-thread protection, some objects will incur overhead that they do not require.

An alternative approach that doesn't require the standard vector class to be modified is to "wrap" the standard vector in a separate class, as follows:

```
template <class T>
class mt_vector
{
   public:
     void push_back (const T& value_)
     {
       lock.obtain ();
       v.push_back (value_);
       lock.release ();
     }

   private:
     mutex lock; // For locking critical sections.
     vector <T> v; // Instance of standard class.
};
```

One problem with both of the previous approaches is that there are many situations where multi-thread safe operations must occur over more than one function class. That is, *transaction*-level locking is required instead of just *function*-level locking.

An alternative approach uses a *monitor* to read- or write-lock an object for an arbitrary period of time, without having to modify the object's class in any way. A monitor is an object that is specially designed to moderate coordinated access to another object in a multi-threaded environment.

A `monitor` class can be built using standard computer science semaphore theory, and has the following interface specifications:

```
template <class T>
class monitor
{
  public:
    // Construct myself to monitor object_.
    monitor (T& object_);

    // Return a reference to the object that I monitor.
    T& operator * ();

    // Return a reference to the object that I monitor.
    const T& operator * () const;

    // Return a pointer to the object that I monitor.
    T* operator -> ();

    // Return a pointer to the object that I monitor.
    const T* operator -> () const;

    // Block until a read lock is obtained.
    void read_lock () const;

    // Release a read lock.
    void read_unlock () const;

    // Block until a write lock is obtained.
    void write_lock ();

    // Release a write lock.
    void write_unlock ();

  protected:
    T& my_object; // Reference to the object that I monitor.
};
```

To lock an object using a monitor, the following steps would be performed:

1. Define a monitor with the type of the object to be locked as its template parameter and the object to be locked as its single constructor argument.

2. To obtain a write lock on the monitor's object, use write_lock(). Only one thread may have a write lock at any given time. To release the write lock, use write_unlock().

3. To obtain a read lock on the monitor's object, use read_lock(). Any number of threads may have a read lock at any given time. To release a read lock, use read_unlock().

4. To access the monitor's object, use either the * or the -> operator. The * operator returns a reference to the object, whereas the -> operator returns a pointer to the object.

The following example shows how some writers and reader could coordinate their access to a shared vector using a monitor object:

```
vector <int> v; // Shared vector.
monitor< vector <int> > mt_v (v); // Monitor the shared vector.



. . .
// A writer executes the following piece of code in its own
// thread.
mt_v.write_lock (); // Obtain a write lock on the shared vector.
mt_v->push_back (42); // Add an element.
mt_v->push_back (21); // Add an element.
sort (mt_v->begin (), mt_v->end () ); // Sort the vector.
my_v.write_unlock (); // Release the write lock.
. . .



. . .
// A reader executes the following piece of code in its own
// thread.
mt_v.read_lock (); // Obtain a read lock on the shared vector.
// Read vector's size.
cout << "size = " << mt_v->size () << endl;
// Read empty status.
cout << "empty = " << mt_v->empty () << endl; //
my_v.read_unlock (); // Release the read lock.
. . .
```

At least one of the commercially available STL implementations includes a comprehensive set of monitor and synchronization classes[8].

---

[8] See the appendix for more details.

Allocators

In order to accomodate varying mechanisms for memory allocation, STL does not explicitly use the standard `new()` and `delete()` operators anywhere in the library. Instead, all STL containers use special objects called *allocators* to allocate and deallocate storage. The last template parameter of each STL container class specifies an Allocator class. The default value of this Allocator is the class `allocator`, which allocates storage space from the regular C++ heap. This may be replaced at instantation time by a different allocator class that allocates storage from shared memory, persistent storage, or some other medium.

Every allocator class has must support a standard interface that includes the following functions:

- `T* allocate( size_t n )`, which returns a pointer to a contiguous array of 'n' objects of type 'T'.

- `void deallocate( T* ptr )`, which deallocates the storage that was previously allocated at address 'ptr'.

The following example assumes that a custom allocator called `Shared Allocator` that adheres to the standard interface is declared in the header file `<shralloc.h>` . `SharedAllocator` obtains storage from shared memory instead of from the heap.

```
#include <vector.h>
#include <shralloc.h>
#include <iostream.h>

int main ()
{
  // Construct a vector that uses the default allocator class.
  vector<int> v1;
  v1.push_back( 4 ); // Storage for int comes from heap.

  // Construct a vector that uses the custom allocator class.
  vector<int, SharedAllocator> v2;
  v2.push_back( 4 ); // Storage for int comes from shared memory.

  return 0;
}
```

Further details of allocators are beyond the scope of this book.

Class Catalog

Class Catalog Introduction

This section contains a concise description of every STL class in alphabetical order. Every entry contains the following information:

- *A Description.* This description is a brief overview; for more information about the class and examples of its usage, consult its corresponding chapter.

- *A Declaration.* This lists the name of the header file that contains the declaration of the class, together with a declaration that shows the inheritance and template structure of the class (if any).

- *A list of constructors and destructors.* For convenience, these functions are grouped at the start of the member function list.

- *A list of member functions.* The class's public functions are presented in alphabetical order, starting with the operator functions. Inherited functions are not shown. Static and non-static functions are combined into the same list. If a function is virtual or static, a comment precedes the function signature that indicates these attributes.

back_insert_iterator , back_inserter

Description
A `back_insert_iterator` is an iterator that always inserts at the end of its associated container.

Declaration
```
#include <iterator.h>
template<Container>
class back_insert_iterator : public output_iterator
```

Adapter
```
template<class Container>
back_insert_iterator<Container>
back_inserter (Container& container_)
```

Constructor   *back_insert_iterator (Container& container_)*
Construct myself to be associated with container_.

=   *back_insert_iterator<Container>&*
                operator = (const value_type& value_)
                Insert a copy of value_ at the end of my associated container.

*   *back_insert_iterator<Container>& operator * ()*
                Return a reference to myself.

++   *back_insert_iterator<Container>& operator ++ ()*
                Return a reference to myself.

++   *back_insert_iterator<Container> operator ++ (int)*
                Return a copy of myself.

Example <binsert1.cpp>

```
#include <vector.h>
#include <iterator.h>
#include <iostream.h>

char* array [] = { "laurie", "jennifer", "leisa" };

int main ()
{
  vector<char*> names;
  copy (array, array + 3,
    back_insert_iterator<vector <char*> > (names));
  vector<char*>::iterator i;
  for (i = names.begin (); i != names.end (); i++)
    cout << *i << endl;
  return 0;
}
```

laurie
jennifer
leisa

Example <binsert2.cpp>

```
#include <vector.h>
#include <iterator.h>
#include <iostream.h>

char* array [] = { "laurie", "jennifer", "leisa" };

int main ()
{
  vector<char*> names;
  copy (array, array + 3, back_inserter (names));
  vector<char*>::iterator i;
  for (i = names.begin (); i != names.end (); i++)
    cout << *i << endl;
  return 0;
}
```

```
laurie
jennifer
leisa
```

binary_compose, compose2

Description

`binary_compose` is a unary function object that returns the result of executing its three operations in a specific sequence. Its associated adapter function `compose2` allows you to conveniently construct a `binary_compose` object directly from three functions.

Declaration

```
#include <functional.h>
template<class Operation1, class Operation2, class Operation3>
class binary_compose : public unary_function
  <Operation2::argument_type,Operation1::result_type>
```

Adapter

```
template <class Operation1, class Operation2, class Operation3>
binary_compose<Operation1, Operation2, Operation3>
compose2
(
  const Operation1& op1,
  const Operation2& op2,
  const Operation3& op3
)
```

Constructor   *binary_compose (const Operation1& op1_, const Operation2& op2_, const Operation3& op3)*
Construct myself with associated operators op1_, op2_, and op3_.

()   *Operation1::result_type operator ()*
(const Operation2::argument_type& x_) const
Return op1_ (op2_ (x_), op3_ (x_)).

Example <bcompos1.cpp>

```
#include <iostream.h>
#include <functional.h>

struct odd : public unary_function<int, bool>
{
  odd () {}
  bool operator () (int n_) const { return (n_ % 2) == 1; }
};

struct positive : public unary_function<int, bool>
{
```

```
    positive () {}
    bool operator () (int n_) const { return n_ >= 0; }
};

int array [6] = { -2, -1, 0, 1, 2, 3 };

int main ()
{
  binary_compose<logical_and<bool>, odd, positive>
    b (logical_and<bool> (), odd (), positive ());
  int* p = find_if (array, array + 6, b);
  if (p != array + 6)
    cout << *p << " is odd and positive" << endl;
  return 0;
}
```

Example <bcompos2.cpp>

```
#include <iostream.h>
#include <functional.h>

struct odd : public unary_function<int, bool>
{
  odd () {}
  bool operator () (int n_) const { return (n_ % 2) == 1; }
};

struct positive : public unary_function<int, bool>
{
  positive () {}
  bool operator () (int n_) const { return n_ >= 0; }
};

int array [6] = { -2, -1 , 0, 1, 2, 3 };

int main ()
{
  int* p = find_if (array, array + 6,
    compose2 (logical_and<bool> (), odd (), positive ()));
  if (p != array + 6)
    cout << *p << " is odd and positive" << endl;
  return 0;
}
```

binary_function

Description

binary_function is the abstract base structure of all binary function objects. It defines three useful typedefs that are used by most of its derived classes.

Declaration

```
#include <functional.h>
```

```
template<class Arg1, class Arg2, class Result>
struct binary_function
{
   typedef Arg1 first_argument_type;
   typedef Arg2 second_argument_type;
   typedef Result result_type;
};
```

binary_negate, not2

Description

binary_negate is a binary function object that returns the logical negation of executing its binary predicate. Its associated adapter function not2
allows you to conveniently construct a binary_negate object directly from
a predicate.

Declaration

```
#include <functional.h>
template<class Predicate>
class binary_negate : public binary_function
   <Predicate::first_argument_type, Predicate::second_argument_type,
   bool>
```

Adapter

```
template<class Predicate>
binary_negate<Predicate> not2(const Predicate& pred_);
```

Constructor   *binary_negate (const Predicate& predicate_)*
                     Construct myself with predicate predicate_

()   *bool operator() (const first_argument_type& x_,*
                     const second_argument_type& y_) const
                     Return the result of predicate_ (x_, y_)

Example <bnegate1.cpp>

```
#include <functional.h>
#include <algorithm.h>
#include <iostream.h>

int array [4] = { 4, 9, 7, 1 };

int main ()
{
  sort (array, array + 4,
    binary_negate<greater<int> > (greater<int> ()));
  for (int i = 0; i < 4; i++)
    cout << array[i] << endl;
  return 0;
}
```

```
1
4
7
9
```

Example <bnegate2.cpp>

```cpp
#include <functional.h>
#include <algorithm.h>
#include <iostream.h>

int array [4] = { 4, 9, 7, 1 };

int main ()
{
  sort (array, array + 4, not2 (greater<int> ()));
  for (int i = 0; i < 4; i++)
    cout << array[i] << endl;
  return 0;
}
```

```
1
4
7
9
```

binder1st, bind1st

Description

binder1st is a unary function object that allows you to apply a binary function to an operand and a predefined value. Its associated adapter function
bind1st allows you to conveniently construct a binder1st object directly
from a function and a value. The reason that it's called binder1st is that the
operand is used as the 1st parameter to the binary function since the 2nd
parameter is supplied. Use binder2nd if you wish the operand to be used as
the 2nd parameter.

Declaration

```cpp
#include <functional.h>
template<class Operation>
class binder1st : public unary_function
  <Operation::second_argument_type,Operation::result_type>
```

Adapter

```cpp
template <class Operation, class T>
binder1st<Operation> bind1st (const Operation& op_, const T& x_)
```

Constructor *binder1st (const Operation& op_,*
                 const Operation::first_argument_type& value_)
                 Construct myself to be associated with operation op_ and value
                 value_.

()   *Operation::result_type operator* ()
                              (const Operation::first_argument_type& x_) const
                              Return op_ (value_, x_).

Example <bind1st.cpp>

```
#include <functional.h>
#include <algorithm.h>
#include <iostream.h>

int array [3] = { 1, 2, 3 };

int main ()
{
  int* p = remove_if (array, array + 3,
    binder1st<less<int> > (less<int> (), 2));
  for (int* i = array; i != p; i++)
    cout << *i << endl;
  return 0;
}
```

2
3

Example <bind1st2.cpp>

```
#include <functional.h>
#include <algorithm.h>
#include <iostream.h>

int array [3] = { 1, 2, 3 };

int main ()
{
  int* p = remove_if (array, array + 3, bind1st(less<int> (), 2));
  for (int* i = array; i != p; i++)
    cout << "** " << *i << endl;
  return 0;
}
```

2
3

binder2nd, bind2nd

Description

binder2nd is a unary function object that allows you to apply a binary function to a predefined value and another operand. Its associated adapter function bind2nd allows you to conveniently construct a binder2nd object directly from a function and a value. The reason that it's called binder2nd is

that the operand is used as the 2nd parameter to the binary function since the
1st parameter is supplied. Use `binder1st` if you wish the operand to be used
as the 1st parameter.

Declaration
```
#include <functional.h>
template<class Operation>
class binder2nd : public unary_function
   <Operation::first_argument_type,Operation::result_type>
```

Adapter
```
template <class Operation, class T>
binder2nd<Operation> bind2nd (const Operation& op_, const T& x_)
```

Constructor   *binder2nd (const Operation& op_, const*
Operation::second_argument_type& value_)
Construct myself to be associated with operation op_ and value
value_.

()   *Operation::result_type operator ()*
(const Operation::first_argument_type& x_) const
Return op_ (x_, value_).

Example <bind2nd1.cpp>

```
#include <functional.h>
#include <algorithm.h>
#include <iostream.h>

int array [3] = { 1, 2, 3 };

int main ()
{
  replace_if (array, array + 3,
    binder2nd<greater<int> > (greater<int> (), 2), 4);
  for (int i = 0; i < 3; i++)
    cout << array[i] << endl;
  return 0;
}

1
2
4
```

Example <bind2nd2.cpp>

```
#include <functional.h>
#include <algorithm.h>
#include <iostream.h>

int array [3] = { 1, 2, 3 };
```

```
int main ()
{
  replace_if (array, array + 3, bind2nd(greater<int> (), 2), 4);
  for (int i = 0; i < 3; i++)
    cout << array[i] << endl;
  return 0;
}
```

deque

Description
A deque is a sequential container that is optimized for fast indexed-based access and efficient insertion at either of its extremities.

Declaration
```
#include <deque.h>
template<class T>
class deque
```

Constructor   *deque ()*
                    Construct myself to be empty.

Constructor   *deque (size_type n_)*
                    Construct me to contain n_ elements set to their default value.

Constructor   *deque (size_type n_, const T& value_)*
                    Construct me to contain n_ copies of value_.

Constructor   *deque (const T* first_, const T* last_)*
                    Construct me to contain copies of all of the elements in the range [first_, last_).

Constructor   *deque (const deque<T>& deque_)*
                    Construct myself to be a copy of deque_.

Destructor   *~deque ()*
                    Destroy myself, erasing all of my items.

=   *deque<T>& operator = (const deque<T>& deque_)*
                    Replace my contents by a copy of deque_'s.

==   *bool operator == (const deque<T>& deque_) const*
                    Return true if I contain the same items in the same order as deque_.

<   *bool operator < (const deque<T>& deque_) const*
                    Return true if I'm lexigraphically less than deque_.

[]   *T& operator [] (int index_)*
                  Return a reference to my index_th element.

[]   *const T& operator [] (int index_) const*
                  Return a reference to my index_th element.

back   *T& back ()*
                  Return a reference to my last element.

back   *const T& back () const*
                  Return a reference to my last element.

begin   *iterator begin ()*
                  Return an iterator positioned at my first item.

begin   *const_iterator begin () const*
                  Return an iterator positioned at my first item.

empty   *bool empty () const*
                  Return true if I contain no entries.

end   *iterator end ()*
                  Return an iterator positioned immediately after my last item.

end   *const_iterator end () const*
                  Return an iterator positioned immediately after my last item.

erase   *void erase (iterator pos_)*
                  Erase the element at pos_.

erase   *void erase (iterator first_, iterator last_)*
                  Erase the elements in range [first_, last_)

front   *T& front ()*
                  Return a reference to my first element.

front   *const T& front () const*
                  Return a reference to my first element.

insert   *iterator insert (iterator pos, const T& value_)*
Insert value_ at pos_ and return an iterator pointing to the new element's position.

insert   *void insert (iterator pos_, size_type n_, const T& value_)*
Insert n_ copies of value_ at pos_.

insert   *void insert (iterator pos_, const T* first_, const T* last_)*
Insert copies of the elements in the range [first_, last_) at pos_.

max_size   *size_type max_size () const*
Return the maximum number of entries that I can contain.

push_back   *void push_back (const T& value_)*
Add value_ at my end.

push_front *void push_front (const T& value_)*
Insert a copy of value_ in front of my first element.

pop_back   *void pop_back ()*
Erase my last element.

pop_front   *void pop_front ()*
Erase my first element.

rbegin   *reverse_iterator rbegin ()*
Return a reverse iterator positioned at my last item.

rbegin   *const_reverse_iterator rbegin () const*
Return a reverse iterator positioned at my last item.

rend   *reverse_iterator rend ()*
Return a reverse_iterator positioned immediately before my first item.

rend   *const_reverse_iterator rend () const*
                        Return a reverse_iterator positioned immediately before my
                        first item.

size   *size_type size () const*
                        Return the number of entries that I contain.

swap   *void swap (deque<T>& deque_)*
                        Swap my contents with deque_'s.

divides

Description

divides is a binary function object that returns the result of dividing its two
operands.

Declaration
```
#include <functional.h>
template<class T>
struct divides : binary_function<T, T, T>
```

()   *T operator () (const T& x_, const T& y_) const*
                        Return x_ / y_.

Example <divides.cpp>

```
#include <functional.h>
#include <algorithm.h>
#include <iostream.h>

int input [3] = { 2, 3, 4 };

int main ()
{
   int result = accumulate (input, input + 4, 48, divides<int>
   ());
   cout << "result = " << result << endl;
   return 0;
}
```

result = 2

equal_to

Description

equal_to is a binary function object that returns true if its operands match using ==.

Declaration

```
#include <functional.h>
template<class T>
struct equal_to : binary_function<T, T, bool>
```

()   *bool operator () (const T& x_, const T& y_) const*
                   Return x_ == y_.

Example <equalto.cpp>

```
#include <functional.h>
#include <algorithm.h>
#include <iostream.h>

int input1 [4] = { 1, 7, 2, 2 };
int input2 [4] = { 1, 6, 2, 3 };

int main ()
{
   int output [4];
   transform (input1, input1 + 4, input2, output, equal_to<int>
   ());
   for (int i = 0; i < 4; i++)
     cout << output[i] << endl;
   return 0;
}

1
0
1
0
```

front_insert_iterator, front_inserter

Description

A front_insert_iterator is an iterator that always inserts an item at the front of its associated container.

Declaration

```
#include <iterator.h>
template<Container>
class front_insert_iterator : public output_iterator
```

Adapter

```
template<class Container>
```

```
front_insert_iterator<Container>
front_inserter (Container& container_)
```

Constructor   *front_insert_iterator (Container& container_)*
                   Construct myself to be associated with container_.

=   *front_insert_iterator<Container>&*
                   operator = (const value_type& value_)
                   Insert a copy of value_ at the front of my associated
                   container.

*   *front_insert_iterator<Container>& operator * ()*
                   Return a reference to myself.

++   *front_insert_iterator<Container>& operator ++ ()*
                   Return a reference to myself.

++   *front_insert_iterator<Container> operator ++ (int)*
                   Return a copy of myself.

Example <finsert1.cpp>

```cpp
#include <deque.h>
#include <iterator.h>
#include <iostream.h>

char* array [] = { "laurie", "jennifer", "leisa" };

int main ()
{
  deque<char*> names; // Can't use a vector.
  copy (array, array + 3,
    front_insert_iterator<deque <char*> > (names));
  deque<char*>::iterator i;
  for (i = names.begin (); i != names.end (); i++)
    cout << *i << endl;
  return 0;
}
```

leisa
jennifer
laurie

Example <finsert2.cpp>

```cpp
#include <deque.h>
#include <iterator.h>
#include <iostream.h>

char* array [] = { "laurie", "jennifer", "leisa" };
```

```
int main ()
{
  deque<char*> names;
  copy (array, array + 3, front_inserter (names));
  deque<char*>::iterator i;
  for (i = names.begin (); i != names.end (); i++)
    cout << *i << endl;
  return 0;
}
```

leisa
jennifer
laurie

greater

Description

greater is a binary function object that returns true if its first operand is greater than its second operand.

Declaration

```
#include <functional.h>
template<class T>
struct greater : binary_function<T, T, bool>
```

()   *bool operator () (const T& x_, const T& y_) const*
                        Return $x_ > y_$.

Example <greater.cpp>

```
#include <functional.h>
#include <algorithm.h>
#include <iostream.h>

int array [4] = { 3, 1, 4, 2 };

int main ()
{
  sort (array, array + 4, greater<int> ());
  for (int i = 0; i < 4; i++)
    cout << array[i] << endl;
  return 0;
}
```

4
3
2
1

greater_equal

Description

greater_equal is a binary function object that returns true if its first operand is greater than or equal to its second operand.

Declaration

```
#include <functional.h>
template<class T>
struct greater_equal : binary_function<T, T, bool>
```

()   *bool operator () (const T& x_, const T& y_) const*
                                Return x_ >= y_.

Example <greateq.cpp>

```
#include <functional.h>
#include <algorithm.h>
#include <iostream.h>

int array [4] = { 3, 1, 4, 2 };

int main ()
{
  sort (array, array + 4, greater_equal<int> ());
  for (int i = 0; i < 4; i++)
    cout << array[i] << endl;
  return 0;
}

4
3
2
1
```

insert_iterator, inserter

Description

An insert_iterator is an iterator that inserts items using an auxiliary iterator.

Declaration

```
#include <iterator.h>
template<Container>
class insert_iterator : public output_iterator
```

Adapter

```
template<class Container, class Iterator>
insert_iterator<Container>
inserter (Container& c_, Iterator iter_)
```

Constructor   *insert_iterator (Container& container_,Container::*
                    iterator iter_) :

=   *insert_iterator<Container>& operator = (const value_type&*
                    value_)
                    Insert a copy of value_ using the iterator iter_ that I was con-
                    structed with.

*   *insert_iterator<Container>& operator * ()*
                    Return a reference to myself.

++   *insert_iterator<Container>& operator ++ ()*
                    Return a reference to myself.

++   *insert_iterator<Container> operator ++ (int)*
                    Return a copy of myself.

Example <insert1.cpp>

```cpp
#include <deque.h>
#include <iterator.h>
#include <iostream.h>

char* array1 [] = { "laurie", "jennifer", "leisa" };
char* array2 [] = { "amanda", "saskia", "carrie" };

int main ()
{
  deque<char*> names (array1, array1 + 3);
  deque<char*>::iterator i = names.begin () + 2;
  copy (array2, array2 + 3,
    insert_iterator<deque <char*> > (names, i));
  deque<char*>::iterator j;
  for (j = names.begin (); j != names.end (); j++)
  cout << *j << endl;
  return 0;
}
```

laurie
jennifer
amanda
saskia
carrie
leisa

Example <insert2.cpp>

```cpp
#include <deque.h>
#include <iterator.h>
#include <iostream.h>

char* array1 [] = { "laurie", "jennifer", "leisa" };
```

```
   char* array2 [] = { "amanda", "saskia", "carrie" };

   int main ()
   {
     deque<char*> names (array1, array1 + 3);
     deque<char*>::iterator i = names.begin () + 2;
     copy (array2, array2 + 3, inserter (names, i));
     deque<char*>::iterator j;
     for (j = names.begin (); j != names.end (); j++)
       cout << *j << endl;
     return 0;
   }
```

laurie
jennifer
amanda
saskia
carrie
leisa

istream_iterator

Description

An `istream_iterator` is an iterator that reads items in a typesafe manner
from a standard input stream.

Declaration
```
#include <iterator.h>
template<class T, class Distance>
class istream_iterator : public input_iterator<T, Distance>
```

Constructor   *istream_iterator ()*
                  Construct myself to serve as a past-the-end value.

Constructor   *istream_iterator (istream& stream_)*
                  Construct myself to be associated with the input stream
                  stream_ and cache my first element.

*   *const T& operator * () const*
                  Return a reference to my currently cached input item.

++   *istream_iterator<T, Distance>& operator ++ ()*
                  Read and cache the next item in my input stream. Return a
                  reference to myself.

++   *istream_iterator<T, Distance> operator ++ (int)*
                  Read and cache the next item in my input stream. Return a
                  copy of my previous value.

==   *bool operator == (const istream_iterator<T, Distance>& iter_)*

> *const*
> Return true if I have the same stream and state as iter_.

!=   *bool operator != (const istream_iterator<T, Distance>& x_)*
                const
                Return true if I don't have the same stream or state
                as iter_.

Example <istmit1.cpp>

```cpp
#include <iterator.h>
#include <iostream.h>

int main ()
{
  char buffer [100];
  int i = 0;
  cin.unsetf(ios::skipws); // Disable white-space skipping.
  cout << "Please enter a string: ";
  istream_iterator<char, ptrdiff_t> s (cin);
  while (*s != '\n')
    buffer[i++] = *s++;
  buffer[i] = '\0'; // Null terminate buffer.
  cout << "read " << buffer << endl;  char buffer [100];
  return 0;
}
```

Please enter a string: truth
read truth

Example <istmit2.cpp>

```cpp
#include <iostream.h>
#include <fstream.h>
#include <vector.h>
#include <iterator.h>

typedef vector<char> Line;

void printLine (const Line* line_)
{
  vector<char>::const_iterator i;
  for (i = line_->begin (); i != line_->end (); i++)
    cout << *i;
  cout << endl;
}

int main ()
{
  Line buffer;
  vector<Line*> lines;
  ifstream s ("data.txt");
  s.unsetf (ios::skipws); // Disable white-space skipping.
  istream_iterator<char, ptrdiff_t> it1 (s); // Position at start.
```

```
    istream_iterator<char, ptrdiff_t> it2; // Past-the-end marker
    copy (it1, it2, back_inserter (buffer));
    Line::iterator i = buffer.begin ();
    Line::iterator p;
    while (i != buffer.end ())
    {
      p = find (i, buffer.end (), '\n');
      lines.push_back (new Line (i, p));
      i = ++p;
    }
    sort (lines.begin (), lines.end (), less_p<Line*> ());
    cout << "Read " << lines.size () << " lines" << endl;
    vector<Line*>::iterator j;
    for (j = lines.begin (); j != lines.end (); j++)
      printLine (*j);
    os_release (lines); // Release memory.
    return 0;
}
```

data.txt:

cat
dog
ape

read 3 lines
ape
cat
dog

less

Description

less is a binary function object that returns true if its first operand is less than its second operand.

Declaration
```
#include <functional.h>
template<class T>
struct less : binary_function<T, T, bool>
```

()   *bool operator () (const T& x_, const T& y_) const*
                      Return x_ < y_.

Example <less.cpp>

```
#include <functional.h>
#include <algorithm.h>
#include <iostream.h>

int array [4] = { 3, 1, 4, 2 };
```

```
int main ()
{
  sort (array, array + 4, less<int> ());
  for (int i = 0; i < 4; i++)
    cout << array[i] << endl;
  return 0;
}
```

1
2
3
4

less_equal

Description
less_equal is a binary function object that returns true if its first operand is less than or equal to its second operand.

Declaration
```
#include <functional.h>
template<class T>
struct less_equal : binary_function<T, T, bool>
```

()   *bool operator () (const T& x_, const T& y_) const*
                        Return x_ <= y_.

Example <lesseq.cpp>

```
#include <functional.h>
#include <algorithm.h>
#include <iostream.h>

int array [4] = { 3, 1, 4, 2 };

int main ()
{
  sort (array, array + 4, less_equal<int> ());
  for (int i = 0; i < 4; i++)
    cout << array[i] << endl;
  return 0;
}
```

1
2
3
4

list

Description
A list is a sequential container that is optimized for insertion and erasure at arbitrary points in its structure at the expense of giving up indexed-based access.

Declaration
```
#include <list.h>
template<class T>
class list
```

Constructor   *list ()*
Construct myself to be empty.

Constructor   *list (size_type n_)*
Construct me to contain n_ elements set to their default value.

Constructor   *list (size_type n_, const T& value_)*
Construct me to contain n_ copies of value_.

Constructor   *list (const T* first_, const T* last_)*
Construct me to contain copies of all of the elements in the range [first_, last_).

Constructor   *list (const list<T>& list_)*
Construct myself to be a copy of list_.

Destructor   *~list ()*
Destroy myself, erasing all of my items.

=   *list<T>& operator = (const list<T>& list_)*
Replace my contents by a copy of list_'s.

==   *bool operator == (const list<T>& list_) const*
Return true if I contain the same items in the same order as list_.

<   *bool operator < (const list<T>& list_) const*
Return true if I'm lexigraphically less than list_.

back   *T& back ()*
Return a reference to my last element.

back
const T& back () const
Return a reference to my last element.

begin
iterator begin ()
Return an iterator positioned at my first item.

begin
const_iterator begin () const
Return an iterator positioned at my first item.

empty
bool empty () const
Return true if I contain no entries.

end
iterator end ()
Return an iterator positioned immediately after my last item.

end
const_iterator end () const
Return an iterator positioned immediately after my last item.

erase
void erase (iterator pos_)
Erase the element at pos_.

erase
void erase (iterator first_, iterator last_)
Erase the elements in range [first_, last_)

front
T& front ()
Return a reference to my first element.

front
const T& front () const
Return a reference to my first element.

insert
iterator insert (iterator pos, const T& value_)
Insert a copy of value_ at pos_ and return an iterator pointing to the new element's position.

insert
void insert (iterator pos_, size_type n_, const T& value_)
Insert n_ copies of value_ at pos_.

insert
void insert (iterator pos_, const T first_, const T* last_)*
Insert copies of the elements in the range [first_, last_) at pos_.

max_size   *size_type max_size () const*
                      Return the maximum number of entries that I can
                      contain.

merge   *void merge (const list<T>& list_)*
                      Move the elements of list_ into myself and place them so that
                      all of my elements are sorted using the < operator. This opera-
                      tion assumes that both myself and list_ were already sorted
                      using operator <.

push_back   *void push_back (const T& value_)*
                      Add value_ at my end.

push_front   *void push_front (const T& value_)*
                      Insert a copy of value_ in front of my first element.

pop_back   *void pop_back ()*
                      Erase my last element.

pop_front   *void pop_front ()*
                      Erase my first element.

rbegin   *reverse_iterator rbegin ()*
                      Return a reverse iterator positioned at my last item.

rbegin   *const_reverse_iterator rbegin () const*
                      Return a reverse iterator positioned at my last item.

remove   *void remove (const T& value_)*
                      Erase all elements that match value_, using == to
                      perform the comparison.

rend   *reverse_iterator rend ()*
                      Return a reverse_iterator positioned immediately before my
                      first item.

rend   *const_reverse_iterator rend () const*
                      Return a reverse_iterator positioned immediately before my
                      first item.

reverse	*void reverse ()* Reverse the order of my elements. The time complexity is O(N).
size	*size_type size () const* Return the number of entries that I contain.
sort	*void sort ()* Sort my elements using operator <. The time complexity is O(NlogN).
splice	*void splice (iterator pos_, list<T>& list_)* Remove all of the elements in list_ and insert them at position pos_.
splice	*void splice (iterator to_, list<T>& list_, iterator from_)* Remove the element in list_ at position from_ and insert it at position to_.
splice	*void splice (iterator pos_, list<T>& list_, iterator first_, iterator last_)* Remove the elements from list_ in the range [first_, last_) and insert them at position pos_.
swap	*void swap (list<T>& list_)* Swap my contents with list_'s.
unique	*void unique ()* Replace all repeating sequences of a single element by a single occurrence of that element.

logical_and

Description
logical_and is a binary function object that returns true if both of its operands are true.

Declaration
```
#include <functional.h>
template<class T>
struct logical_and : binary_function<T, T, bool>
```

()   *bool operator () (const T& x_, const T& y_) const*
                     Return (x_ && y_).

Example <logicand.cpp>

```
#include <functional.h>
#include <algorithm.h>
#include <iostream.h>

int input1 [4] = { 1, 1, 0, 1 };
int input2 [4] = { 0, 1, 0, 0 };

int main ()
{
  int output [4];
  transform (input1, input1 + 4, input2, output,
    logical_and<bool> ());
  for (int i = 0; i < 4; i++)
    cout << output[i] << endl;
  return 0;
}

0
1
0
0
```

logical_not

Description

logical_not is a unary function object that returns true if its operand is zero (false).

Declaration

```
#include <functional.h>
template<class T>
struct logical_not : unary_function<T, bool>
```

()   *bool operator () (const T& x_) const*
                     Return !x_.

Example <logicnot.cpp>

```
#include <functional.h>
#include <algorithm.h>
#include <iostream.h>

int array [7] = { 1, 0, 0, 1, 1, 1, 1 };

int main ()
{
  int n = 0;
```

```
        count_if (array, array + 7, logical_not<int> (), n);
        cout << "count = " << n << endl;
        return 0;
    }
```

```
    count = 2
```

logical_or

Description

logical_or is a binary function object that returns true if either of its operands are true.

Declaration

```
    #include <functional.h>
    template<class T>
    struct logical_or : binary_function<T, T, bool>
```

()   *bool operator () (const T& x_, const T& y_) const*
                Return (x_ || y_).

Example <logicor.cpp>

```
    #include <functional.h>
    #include <algorithm.h>
    #include <iostream.h>

    int input1 [4] = { 1, 0, 0, 1 };
    int input2 [4] = { 0, 1, 0, 0 };

    int main ()
    {
        int output [4];
        transform (input1, input1 + 4, input2, output,
            logical_or<bool> ());
        for (int i = 0; i < 4; i++)
            cout << output[i] << endl;
        return 0;
    }
```

```
    1
    1
    0
    1
```

map

Description

A map is an associative container that manages a set of ordered key/value pairs. The pairs are ordered by key, based on a user-supplied comparitor func-

tion. Only one value may be associated with a particular key. A map's underlying data structure allows you to very efficiently find the value associated
with a particular key.

Declaration

```
#include <map.h>
template<class Key, class Value, class Compare>
class map
```

Constructor   *map ()*
Construct myself to be an empty map that orders its keys
using the compare function specified when my template was
instantiated.

Constructor   *map (const Compare& compare_)*
Construct myself to be an empty map that orders its keys using the compare function compare_.

Constructor   *map (const value_type* first_, const value_type* last_)*
Construct myself to contain copies of the key/value pairs in the
range [first_, last_), using the compare function specified when
my template was instantiated to order my keys.

Constructor   *map (const value_type* first_, const value_type* last_,*
*const Compare& compare_*
Construct myself to contain copies of the key/value pairs in the
range [first_, last_), using compare_ to order my keys.

Constructor   *map (const map<Key,Value,Compare>& map_)*
Construct myself to be a copy of map_.

Destructor   *~map ()*
Destroy myself, erasing all of my key/value pairs.

=   *map<Key,Value,Compare>&*
operator = (const map<Key,Value,Compare>& map_)
Replace my contents by a copy of map_'s.

==   *bool operator == (const map<Key,Value,Compare>& map_)*

map   137

const
Return true if I contain the same items in the same order as map_.

<
*bool operator < (const map<Key,Value,Compare>& map_)
const*
Return true if I'm lexigraphically less than map_.

[]
Value& operator [] (const Key& key_)
If no value is associated with key_, associate key_ with a default-constructed value and return a reference to this new value, otherwise return a reference to the value already associated with key_.

begin
iterator begin ()
Return an iterator positioned at my first key/value pair.

begin
const_iterator begin () const
Return an iterator positioned at my first key/value pair.

count
size_type count (const Key& key_) const
Return the number of key/value pairs that I contain whose key matches key_.

empty
bool empty () const
Return true if I contain no entries.

end
iterator end ()
Return an iterator positioned immediately after my last key/value pair.

end
const_iterator end () const
Return an iterator positioned immediately after my last key/value pair.

equal_range
pair <iterator, iterator> equal_range (const Key& key_)
Return a pair of iterators whose first element is equal to lower_bound() and whose second element is equal to upper_bound().

equal_range   *pair <const_iterator, const_iterator>*
                    equal_range (const Key& key_) const
                    Return a pair of iterators whose first element is equal to lower_bound() and whose second element is equal to upper_bound().

erase   *void erase (iterator pos_)*
                    Erase the key/value pair at pos_.

erase   *void erase (iterator first_, iterator last_)*
                    Erase the key/value pairs in range [first_, last_)

erase   *size_type erase (const Key& key_)*
                    Erase all key/value pairs whose key matches key_ and return the number of elements that were erased.

find   *iterator find (const Key& key_) const*
                    If I contain a key/value pair whose key matches key_, return an iterator positioned at the matching pair, otherwise return an iterator positioned at end().

insert   *pair <iterator, bool> insert (const value_type& pair_)*
                    If I don't contain a key/value pair whose key matches that of pair_, insert a copy of pair_ and return a pair whose first element is an iterator positioned at the new key/value pair and whose second element is true. If I already contain a key/value pair whose key matches that of pair_, return a pair whose first element is an iterator positioned at the existing key/value pair and whose second element is false.

insert   *void insert (const value_type* first_, const value_type* last_)*
                    Insert copies of the key/value pairs in the range [first_, last_).

insert   *iterator insert (iterator pos_, const value_type& pair_)*
                    Insert a copy of value_type if I don't already contain a key/value pair whose key that matches its key, using pos_ as a hint on where to start searching for the correct place to insert.

map   139

key_comp   *Compare key_comp () const*
                      Return the comparison object used to compare my keys.

lower_bound   *iterator lower_bound (const Key& key_)*
                      Return an iterator positioned at the first location where a pair
                      with key key_ could be inserted without violating the ordering
                      criteria. If no such location is found, return an iterator posi-
                      tioned at end().

lower_bound   *const_iterator lower_bound (const Key& key_) const*
                      Return an iterator positioned at the first location where a pair
                      with key key_ could be inserted without violating the ordering
                      criteria. If no such location is found, return an iterator posi-
                      tioned at end().

max_size   *size_type max_size () const*
                      Return the maximum number of key/value pairs that I can
                      contain.

rbegin   *reverse_iterator rbegin ()*
                      Return a reverse iterator positioned at my last key/value
                      pair.

rbegin   *const_reverse_iterator rbegin () const*
                      Return a reverse iterator positioned at my last key/value
                      pair.

rend   *reverse_iterator rend ()*
                      Return a reverse_iterator positioned immediately before my
                      first key/value pair.

rend   *const_reverse_iterator rend () const*
                      Return a reverse_iterator positioned immediately before my
                      first key/value pair.

size   *size_type size () const*
                      Return the number of key/value pairs that I contain.

swap   *void swap (map<Key,Value,Compare>& map_)*
                        Swap my contents with map_'s.

upper_bound *iterator upper_bound (const Key& key_)*
                        Return an iterator positioned at the last location where a pair
                        with key key_ could be inserted without violating the ordering
                        criteria. If no such location is found, return an iterator posi-
                        tioned at end().

upper_bound *const_iterator upper_bound (const Key& key_) const*
                        Return an iterator positioned at the last location where a pair
                        with key key_ could be inserted without violating the ordering
                        criteria. If no such location is found, return an iterator posi-
                        tioned at end().

value_comp   *map_compare<Key,Value,Compare> value_comp () const*
                        Return the comparison object used for comparing my key/value
                        pairs.

minus

Description
minus is a binary function object that returns the result of subtracting its
second operand from its first operand.

Declaration
```
#include <functional.h>
template<class T>
struct minus : binary_function<T, T, T>
```

()   *T operator () (const T& x_, const T& y_) const*
                        Return x_ - y_.

Example <minus.cpp>

```
#include <functional.h>
#include <algorithm.h>
```

```
#include <iostream.h>

int input1 [4] = { 1, 5, 7, 8 };
int input2 [4] = { 1, 4, 8, 3 };

int main ()
{
  int output [4];
  transform (input1, input1 + 4, input2, output, minus<int> ());
  for (int i = 0; i < 4; i++)
    cout << output[i] << endl;
  return 0;
}

0
1
-1
5
```

modulus

Description

modulus is a binary function object that returns its second operand in the modulus of the first operand.

Declaration

```
#include <functional.h>
template<class T>
struct modulus : binary_function<T, T, T>
```

()   *T operator () (const T& x_, const T& y_) const*
                 Return x_ % y_.

Example <modulus.cpp>

```
#include <functional.h>
#include <algorithm.h>
#include <iostream.h>

int input1 [4] = { 6, 8, 10, 2 };
int input2 [4] = { 4, 2, 11, 3 };

int main ()
{
  int output [4];
  transform (input1, input1 + 4, input2, output, modulus<int>
  ());
  for (int i = 0; i < 4; i++)
```

```
        cout << output[i] << endl;
    return 0;
}
```

2
0
10
2

multimap

Description

A multimap is an associative container that manages a set of ordered
key/value pairs. The pairs are ordered by key, based on a user-supplied comparitor function. More than one value may be associated with a particular key.
A multimap's underlying data structure allows you to very efficiently find all
of the values associated with a particular key.

Declaration

```
#include <map.h>
template<class Key, class Value, class Compare>
class multimap
```

Constructor   *multimap ()*
Construct myself to be an empty multimap that orders its keys
using the compare function specified when my template was
instantiated.

Constructor   *multimap (const Compare& compare_)*
Construct myself to be an empty multimap that orders its keys
using the compare function compare_.

Constructor   *multimap (const value_type* first_, const value_type* last_)*
Construct myself to contain copies of the key/value pairs in the
range [first_, last_), using the compare function specified when
my template was instantiated to order my keys.

Constructor   *multimap (const value_type* first_, const value_type* last_,*
const Compare& compare_)
Construct myself to contain copies of the key/value pairs in the
range [first_, last_), using compare_ to order my keys.

Constructor   *multimap (const multimap<Key,Value,Compare>&*
multimap_)
Construct myself to be a copy of multimap_.

Destructor	*~multimap ()* Destroy myself, erasing all of my key/value pairs.
=	*multimap<Key,Value,Compare>& operator =* *(const multimap<Key,Value,Compare>& multimap_)* Replace my contents by a copy of multimap_'s.
==	*bool operator ==* *(const multimap<Key,Value,Compare>& multimap_) const* Return true if I contain the same items in the same order as multimap_.
<	*bool operator <* *(const multimap<Key,Value,Compare>& multimap_) const* Return true if I'm lexigraphically less than multimap_.
begin	*iterator begin ()* Return an iterator positioned at my first key/value pair.
begin	*const_iterator begin () const* Return an iterator positioned at my first key/value pair.
count	*size_type count (const Key& key_) const* Return the number of key/value pairs that I contain whose key matches key_.
empty	*bool empty () const* Return true if I contain no entries.
end	*iterator end ()* Return an iterator positioned immediately after my last key/value pair.
end	*const_iterator end () const* Return an iterator positioned immediately after my last key/value pair.

equal_range   *pair <iterator, iterator> equal_range (const Key& key_)*
                     Return a pair of iterators whose first element is equal
                     to lower_bound() and whose second element is equal to
                     upper _bound().

equal_range   *pair <const_iterator, const_iterator>*
                     equal_range (const Key& key_) const
                     Return a pair of iterators whose first element is equal
                     to lower_bound() and whose second element is equal to
                     upper_bound().

erase   *void erase (iterator pos_)*
                     Erase the key/value pair at pos_.

erase   *void erase (iterator first_, iterator last_)*
                     Erase the key/value pairs in range [first_, last_)

erase   *size_type erase (const Key& key_)*
                     Erase all key/value pairs whose key matches key_ and return
                     the number of elements that were erased.

find   *iterator find (const Key& key_) const*
                     If I contain a key/value pair whose key matches key_, return
                     an iterator positioned at the matching pair, otherwise return
                     an iterator positioned at end().

insert   *iterator insert (const value_type & pair)*
                     Insert a copy of the key/value pair pair_, and return an itera-
                     tor to the new key/value pair.

insert   *void insert (const value_type* first_, const value_type* last_)*
                     Insert copies of the key/value pairs in the range [first_, last_).

insert   *iterator insert (iterator pos_, const value_type& pair_)*
                     Insert a copy of value_type if I don't already contain an
                     key/value pair whose key that matches its key, using pos_ as a
                     hint on where to start searching for the correct place to insert.

key_comp   *Compare key_comp () const*
                  Return the comparison object used to compare my keys.

lower_bound   *iterator lower_bound (const Key& key_)*
                  Return an iterator positioned at the first location where a pair
                  with key key_ could be inserted without violating the ordering
                  criteria. If no such location is found, return an iterator posi-
                  tioned at end().

lower_bound   *const_iterator lower_bound (const Key& key_) const*
                  Return an iterator positioned at the first location where a pair
                  with key key_ could be inserted without violating the ordering
                  criteria. If no such location is found, return an iterator posi-
                  tioned at end().

max_size   *size_type max_size () const*
                  Return the maximum number of key/value pairs that I can
                  contain.

rbegin   *reverse_iterator rbegin ()*
                  Return a reverse iterator positioned at my last key/value pair.

rbegin   *const_reverse_iterator rbegin () const*
                  Return a reverse iterator positioned at my last key/value pair.

rend   *reverse_iterator rend ()*
                  Return a reverse_iterator positioned immediately before my
                  first key/value pair.

rend   *const_reverse_iterator rend () const*
                  Return a reverse_iterator positioned immediately before my
                  first key/value pair.

size   *size_type size () const*
                  Return the number of key/value pairs that I contain.

swap   *void swap (multimap<Key,Value,Compare>& multimap_)*
                    Swap my contents with multimap_'s.

upper_bound   *iterator upper_bound (const Key& key_)*
                    Return an iterator positioned at the last location where a pair
                    with key key_ could be inserted without violating the ordering
                    criteria. If no such location is found, return an iterator posi-
                    tioned at end().

upper_bound   *const_iterator upper_bound (const Key& key_) const*
                    Return an iterator positioned at the last location where a pair
                    with key key_ could be inserted without violating the ordering
                    criteria. If no such location is found, return an iterator posi-
                    tioned at end().

value_comp   *map_compare<Key,Value,Compare> value_comp () const*
                    Return the comparison object using for comparing my
                    key/value pairs.

multiset

Description

A multiset is a container that is optimized for fast associative lookup. Items
are matched using their == operator. When an item is inserted into a multiset,
it is stored in a data structure that allows the item to be found very quickly.
Within the data structure, the items are ordered according to a user-defined
comparitor function object. A typical user-supplied function object is less,
which causes the items to be ordered in ascending order. Unlike sets, a multiset can contain multiple copies of the same item.

Declaration

```
#include <set.h>
template<class Key, class Compare>
class multiset
```

Constructor   *multiset ()*
                    Construct myself to be an empty multiset that orders elements
                    using the compare function specified when my template was
                    instantiated.

Constructor   *multiset (const Compare& compare_)*
Construct myself to be an empty multiset that orders elements
using the compare function compare_.

Constructor   *multiset (const Key* first_, const Key* last_)*
Construct myself to contain copies of the elements in the range
[first_, last_), using the compare function specified when my
template was instantiated.

Constructor   *multiset (const Key* first_, const Key* last_,*
const Compare& compare_)
Construct myself to contain copies of the elements in the range
[first_, last_), using compare_ to order the elements.

Constructor   *multiset (const multiset<Key,Compare>& multiset_)*
Construct myself to be a copy of multiset_.

Destructor   *~multiset ()*
Destroy myself, erasing all of my items.

=   *multiset<Key,Compare>&*
operator = (const multiset<Key,Compare>& multiset_)
Replace my contents by a copy of multiset_'s.

==   *bool operator == (const multiset<Key,Compare>& multiset_)*
const
Return true if I contain the same items in the same order as
multiset_.

<   *bool operator < (const multiset<Key,Compare>& multiset_)*
const
Return true if I'm lexigraphically less than multiset_.

begin   *iterator begin () const*
Return an iterator positioned at my first item.

count   *size_type count (const Key& key_) const*
Return the number of elements that I contain that match key_.

empty   *bool empty () const*
Return true if I contain no entries.

end   *iterator end () const*
                       Return an iterator positioned immediately after my last item.

equal_range   *pair <const_iterator, const_iterator>*
                       equal_range (const Key& key_) const
                       Return a pair of iterators whose first element is equal
                       to lower_bound() and whose second element is equal to
                       upper_bound().

erase   *void erase (iterator pos_)*
                       Erase the element at pos_.

erase   *void erase (iterator first_, iterator last_)*
                       Erase the elements in range [first_, last_)

erase   *size_type erase (const Key& key_)*
                       Erase all elements that match value_ and return the number
                       of elements that were erased.

find   *iterator find (const Key& key_) const*
                       If I contain an element that matches value_, return an iterator
                       positioned at the matching element, otherwise return an iter-
                       ator positioned at end().

insert   *iterator insert (const Key& key_)*
                       Insert a copy of value_ and return an iterator positioned at the
                       new element.

insert   *void insert (const Key* first_, const Key* last_)*
                       Insert copies of the elements in the range [first_, last_).

insert   *iterator insert (iterator pos_, const Key& key_)*
                       Insert a copy of value_ and return an iterator positioned at the
                       new element. Use pos_ as a hint on where to start searching
                       for the correct place to insert.

key_comp   *Compare key_comp () const*
                    Return my comparison object.

lower_bound   *iterator lower_bound (const Key& key_) const*
                    Return an iterator positioned at the first location that key_
                    could be inserted without violating the ordering criteria. If no
                    such location is found, return an iterator positioned at end().

max_size   *size_type max_size () const*
                    Return the maximum number of entries that I can contain.

rbegin   *reverse_iterator rbegin () const*
                    Return a reverse iterator positioned at my last item.

rend   *reverse_iterator rend () const*
                    Return a reverse_iterator positioned immediately before my
                    first item.

size   *size_type size () const*
                    Return the number of entries that I contain.

swap   *void swap (multiset<Key,Compare>& multiset_)*
                    Swap my contents with multiset_'s.

upper_bound   *iterator upper_bound (const Key& key_) const*
                    Return an iterator positioned at the last location that key_
                    could be inserted without violating the ordering criteria. If no
                    such location is found return an iterator positioned at end().

value_comp   *Compare value_comp () const*
                    Return my comparison object.

negate

Description
negate is a unary function object that returns the negation of its operand.

Declaration
```
#include <functional.h>
template<class T>
struct negate : unary_function <T, T>
```

()   *T operator () (const T& x_) const*
            Return -x_.

Example <negate.h>

```
#include <functional.h>
#include <algorithm.h>
#include <iostream.h>

int input [3] = { 1, 2, 3 };

int main ()
{
  int output[3];
  transform (input, input + 3, output, negate<int> ());
  for (int i = 0; i < 3; i++)
    cout << output[i] << endl;
  return 0;
}

-1
-2
-3
```

not_equal_to

Description
not_equal_to is a binary function object that returns true if its first operand is not equal to its second operand.

Declaration
```
#include <functional.h>
template<class T>
struct not_equal_to : binary_function <T, T, bool>
```

()   *bool operator () (const T& x_, const T& y_) const*
                  Return x_ != y_.

Example <nequal.cpp>

```
#include <functional.h>
#include <algorithm.h>
#include <iostream.h>

int input1 [4] = { 1, 7, 2, 2 };
int input2 [4] = { 1, 6, 2, 3 };
```

```
int main ()
{
  int output [4];
  transform (input1, input1 + 4, input2, output,
    not_equal_to<int> ());
  for (int i = 0; i < 4; i++)
    cout << output[i] << endl;
  return 0;
}
0
1
0
1
```

ostream_iterator

Description

An ostream_iterator is an iterator that outputs items (with an optional trailer) in a typesafe manner to an output stream.

Declaration

```
#include <iterator.h>
template<class T>
class ostream_iterator : public output_iterator
```

Constructor   *ostream_iterator (ostream& stream_)*
Construct myself to be associated with stream_. Set my trailer to an empty string.

Constructor   *ostream_iterator (ostream& stream_, char* trailer_)*
Construct myself to be associated with stream_. Set my trailer to trailer_.

=   *ostream_iterator<T>& operator = (const T& value_)*
Write value_ together with my trailer to my associated stream.

*   *ostream_iterator<T>& operator * ()*
Return a reference to myself.

++   *ostream_iterator<T>& operator ++ ()*
Return a reference to myself.

++   *ostream_iterator<T> operator ++ (int)*
Return a copy of myself.

Example <ostmit.cpp>

```
#include <iterator.h>
#include <algorithm.h>
```

```
int array [] = { 1, 5, 2, 4 };

int main ()
{
   char* string = "hello";
   ostream_iterator<char> it1 (cout);
   copy (string, string + 5, it1);
   cout << endl;
   ostream_iterator<int> it2 (cout);
   copy (array, array + 4, it2);
   cout << endl;
   return 0;
}
```

hello
1524

pair

Description
A pair is an object that contains two other objects. It is most commonly used for conveniently storing and passing pairs of objects.

Declaration
```
#include <utility.h>
template<class T1, class T2>
class pair
```

Adapter
```
template<class T1, class T2>
pair<T1,T2>
make_pair (const T1& x_, const T2& y_)
```

Constructor   *pair (const T1& a_, const T2& b_)*
Construct myself to contain a copy of a_ as my first item and a copy of b_ as my second item.

==   *bool operator == (const pair<T1,T2>& x_, const pair<T1,T2>& y_)*
Return true if (x_.first == y_.first) and (x_.second == y_.second). This is a templatized non-member function.

<   *bool operator < (const pair<T1,T2>& x_, const pair<T1,T2>& y_)*
Return true if x_ is lexographically less than y_. That is, (x_.first < y_.first) or (x_.first == y_.first && x_.second < y_.second). This is a templatized non-member function.

first   *first*
My first item. This is a public data member, not a function.

second   *second*
                    My second item. This is a public data member, not a function.

plus

Description

plus is a binary function object that returns the sum of its two operands.

Declaration
```
#include <functional.h>
template<class T>
struct plus : binary_function <T, T, T>
```

()   *T operator () (const T& x_, const T& y_) const*
                    Return x_ + y_.

Example <plus.cpp>

```
#include <functional.h>
#include <algorithm.h>
#include <iostream.h>

int input1 [4] = { 1, 6, 11, 8 };
int input2 [4] = { 1, 5, 2, 3 };

int main ()
{
   int total = inner_product (input1, input1 + 4, input2, 0,
      plus<int> (), times<int> ());
   cout << "total = " << total << endl;
   return 0;
}
```

```
total = 77
```

pointer_to_binary_function, ptr_fun

Description

pointer_to_binary_function is an object that allows you to use a regular "C" binary function as a binary function object. When executed, it returns the result of executing the regular "C" function with two operands. Its associated adapter function ptr_fun allows you to conveniently construct a pointer_to_binary_function object directly from a "C" binary function.

Declaration
```
#include <functional.h>
template<class Arg1, class Arg2, class Result>
class pointer_to_binary_function : public binary_function<Arg1, Arg2,
Result>
```

Adapter

```
template <class Arg1, class Arg2, class Result>
pointer_to_binary_function<Arg1, Arg2, Result> ptr_fun
(
   Result (*f_) (Arg1, Arg2)
)
```

Constructor   *pointer_to_binary_function (Result (*f_ (Arg1, Arg2))*
                 Construct myself with an associated function f_.

()   *Result operator () (const Arg1& x_, const Arg2& y_) const*
                 Return f_ (x_, y_)

Example <ptrbinf1.cpp>

```
#include <functional.h>
#include <algorithm.h>
#include <iostream.h>

int sum (int x_, int y_)
{
   return x_ + y_;
}

int input1 [4] = { 7, 2, 3, 5 };
int input2 [4] = { 1, 5, 5, 8 };

int main ()
{
   int output [4];
   transform (input1, input1 + 4, input2, output,
     pointer_to_binary_function<int, int, int> (sum));
   for (int i = 0; i < 4; i++)
     cout << output[i] << endl;
   return 0;
}

8
7
8
13
```

Example <ptrbinf2.cpp>

```
#include <functional.h>
#include <algorithm.h>
#include <iostream.h>

int input1 [4] = { 7, 2, 3, 5 };
int input2 [4] = { 1, 5, 5, 8 };

int main ()
{
```

```
    int output [4];
    transform (input1, input1 + 4, input2, output, ptr_fun (sum));
    for (int i = 0; i < 4; i++)
        cout << output[i] << endl;
    return 0;
}
```

8
7
8
13

pointer_to_unary_function, ptr_fun

Description

`pointer_to_unary_function` is an object that allows you to use a regular "C" unary function as a unary function object. When executed, it returns the result of executing the regular "C" function with an operand. Its associated adapter function `ptr_fun` allows you to conveniently construct a `pointer_ to_unary_function` object directly from a "C" unary function.

Declaration

```
#include <functional.h>
template<class Arg, class Result>
class pointer_to_unary_function : public unary_function<Arg,
Result>
```

Adapter

```
template <class Arg, class Result>
pointer_to_unary_function<Arg, Result> ptr_fun (Result (*f_)(Arg))
```

Constructor   *pointer_to_unary_function (Result (*f_) (Arg))*
              Construct myself with associated unary function f_.

()   *Result operator () (const Arg& x_) const*
              Return f_ (x_).

Example <ptrunf1.cpp>

```
#include <functional.h>
#include <algorithm.h>
#include <iostream.h>

int array [3] = { 1, 2, 3 };

int main ()
{
    int* p = find_if (array, array + 3,
        pointer_to_unary_function<int, bool> (even));
    if (p != array + 3)
        cout << *p << " is even" << endl;
    return 0;
```

```
}
```

2 is even
Example <ptrunf2.cpp>

```
#include <functional.h>
#include <algorithm.h>
#include <iostream.h>

int array [3] = { 1, 2, 3 };

int main ()
{
  int* p = find_if (array, array + 3, ptr_fun(even));
  if (p != array + 3)
    cout << *p << endl;
  return 0;
}
```

2 is even

priority_queue

Description

A `priority_queue` is an adapter that allows you to use any sequential container that has a random access iterator to maintain a sorted collection of items. It allows you to specify a comparator that is used to sort the items.

Declaration
```
#include <queue.h>
template<class Container, class Compare>
class priority_queue
```

Constructor   *priority_queue ()*
Construct myself to be an empty stack.

Destructor   *~priority_queue ()*
Destroy myself, erasing all of my items.

=   *priority_queue<Container,Compare>& operator =*
(const priority_queue<Container,Compare>& priority_queue_)
Replace my contents by a copy of priority_queue_'s.

empty   *bool empty () const*
Return true if I contain no entries.

max_size   *size_type max_size () const*
Return the maximum number of entries that I can contain.

pop	*void pop ()* Erase my top element.
push	*void push (const T& value_)* Push a copy of value_.
size	*size_type size () const* Return the number of entries that I contain.
swap	*void swap (priority_queue<Container,Compare>&* *priority_queue_)* Swap my contents with priority_queue_'s.
top	*T& top ()* Return a reference to my top element.
top	*const T& top () const* Return a reference to my top element.

queue

Description

A queue is an adapter that allows you to use any container that supports
push_back() and pop_front() as a first-in, first-out data structure.

Declaration

```
#include <queue.h>
template<class Container>
class queue
```

Constructor	*queue ()* Construct myself to be an empty queue.
Destructor	*~queue ()* Destroy myself, erasing all of my items.
=	*queue<Container>& operator = (const queue<Container>&* *queue_)* Replace my contents by a copy of queue_'s.
==	*bool operator == (const queue<Container>& queue_) const* Return true if I contain the same items in the same order as queue_.

<   *bool operator < (const queue<Container>& queue_) const*
                      Return true if I'm lexigraphically less than queue_.

back   *T& back ()*
                      Return a reference to my last element.

back   *const T& back () const*
                      Return a reference to my last element.

empty   *bool empty () const*
                      Return true if I contain no entries.

front   *T& front ()*
                      Return a reference to my first element.

front   *const T& front () const*
                      Return a reference to my first element.

max_size   *size_type max_size () const*
                      Return the maximum number of entries that I can contain.

pop   *void pop ()*
                      Erase my top element.

push   *void push (const T& value_)*
                      Push a copy of value_.

size   *size_type size () const*
                      Return the number of entries that I contain.

swap   *void swap (queue<Container>& queue_)*
                      Swap my contents with queue_'s.

raw_storage_iterator

Description

A `raw_storage_iterator` is an iterator that allows you to directly construct objects in raw storage.

Declaration

```
#include <iterator.h>
template<class OutputIterator, class T>
class raw_storage_iterator : public output_iterator
```

Constructor   *raw_storage_iterator (OutputIterator iterator_)*
Construct myself to be associated with iterator_.

*   *raw_storage_iterator<OutputIterator, T>& operator * ()*
Return a reference to myself.

=   *raw_storage_iterator<OutputIterator, T>& operator = (const*
T& x_)
Construct a copy of x_ using my associated iterator.

++   *raw_storage_iterator<OutputIterator, T>& operator ++ ()*
Advance my associated iterator.

++   *raw_storage_iterator<OutputIterator, T> operator ++ (int)*
Advance my associated iterator.

Example <rawiter.cpp>

```cpp
#include <iterator.h>
#include <iostream.h>

class X
{
  public:
    X (int i_ = 0) : i (i_) {}
    int i;
};

ostream& operator << (ostream& stream_, const X& x_)
{
  return stream_ << x_.i;
}

int main ()
{
  X* p = (X*) ::new (sizeof (X) * 5); // Allocate raw memory.
  X* q = p;
  raw_storage_iterator<X*, X> r (q);
  for (int i = 0; i < 5; i++)
    *r++ = X (i);
  for (i = 0; i < 5; i++)
    cout << *p++ << endl;
  return 0;
}

0
1
2
3
4
```

reverse_bidirectional_iterator

Description

A `reverse_bidirectional_iterator` allows a bidirectional iterator to be used as a reverse iterator.

Declaration

```
#include <iterator.h>
template <class BidirectionalIterator, class T, class Reference,
   class Distance>
class reverse_bidirectional_iterator :
   public bidirectional_iterator<T, Distance>
```

Constructor   *reverse_bidirectional_iterator ()*
Construct myself to serve as a past-the-end marker.

Constructor   *reverse_bidirectional_iterator (BidirectionalIterator iterator_)*
Construct myself to be associated with iterator_.

base   *BidirectionalIterator base ()*
Return a copy of my associated iterator.

*   *Reference operator * ()*
Return a reference to the item referenced by my associated iterator.

++   *reverse_bidirectional_iterator <BidirectionalIterator, T, Reference, Distance>& operator ++ ()*
Retreat my associated iterator by one and return a reference to my new value.

++   *reverse_bidirectional_iterator <BidirectionalIterator, T, Reference, Distance> operator ++ (int)*
Retreat my associated iterator by one and return a copy of my previous value.

--   *reverse_bidirectional_iterator <BidirectionalIterator, T, Reference, Distance>& operator -- ()*
Advance my associated iterator and return a reference to my new value.

--   *reverse_bidirectional_iterator <BidirectionalIterator, T, Reference, Distance> operator -- (int)*
Advance my associated iterator and return a copy of my previous value.

==   *bool operator ==*
               (constreverse_bidirectional_iterator <BidirectionalIterator,T,
               Reference, Distance>& iterator_) const
               Return true if my associated iterator is in the same state as
               iterator_'s.

!=   *bool operator != (*
               const reverse_bidirectional_iterator<BidirectionalIterator,T,
               Reference, Distance>& iterator_) const
               Return true if my associated iterator is not in the same state
               as iterator_'s.

Example <revbit1.cpp>

```
#include <vector.h>
#include <iterator.h>
#include <iostream.h>

int array [] = { 1, 5, 2, 3 };

int main ()
{
  vector<int> v (array, array + 4);
  reverse_bidirectional_iterator<vector<int>::iterator, int,
    vector<int>::reference, vector<int>::difference_type>
    r (v.end ());
  while (r != v.begin ())
    cout << *r++ << endl;
  return 0;
}

3
2
5
1
```

Example <revbit2.cpp>

```
#include <stl.h>
#include <iostream.h>

int array [] = { 1, 5, 2, 3 };

int main ()
{
  vector<int> v (array, array + 4);
  vector<int>::reverse_iterator r;
  for (r = v.rbegin (); r != v.rend (); r++)
    cout << *r << endl;
  return 0;
}
```

3
2
5
1

reverse_iterator

Description
A reverse_iterator is an iterator that allows you to reverse the polarity of
an existing random access iterator.

Declaration
```
#include <iterator.h>
template <class RandomAccessIterator,class T, class Reference,
   class Distance>
class stl_reverse_iterator : public
   random_access_iterator<T, Distance>
```

Constructor   *reverse_iterator ()*
Construct myself to act as a past-the-end value.

Constructor   *reverse_iterator (RandomAccessIterator iterator_)*
Construct myself to be associated with iterator_.

base   *RandomAccessIterator base ()*
Return a copy of my associated iterator.

*   *Reference operator * ()*
Return a reference to the item referenced by my associated
iterator.

++   *reverse_iterator<RandomAccessIterator, T, Reference,
Distance>& operator++ ()*
Retreat my associated iterator by one and a reference to
myself.

++   *reverse_iterator<RandomAccessIterator, T, Reference,
Distance>operator ++ (int)*
Retreat my associated iterator by one and return a copy of my
old value.

--   *reverse_iterator<RandomAccessIterator, T, Reference,
Distance>& operator -- ()*
Advance my associated iterator and return a reference to
myself.

--   *reverse_iterator<RandomAccessIterator, T, Reference,
Distance>operator -- (int)*

Advance my associated iterator and return a copy of my old value.

+   *reverse_iterator<RandomAccessIterator, T, Reference, Distance>operator + (Distance n_) const*
Return a copy of my associated iterator retreated by n_ positions.

+= *reverse_iterator<RandomAccessIterator, T, Reference, Distance>& operator += (Distance n_)*
Retreat my associated iterator by n_ positions and return a reference to myself.

-   *reverse_iterator<RandomAccessIterator, T, Reference, Distance>operator - (Distance n_) const*
Return a copy of my associated iterator advanced by n_ positions.

-= *reverse_iterator<RandomAccessIterator, T, Reference, Distance>& operator -= (Distance n_)*
Advance my associated iterator by n_ positions and return a reference to myself.

[] *Reference operator [] (Distance n_)*
Return a reference to the item that is n_ positions behind my associated iterator.

== *bool operator == (const reverse_iterator<RandomAccessIterator, T, Reference, Distance>& x_)const*
Return true if my associated iterator is in the same state as x_'s.

!= *bool operator != (const reverse_iterator<RandomAccessIterator, T, Reference, Distance>& x_)const*
Return true if my associated iterator is not in the same state as x_'s.

<   *bool operator < (const reverse_iterator<RandomAccessIterator, T, Reference, Distance>& x_const*
Return true if x_'s associated iterator is less than my own.

-   *Distance operator - (const reverse_iterator<RandomAccessIterator, T, Reference, Distance>& x_)const*

Return the distance between x_'s associated iterator and
my own.

+
> *friend reverse_iterator*
> *<RandomAccessIterator, T, Reference,Distance> operator +*
> *(*
> *Distance n_,*
> *const reverse_iterator<RandomAccessIterator, T, Reference,*
> *Distance>& x_*
> *)*
>
> Return a reverse_iterator whose associated iterator is n_ posi-
> tions behind by associated iterator.

Example <reviter1.cpp>

```
#include <vector.h>
#include <iterator.h>
#include <iostream.h>

int array [] = { 1, 5, 2, 3 };

int main ()
{
  vector<int> v (array, array + 4);
  reverse_iterator<vector<int>::iterator, int,
    vector<int>::reference, vector<int>::difference_type>
    r (v.end ());
  while (r != v.begin ())
    cout << *r++ << endl;
  return 0;
}

3
2
5
1
```

Example <reviter2.cpp>

```
#include <vector.h>
#include <iterator.h>
#include <iostream.h>

int array [] = { 1, 5, 2, 3 };

int main ()
{
  vector<int> v (array, array + 4);
  vector<int>::reverse_iterator r;
  for (r = v.rbegin (); r != v.rend (); r++)
    cout << *r << endl;
  return 0;
}
```

3
2
5
1

set

Description

A set is a container that is optimized for fast associative lookup. Items are matched using their == operator. When an item is inserted into a set, it is stored in a data structure that allows the item to be found very quickly. Within the data structure, the items are ordered according to a user-defined comparitor function object. A typical user-supplied function object is less, which causes the items to be ordered in ascending order. Unlike multisets, a set cannot contain multiple copies of the same item.

Declaration

```
#include <set.h>
template<class Key, class Compare>
class set
```

Constructor   *set ()*
Construct myself to be an empty set that orders elements using the compare function specified when my template was instantiated.

Constructor   *set (const Compare& compare_)*
Construct myself to be an empty set that orders elements using the compare function compare_.

Constructor   *set (const Key* first_, const Key* last_)*
Construct myself to contain copies of the elements in the range [first_, last_), using the compare function specified when my template was instantiated.

Constructor   *set (const Key* first_, const Key* last_, const Compare& compare_)*
Construct myself to contain copies of the elements in the range [first_, last_), using compare_ to order the elements.

Constructor   *set (const set<Key,Compare>& set_)*
Construct myself to be a copy of set_.

Destructor   *~set ()*
                   Destroy myself, erasing all of my items.

=   *set<Key,Compare>& operator = (const set<Key,Compare>&*
                   set_)
                   Replace my contents by a copy of set_'s.

==   *bool operator == (const set<Key,Compare>& set_) const*
                   Return true if I contain the same items in the same order as
                   set_.

<   *bool operator < (const set<Key,Compare>& set_) const*
                   Return true if I'm lexigraphically less than set_.

begin   *iterator begin () const*
                   Return an iterator positioned at my first item.

count   *size_type count (const Key& key_) const*
                   Return the number of elements that I contain that match
                   key_.

empty   *bool empty () const*
                   Return true if I contain no entries.

end   *iterator end () const*
                   Return an iterator positioned immediately after my last item.

erase   *void erase (iterator pos_)*
                   Erase the element at pos_.

erase   *void erase (iterator first_, iterator last_)*
                   Erase the elements in range [first_, last_)

erase   *size_type erase (const Key& key_)*
                   Erase all elements that match key_ and return the number of
                   elements that were erased.

find   *iterator find (const Key& key_) const*
                   If I contain an element that matches key_, return an iterator

positioned at the matching element, otherwise return an iterator positioned at end().

insert   *pair <const_iterator, bool> insert (const Key& key_)*
                        If I don't contain an element that matches key_, insert a copy
                        of key_ and return a pair whose first element is an iterator
                        positioned at the new element and whose second element is
                        true. If I already contain an element that matches key_, return
                        a pair whose first element is an iterator positioned at the exist-
                        ing element and whose second element is false.

insert   *void insert (const Key* first_, const Key* last_)*
                        Insert copies of the elements in the range [first_, last_).

insert   *iterator insert (iterator pos_, const Key& key_)*
                        Insert a copy of key_ if I don't already contain an element that
                        matches it, using pos_ as a hint on where to start searching for
                        the correct place to insert.

key_comp   *Compare key_comp () const*
                        Return my comparison object.

lower_bound   *iterator lower_bound (const Key& key_) const*
                        Return an iterator positioned at the first location that key_
                        could be inserted without violating the ordering criteria. If no
                        such location is found, return an iterator positioned at end().

max_size   *size_type max_size () const*
                        Return the maximum number of entries that I can contain.

rbegin   *reverse_iterator rbegin () const*
                        Return a reverse iterator positioned at my last item.

rend   *reverse_iterator rend () const*
                        Return a reverse_iterator positioned immediately before my
                        first item.

size   *size_type size () const*
                        Return the number of entries that I contain.

swap   *void swap (set<Key,Compare>& set_)*
                            Swap my contents with set_'s.

upper_bound   *iterator upper_bound (const Key& value_) const*
                            Return an iterator positioned at the last location that key_
                            could be inserted without violating the ordering criteria. If no
                            such location is found return an iterator positioned at end().

value_comp   *Compare value_comp () const*
                            Return my comparison object.

stack

Description

A `stack` is an adapter that allows you to use any container that supports
`push_back()` and `pop_back()` as a first-in, last-out data structure.

Declaration
```
#include <stack.h>
template<class Container>
class stack
```


Constructor   *stack ()*
                            Construct myself to be an empty stack.

Destructor   *~stack ()*
                            Destroy myself, erasing all of my items.

=   *stack<Container>& operator = (const stack<Container>&
                            stack_)*
                            Replace my contents by a copy of stack_'s.

==   *bool operator == (const stack<Container>& stack_) const*
                            Return true if I contain the same items in the same order as
                            stack_.

<   *bool operator < (const stack<Container>& stack_) const*
                            Return true if I'm lexigraphically less than stack_.

empty   *bool empty () const*
                   Return true if I contain no entries.

max_size   *size_type max_size () const*
                   Return the maximum number of entries that I can contain.

pop   *void pop ()*
                   Erase my top element.

push   *void push (const_reference& value_)*
                   Push a copy of value_.

size   *size_type size () const*
                   Return the number of entries that I contain.

swap   *void swap (stack<Container>& stack_)*
                   Swap my contents with stack_'s.

top   *reference& top ()*
                   Return a reference to my top element.

top   *const_reference& top () const*
                   Return a reference to my top element.

string

Description
The ANSI templatized string.

Declaration
```
#include <string.h>
template< class CHAR_T, class TRAITS >
class basic_string;
```

```
typedef basic_string< char, string_char_traits > string
typedef basic_string< wchar_t, string_char_traits > wstring
```

Constructor   *string()*
Construct myself to be an empty string.

Constructor   *string(const char* str)*
Construct myself to be a copy of 'str'.

Constructor   *string(const string& str, size_t pos, size_t n)*
Construct myself to be a string whose length is the smaller of
'n' and 'str'.size() - 'pos', and whose contents start at 'string'
+ 'pos'.

Constructor   *string(const char* str, size_t n)*
Construct myself to be a copy of the array of 'n' characters
whose first element is located at str.

Constructor   *string(char c, size_t n)*
Construct myself to be string consisting of 'n' copies of 'c'.

Constructor   *string(const string& str)*
Construct myself to be a copy of 'str'.

Destructor   *~string()*
Destroy myself, deallocating my contents if necessary.

=   *string& operator=(const string& str)*
Assign myself from 'str'. Return a reference to myself.

=   *string& operator=(const char* str)*
Assign myself from 'str'. Return a reference to myself.

=   *string& operator=(char c)*
Assign myself to be a string that contains the single character
'c'. Return a reference to myself.

+=   *string& operator+=(const string& str)*
Append a copy of 'str' to myself. Return a reference to myself.

+=   *string& operator+=(const char* str)*
Append a copy of 'str' to myself. Return a reference to myself.

+=   *string& operator+=(char c)*
Append 'c' to myself. Return a reference to myself.

[]	*char& operator[](size_t pos)* Return the character at index 'pos'.

[]	*char operator[](size_t pos) const* Return the character at index 'pos'.

append	*string& append(const char* str)* Append a copy of 'str' to myself. Return a reference to myself.

append	*string& append(const string& str, size_t pos = 0,* *size_t n = NPOS)* Append to myself a string whose length is the smaller of 'n' and 'str'.size() and whose contents begin at location 'str' + 'pos'. Return a reference to myself.

append	*string& append(const char* str, size_t n)* Append an array of 'n' characters whose first element is located at 'str'. Return a reference to myself.

append	*string& append(char c, size_t n = 1)* Append 'n' copies of 'c' to myself. Return a reference to myself.

assign	*os_string& assign(const os_string& str)* Assign 'str' to myself. Return a reference to myself.

assign	*string& assign(const string& str, size_t pos, size_t n = NPOS)* Assign myself to be a string whose length is the smaller of 'n' and 'str'.size() and whose contents are copied from the location 'str' + 'pos'. Return a reference to myself.

assign	*string& assign(const char* str, size_t n)* Assign myself to be an array of 'n' characters whose first element is located at 'str'. Return a reference to myself.

assign	*string& assign(const char* str)* Assign myself to be a copy of 'str'. Return a reference to myself.

assign	*string& assign(char c, size_t n = 1)* Assign myself to be a string consisting of 'n' copies of 'c'. Return a reference to myself.

c_str	*const char* c_str() const* Return a pointer to a string of length size() + 1, whose first size() characters are equal to the string that I control and

whose last character is equal to TRAITS::eos(). The returned pointer should be considered invalid when any non-const function is invoked upon me.

compare   *compare(const string& str, size_t pos = 0, size_t n = NPOS)*
                     const
                     Return the result of comparing the string whose length is the smaller of 'n' and size() - 'pos' and whose contents start at index 'pos' of myself against 'str'.

compare   *int compare(char* str, size_t pos, size_t n) const*
                     Return the result of comparing the string whose length is the smaller of 'n' and size() - 'pos' and whose contents start at index 'pos' of myself against 'str'.

copy   *size_t copy(char* str, size_t n, size_t pos = 0) const*
                     Copy the character sequence whose length is the smaller of 'n' and size() - 'pos' from myself to 'str', without adding a null character. Return the number of characters copied.

data   *const char* data() const*
                     If I am empty, return a null pointer; otherwise, return a pointer to my data area. Note that unlike c_str(), this data will not be null-terminated. This data can become invalid when a non-const function or c_str() is executed on myself.

empty   *bool empty() const*
                     Return true if I don't contain any characters.

exchange   *oid exchange(string& str)*
                     Swap contents with 'str'.

find   *size_t find(const string& str, size_t pos) const*
                     Starting the search from index 'pos' of myself, return the index of the first occurrence of 'str', or NPOS if no such index exists.

find   *size_t find(const char* str, size_t pos, size_t n) const*
                     The search string is the first 'n' characters of 'string'. Starting the search from index 'pos' of myself, return the index of the first occurrence of this search string, or NPOS if no such index exists.

find   *size_t find(const char* str, size_t pos) const*
                     Starting the search from index 'pos' of myself, return the index of the first occurrence of 'str', or NPOS if no such index exists.

find_first_not_of   *size_t find_first_not_of(const string& str, size_t pos) const*
Starting the search from index 'pos' of myself, return the index of the first character that doesn't occur in 'str'. If no such index exists, return NPOS.

find_first_not_of   *size_t find_first_not_of(const char& c, size_t pos) const*
Starting the search from index 'pos' of myself, return the index of the first character that is not equal to 'c'. If no such index exists, return NPOS.

find_first_not_of   *size_t find_first_not_of(const char* str, size_t pos, size_t n) const*
The search string is the first 'n' characters of 'str'. Starting the search from index 'pos' of myself, return the index of the first character that doesn't occur in the search string. If no such index exists, return NPOS.

find_first_not_of   *size_t find_first_not_of(const char* str, size_t pos) const*
Starting the search from index 'pos' of myself, return the index of the first character that doesn't occur in 'str'. If no such index exists, return NPOS.

find_first_of   *size_t find_first_of(const string& str, size_t pos) const*
Starting the search from index 'pos' of myself, return the index of the first character that occurs in 'str'. If no such index exists, return NPOS.

find_first_of   *size_t find_first_of(const char& c, size_t pos) const*
Starting the search from index 'pos' of myself, return the index of the first character that is equal to 'c'. If no such index exists, return NPOS.

find_first_of   *size_t find_first_of(const char* str, size_t pos, size_t n) const*
The search string is the first 'n' characters of 'str'. Starting the search from index 'pos' of myself, return the index of the first character that occurs in the search string. If no such index exists, return NPOS.

find_first_of   *size_t find_first_of(const char* str, size_t pos) const*
Starting the search from index 'pos' of myself, return the index of the first character that occurs in 'str'. If no such index exists, return NPOS.

find_last_not_of   *size_t find_last_not_of(const string& str, size_t pos)*
                           const
                           Starting the search from index 'pos' of myself, return the
                           index of the last character that doesn't occur in 'str'. If no
                           such index exists, return NPOS.

find_last_not_of   *size_t find_last_not_of(const char& c, size_t pos) const*
                           Starting the search from index 'pos' of myself, return the
                           index of the last character that is not equal to 'c'. If no
                           such index exists, return NPOS.

find_last_not_of   *size_t find_last_not_of(const char* s, size_t pos, size_t n*
) const
                           The search string is the first 'n' characters of 'string'.
                           Starting the search from index 'pos' of myself, return the
                           index of the last character that doesn't occur in the search
                           string. If no such index exists, return NPOS.

find_last_not_of   *size_t find_last_not_of(const char* str, size_t pos) const*
                           Starting the search from index 'pos' of myself, return the
                           index of the last character that doesn't occur in 'str'. If no
                           such index exists, return NPOS.

find_last_of   *size_t find_last_of(const string& str, size_t pos) const*
                           Starting the search from index 'pos' of myself, return the
                           index of the last character that occurs in 'str'. If no such
                           index exists, return NPOS.

find_last_of   *size_t find_last_of(const char& c, size_t pos) const*
                           Starting the search from index 'pos' of myself, return the
                           index of the last character that is equal to 'c'. If no such
                           index exists, return NPOS.

find_last_of   *size_t find_last_of(const char* str, size_t pos, size_t n)*
                           const
                           The search string is the first 'n' characters of 'str'. Start-
                           ing the search from index 'pos' of myself, return the index
                           of the last character that occurs in the search string. If no
                           such index exists, return NPOS.

find_last_of   *size_t find_last_of(const char* str, size_t pos) const*
                           Starting the search from index 'pos' of myself, return the
                           index of the last character that occurs in 'str'. If no such
                           index exists, return NPOS.

insert   *os_string& insert(size_t pos, const char* str)*
                         Insert a copy of 'str' at index 'pos'. Return a reference to myself.

insert   *string& insert(size_t pos1, const string& str, size_t pos2 = 0,*
                         size_t n = NPOS)
                         Insert at index 'pos1' a string whose length is the smaller of 'n'
                         and 'str'.size() and whose contents begin at location 'str' +
                         'pos2'. Return a reference to myself.

insert   *string& insert(size_t pos, const char* str, size_t n)*
                         Insert at index 'pos' an array of 'n' characters whose first ele-
                         ment is located at 'str'. Return a reference to myself.

insert   *string& insert(size_t pos, char c, size_t n = 1)*
                         Insert at index 'pos' a string consisting of 'n' copies of 'c'. Re-
                         turn a reference to myself.

length   *size_t length() const*
                         Return the number of characters that I contain.

remove   *string& remove()*
                         Become an empty string. Return a reference to myself.

remove   *string& remove(size_t pos, size_t n = NPOS)*
                         Remove the character sequence starting at index 'pos' whose
                         length is the smaller of 'n' and size() - 'pos'. Return a reference
                         to myself.

replace   *string& replace(size_t pos1, size_t n1, const string& str,*
                         size_t pos2 = 0, size_t n2 = NPOS)
                         Target the character sequence starting at index 'pos1' whose
                         length is the smaller of 'n1' and size() - 'pos1'. Replace this tar-
                         get with the character sequence starting at index 'pos2' whose
                         length is the smaller of 'n2' and 'str'.size() - 'pos2'. Return a
                         reference to myself.

replace   *string& replace(size_t pos, size_t n1, const char* str,*
                         size_t n2)
                         Target the character sequence starting at index 'pos' whose
                         length is the smaller of 'n1' and size() - 'pos'. Replace this tar-
                         get with an array of 'n2' characters whose first element is
                         located at 'str'. Return a reference to myself.

replace *string& replace(size_t pos, size_t n1, char c, size_t n2 = 1)*
Target the character sequence starting at index 'pos' whose length is the smaller of 'n1' and size() - 'pos'. Replace this target with a string consisting of 'n2' copies of 'c'. Return a reference to myself.

replace *string& replace(size_t pos, size_t n1, const char* str)*
Target the character sequence starting at index 'pos' whose length is the smaller of 'n1' and size() - 'pos'. Replace this target with a copy of 'str'. Return a reference to myself.

reserve *size_t reserve() const*
Return the number of characters that I can hold without reallocating my internal storage.

reserve *void reserve(size_t size)*
If necessary, expand my internal storage so that it can hold at least 'size' characters.

resize *void resize(size_t n, char c)*
If my size is less than 'n', append 'n' - size() copies of 'c' to myself, otherwise, truncate myself to become 'n' characters long.

resize *void resize(size_t n)*
If my size is less than 'n', append 'n' - size() copies of the null character to myself; otherwise, truncate myself to become 'n' characters long.

rfind *size_t rfind(const string& str, size_t pos) const*
Starting the search from index 'pos' of myself, return the index of the last occurrence of 'str', or NPOS if no such index exists.

rfind *size_t rfind(const char* str, size_t pos, size_t n) const*
The search string is the first 'n' characters of 'str'. Starting the search from index 'pos' of myself, return the index of the last occurrence of this search string, or NPOS if no such index exists.

rfind *size_t rfind(const char* str, size_t pos) const*
Starting the search from index 'pos' of myself, return the index of the last occurrence of 'str', or NPOS if no such substring is found.

size	*size_t size() const*
	Return the number of characters that I contain.
substr	*string substr(size_t pos = 0, size_t n = NPOS) const*
	Return a string whose length is the smaller of 'n' and size() - 'pos' and whose contents are copied from index 'pos' of myself.

Non-Member Functions:

+	*string operator+(const string& s1, const string& s2)*
	Returns the result of catenating together the two arguments.
+	*string operator+(const char* s1, const string s2)*
	Returns the result of catenating together the two arguments.
+	*string operator+(const char c, const string& s)*
	Returns the result of catenating together the two arguments.
+	*string operator+(const string& s1, const char* s2)*
	Returns the result of catenating together the two arguments.
+	*string operator+(const string& s, const char c)*
	Returns the result of catenating together the two arguments.
>,<,>=,<=,==,!=	*various relational operators*
	A full complement of relational operators are provided, which make the use of compare() much simpler.

times

Description

times is a binary function object that returns the product of its two operands.

Declaration

```
#include <functional.h>
template<class T>
struct times : binary_function<T, T, T>
```

()	*bool operator () (const T& x_, const T& y_) const*
	Return x_ * y_.

Example <times.cpp>

```
#include <functional.h>
#include <algorithm.h>
#include <iostream.h>
```

```
int input [4] = { 1, 5, 7, 2 };

int main ()
{
   int total = accumulate (input, input + 4, 1, times<int> ());
   cout << "total = " << total << endl;
   return 0;
}

total = 70
```

unary_compose, compos1

Description
unary_compose is a unary function object that returns the result of executing its two operations in a specific sequence. Its associated adapter function compose1 allows you to conveniently construct a unary_compose object directly from two functions.

Declaration
```
#include <functional.h>
template<class Operation1, class Operation2 >
class unary_compose : public unary_function
   <Operation2::argument_type, Operation1::result_type>
```

Adapter
```
template <class Operation1, class Operation2>
binary_compose<Operation1, Operation2>
compose1 (const Operation1& op1, const Operation2& op2)
```

Constructor   *unary_compose (const Operation1& op1_, const Operation2& op2_)*
Construct myself with associated operators op1_ and op2_.

()   *Operation1::result_type operator ()*
(const Operation2::argument_type& x_) const
Return op1_ (op2_ (x)).

Example <ucompos1.cpp>

```
#include <iostream.h>
#include <math.h>
#include <functional.h>
#include <algorithm.h>

struct square_root : public unary_function<double, double>
{
   square_root () {}
   double operator () (double x_) const { return sqrt (x_); }
};
```

```
   int input [3] = { -1, -4, -16 };

   int main ()
   {
      int output [3];
      transform (input, input + 3, output,
        unary_compose<square_root, negate<int> > (square_root (),
        negate<int> ()));
      for (int i = 0; i < 3; i++)
        cout << output[i] << endl;
      return 0;
   }
```

1
2
4

Example <ucompos2.cpp>

```
#include <iostream.h>
#include <math.h>
#include <functional.h>
#include <algorithm.h>

struct square_root : public unary_function<double, double>
{
   square_root () {}
   double operator () (double x_) const { return sqrt (x_); }
};

int input [3] = { -1, -4, -16 };

int main ()
{
   int output [3];
   transform (input, input + 3, output,
     compose1 (square_root (), negate<int> ()));
   for (int i = 0; i < 3; i++)
     cout << output[i] << endl;
   return 0;
}
```

1
2
4

unary_function

Description

unary_function is the abstract base structure of all unary function objects.
It defines two useful typedefs that are used by most of its derived classes.

Declaration

```
#include <functional.h>
template<class Arg, class Result>
struct unary_function
{
   typedef Arg argument_type;
   typedef Result result_type;
};
```

unary_negate, not1

Description

unary_negate is a unary function object that returns the logical negation of executing its unary predicate. Its associated adapter function not1 allows you to conveniently construct a unary_negate object directly from a predicate.

Declaration

```
#include <functional.h>
template<class Predicate>
class unary_negate : public unary_function
   <Predicate::argument_type, bool>
```

Adapter

```
template <class Predicate>
unary_negate<Predicate> not1(const Predicate& pred_);
```

Constructor   *unary_negate (const Predicate& pred_)*
                     Construct myself with predicate pred_

()   *bool operator() (const argument_type& x_) const*
                     Return the result of pred_ (x_)

Example <unegate1.cpp>

```
#include <iostream.h>
#include <functional.h>
#include <algorithm.h>

struct odd : public unary_function<int, bool>
{
   odd () {}
   bool operator () (int n_) const { return (n_ % 2) == 1; }
};
int array [3] = { 1, 2, 3 };

int main ()
{
   int* p = find_if (array, array + 3, unary_negate<odd> (odd
   ()));
   if (p != array + 3)
      cout << *p << endl;
```

```
      return 0;
}
```

2 is not odd

Example <unegate2.cpp>

```
#include <iostream.h>
#include <functional.h>
#include <algorithm.h>

struct odd : public unary_function<int, bool>
{
  odd (_) {}
  bool operator () (int n_) const { return (n_ % 2) == 1; }
};

int array [3] = { 1, 2, 3 };

int main ()
{
  int* p = find_if (array, array + 3, not1 (odd ()));
  if (p != array + 3)
    cout << *p << endl;
  return 0;
}
```

2 is not odd

vector

Description

A vector is a sequential container that is very similar to a regular "C" array except that it can expand to accomodate new elements.

Declaration

```
#include <vector.h>
template<class T>
class vector
```

Constructor   *vector ()*
                    Construct myself to be empty.

Constructor   *vector (size_type n_)*
                    Construct me to contain n_ elements set to their default value.

Constructor   *vector (size_type n_, const T& value_)*
                    Construct me to contain n_ copies of value_.

Constructor   *vector (const T* first_, const T* last_)*
                   Construct me to contain copies of all of the elements in the
                   range [first_, last_).

Constructor   *vector (const vector<T>& vector_)*
                   Construct myself to be a copy of vector_.

Destructor   *~vector ()*
                   Destroy myself, erasing all of my items.

=   *vector<T>& operator = (const vector<T>& vector_)*
                   Replace my contents by a copy of vector_'s.

==   *bool operator == (const vector<T>& vector_) const*
                   Return true if I contain the same items in the same order as
                   vector_.

<   *bool operator < (const vector<T>& vector_) const*
                   Return true if I'm lexigraphically less than vector_.

[]   *T& operator [] (int index_)*
                   Return a reference to my index_th element.

[]   *const T& operator [] (int index_) const*
                   Return a reference to my index_th element.

back   *T& back ()*
                   Return a reference to my last element.

back   *const T& back () const*
                   Return a reference to my last element.

begin   *iterator begin ()*
                   Return an iterator positioned at my first item.

begin   *const_iterator begin () const*
                   Return an iterator positioned at my first item.

capacity   *size_type capacity () const*
                   Return the number of elements that I can contain without
                   allocating more memory.

empty   *bool empty () const*
                   Return true if I contain no entries.

end   *iterator end ()*
         Return an iterator positioned immediately after my last item.

end   *const_iterator end () const*
         Return an iterator positioned immediately after my last item.

erase   *void erase (iterator pos_)*
         Erase the element at pos_.

erase   *void erase (iterator first_, iterator last_)*
         Erase the elements in range [first_, last_)

front   *T& front ()*
         Return a reference to my first element.

front   *const T& front () const*
         Return a reference to my first element.

insert   *iterator insert (iterator pos, const T& value_)*
         Insert value_ at pos_ and return an iterator pointing to the
         new element's position.

insert   *void insert (iterator pos_, size_type n_, const T& value_)*
         Insert n_ copies of value_ at pos_.

insert   *void insert (iterator pos_, const T* first_, const T* last_)*
         Insert copies of the elements in the range [first_, last_) at pos_.

max_size *size_type max_size () const*
         Return the maximum number of entries that I can contain.

push_back *void push_back (const T& value_)*
         Add value_ at my end.

pop_back *void pop_back ()*
         Erase my last element.

rbegin   *reverse_iterator rbegin ()*
         Return a reverse iterator positioned at my last item.

rbegin   *const_reverse_iterator rbegin () const*
         Return a reverse iterator positioned at my last item.

rend   *reverse_iterator rend ()*
                      Return a reverse_iterator positioned immediately before my
                      first item.

rend   *const_reverse_iterator rend () const*
                      Return a reverse_iterator positioned immediately before my
                      first item.

reserve   *void reserve (size_type n_)*
                      Pre-allocate enough space to hold up to n_ elements. This oper-
                      ation does not change the value returned by size().

size   *size_type size () const*
                      Return the number of entries that I contain.

swap   *void swap (vector<T>& vector_)*
                      Swap my contents with vector_'s.

Algorithm Catalog

Algorithm Catalog Introduction

This section contains a concise description of every STL algorithm in alphabetical order. Every entry contains the following information:

- *A Synopsis*. A brief description of the algorithm.

- *The Signatures*. The declaration of the algorithm.

- *A Description*. A full description of the algorithm together with special notes and/or hints on usage.

- *The Complexity*. The space and time complexity of the algorithm.

- *One or more Examples.*

The algorithm catalog also contains descriptions of the public domain "helper" algorithms from ObjectSpace, Inc. These algorithms begin with an os_ prefix. It is assumed that the ObjectSpace header file <helper.h> has been placed in a standard directory. For information about how to obtain these algorithms, consult the Appendix section.

accumulate

Synopsis
Sum the values in a range.

Signatures
```
#include <algorithm.h>
template<class InputIterator, class T>
T accumulate (InputIterator first_, InputIterator last_, T init_)

template<InputIterator, T, BinaryOperation>
T accumulate
(
   InputIterator first_,
   InputIterator last_,
   T init_,
   BinaryOperation binary_op_
)
```

Description

Add the value of each element in the range [first_, last_) to init_ and return the new value of init_. Note that init_ is not automatically initialized prior to this operation. The first version uses operator+ to perform the addition, whereas the second version uses the binary function binary_op_.

Complexity

Time complexity is linear. Space complexity is constant.

Example <accum1.cpp>

```cpp
#include <algorithm.h>
#include <vector.h>
#include <iostream.h>

int main ()
{
  vector <int> v (5);
  for (int i = 0; i < v.size (); i++)
    v[i] = i + 1;
  int sum = accumulate (v.begin (), v.end (), 0);
  cout << "Sum = " << sum << endl;
  return 0;
}
```

```
Sum = 15
```

Example <accum2.cpp>

```cpp
#include <algorithm.h>
#include <vector.h>
#include <iostream.h>

int mult (int initial_, int element_)
{
  return initial_ * element_;
}

int main ()
{
  vector <int> v (5);
  for (int i = 0; i < v.size (); i++)
    v[i] = i + 1;
  int prod = accumulate (v.begin (), v.end (), 1, mult);
  cout << "Prod = " << prod << endl;
  return 0;
}
```

```
Prod = 120
```

adjacent_difference

Synopsis
Calculate and sum the difference between adjacent pairs of values.

Signatures
```
#include <algorithm.h>
template<class InputIterator, class OutputIterator>
OutputIterator adjacent_difference
(
  InputIterator first_,
  InputIterator last_,
  OutputIterator result_
)

template
<
  class InputIterator,
  class OutputIterator,
  class BinaryOperation
>
OutputIterator adjacent_difference
(
  InputIterator first_,
  InputIterator last_,
  OutputIterator result_,
  BinaryOperator binary_op_
)
```

Description
Iterate through every element in the range [first_+1..last_) and write the difference between the element and its preceding element to result_. Return an iterator equal to result_ + n where n = last_ - first_. Assignment back into the original range is allowed. The first version of this algorithm uses operator- to calculate the difference, whereas the second version of this algorithm uses the binary function binary_op.

Complexity
Time complexity is linear as operator- or binary_op_ are applied last_ - first_ - 1 times. Space complexity is constant.

Example <adjdiff0.cpp>
```
#include <algorithm.h>
#include <iostream.h>

int numbers[5] = { 1, 2, 4, 8, 16 };

int main ()
{
  int difference[5];
  adjacent_difference (numbers, numbers + 5, difference);
```

```
    for (int i = 0; i < 5; i++)
      cout << numbers[i] << ' ';
    cout << endl;
    for (i = 0; i < 5; i++)
      cout << difference[i] << ' ';
    cout << endl;
    return 0;
  }

  1 2 3 8 16
  1 1 2 4 8
```

Example <adjdiff1.cpp>

```
  #include <algorithm.h>
  #include <vector.h>
  #include <iterator.h>
  #include <iostream.h>

  int main ()
  {
    vector <int> v (10);
    for (int i = 0; i < v.size (); i++)
      v[i] = i * i;
    vector <int> result (v.size ());
    adjacent_difference (v.begin (), v.end (), result.begin ());
    ostream_iterator<int> iter (cout, " ");
    copy (v.begin (), v.end (), iter);
    cout << endl;
    copy (result.begin (), result.end (), iter);
    cout << endl;
    return 0;
  }

  0 1 4 9 16 25 36 49 64 81
  0 1 3 5 7 9 11 13 15 17
```

Example <adjdiff2.cpp>

```
  #include <algorithm.h>
  #include <vector.h>
  #include <iterator.h>
  #include <iostream.h>

  int mult (int a_, int b_)
  {
    return a_ * b_;
  }

  int main ()
  {
    vector <int> v (10);
    for (int i = 0; i < v.size (); i++)
      v[i] = i + 1;
```

```
        vector <int> result (v.size ());
        adjacent_difference (v.begin (), v.end (), result.begin (),
        mult);
        ostream_iterator<int> iter (cout, " ");
        copy (v.begin (), v.end (), iter);
        cout << endl;
        copy (result.begin (), result.end (), iter);
        cout << endl;
        return 0;
}

1 2 3 4 5 6 7 8 9 10
1 2 6 12 20 30 42 56 72 90
```

adjacent_find

Synopsis
Locate a consecutive sequence in a range.

Signatures
```
#include <algorithm.h>
template<class InputIterator>
InputIterator adjacent_find
(
   InputIterator first_,
   InputIterator last_
)

template<class InputIterator, class BinaryPredicate>
InputIterator adjacent_find
(
   InputIterator first_,
   InputIterator last_,
   BinaryPredicate binary_pred_
)
```

Description
Return an input iterator positioned at the first pair of matching consecutive elements. If no match is found, return last_. The first version performs matching using operator==, whereas the second version uses the binary function binary_pred_.

Complexity
Time complexity is linear, as a maximum of (last_ - first_) comparisons are performed. Space complexity is constant.

Example <adjfind0.cpp>

```
#include <algorithm.h>
#include <iostream.h>

int numbers1 [5] = { 1, 2, 4, 8, 16 };
```

```cpp
int numbers2 [5] = { 5, 3, 2, 1, 1 };

int main ()
{
  int* location = adjacent_find (numbers1, numbers1 + 5);
  if (location != numbers1 + 5)
    cout
      << "Found adjacent pair of: "
      << *location
      << " at offset "
      << location - numbers1
      << endl;
  else
    cout << "No adjacent pairs" << endl;
  location = adjacent_find (numbers2, numbers2 + 5);
  if (location != numbers2 + 5)
    cout
      << "Found adjacent pair of: "
      << *location
      << " at offset "
      << location - numbers2
      << endl;
  else
    cout << "No adjacent pairs" << endl;
  return 0;
}
```

No adjacent pairs
Found adjacent pair of: 1 at offset 3

Example <adjfind1.cpp>

```cpp
#include <algorithm.h>
#include <vector.h>
#include <iostream.h>

int main ()
{
  typedef vector<int> IntVector;
  IntVector v (10);
  for (int i = 0; i < v.size (); i++)
    v[i] = i;
  IntVector::iterator location;
  location = adjacent_find (v.begin (), v.end ());
  if (location != v.end ())
    cout << "Found adjacent pair of: " << *location << endl;
  else
    cout << "No adjacent pairs" << endl;
  v[6] = 7;
  location = adjacent_find (v.begin (), v.end ());
  if (location != v.end ())
    cout << "Found adjacent pair of: " << *location << endl;
  else
    cout << "No adjacent pairs" << endl;
```

```
      return 0;
   }
```

No adjacent pairs
Found adjacent pair of: 7

Example <adjfind2.cpp>

```
#include <algorithm.h>
#include <vector.h>
#include <iostream.h>
#include <string.h>

typedef vector <char*> CStrVector;

int equal_length (const char* v1_, const char* v2_)
{
   return ::strlen (v1_) == ::strlen(v2_);
}

char* names[] = { "Brett", "Graham", "Jack", "Mike", "Todd" };

int main ()
{
   const int nameCount = sizeof (names)/sizeof(names[0]);
   CStrVector v (nameCount);
   for (int i = 0; i < nameCount; i++)
     v[i] = names[i];
   CStrVector::iterator location;
   location = adjacent_find (v.begin (), v.end (), equal_length);
   if (location != v.end ())
     cout
        << "Found two adjacent strings of equal length: "
        << *location
        << " -and- "
        << *(location + 1)
        << endl;
   else
     cout << "Didn't find two adjacent strings of equal length.";
   return 0;
}
```

Found two adjacent strings of equal length: Jack -and- Mike

binary_search

Synopsis
Locate an item in a sorted sequence.

Signatures
```
#include <algorithm.h>
template<class ForwardIterator, class T>
```

```
bool binary_search
(
  ForwardIterator first_,
  ForwardIterator last_,
  const T& value_
)

template<class ForwardIterator, class T, class Compare>
bool binary_search
(
  ForwardIterator first_,
  ForwardIterator last_,
  const T& value_,
  Compare compare_
)
```

Description

Return true if value_ is in the range [first_..last_). The first version assumes that the elements in [first_..last_) are already sorted using operator <, whereas the second version assumes that the elements are already sorted using the comparison function compare_.

Complexity

Time complexity is O(Log N) for random access iterators and O(N) for all other iterators. Space complexity is constant.

Helper

```
bool os_binary_search (const Container& c_, const T& value_)
```

Example <binsrch1.cpp>

```
#include <algorithm.h>
#include <vector.h>
#include <iostream.h>

int main ()
{
  int vector[100];
  for (int i = 0; i < 100; i++)
    vector[i] = i;
  if (binary_search (vector, vector + 100, 42))
    cout << "found 42" << endl;
  else
    cout << "did not find 42" << endl;
  return 0;
}
```

found 42

Example <binsrch2.cpp>

```
#include <algorithm.h>
#include <iostream.h>
#include <string.h>

bool str_compare (const char* a_, const char* b_)
{
   return ::strcmp (a_, b_) < 0 ? 1 : 0;
}

char* labels[] = { "aa", "dd", "ff", "jj", "ss", "zz" };

int main ()
{
   const unsigned count = sizeof (labels) / sizeof (labels[0]);
   if (binary_search (labels, labels + count, "ff", str_compare))
     cout << "ff is in labels." << endl;
   else
     cout << "ff is not in labels." << endl;
   return 0;
}
```

ff is in labels

copy

Synopsis
Copy a range of items to another area.

Signature
```
#include <algorithm.h>
template<class InputIterator, class OutputIterator>
OutputIterator copy
(
   InputIterator first_,
   InputIterator last_,
   OutputIterator result_
)
```

Description
Copy the elements from the range [first_, last_) into a range of the same size starting at result_, using operator= to replace the existing elements. Return an iterator of the same type as result_ positioned immediately after the last new element.

Complexity
Time complexity is linear, as (last_ - first_) assignments are performed. Space complexity is constant.

Example <copy1.cpp>

```
#include <algorithm.h>
#include <iostream.h>
#include <string.h>

char string[23] = "A string to be copied.";

int main ()
{
  char result[23];
  copy (string, string + 23, result);
  cout << " Src: " << string << "\nDest: " << result << endl;
  return 0;
}
```

```
 Src: A string to be copied.
Dest: A string to be copied.
```

Example <copy2.cpp>

```
#include <algorithm.h>
#include <vector.h>
#include <iterator.h>
#include <iostream.h>

int main ()
{
  vector <int> v (10);
  for (int i = 0; i < v.size (); i++)
    v[i] = i;
  ostream_iterator<int> iter (cout, " ");
  copy (v.begin (), v.end (), iter);
  return 0;
}
```

```
0 1 2 3 4 5 6 7 8 9
```

Example <copy3.cpp>

```
#include <algorithm.h>
#include <vector.h>
#include <iterator.h>
#include <iostream.h>

int main ()
{
  vector <int> v1 (10);
  for (int i = 0; i < v1.size (); i++)
    v1[i] = i;
  vector <int> v2 (10);
  copy (v1.begin (), v1.end (), v2.begin ());
  ostream_iterator<int> iter (cout, " ");
  copy (v2.begin (), v2.end (), iter);
  return 0;
```

```
}
```

```
0 1 2 3 4 5 6 7 8 9
```

Example <copy4.cpp>

```
#include <algorithm.h>
#include <vector.h>
#include <iterator.h>
#include <iostream.h>

int main ()
{
  typedef vector <int> IVec;
  vector <int> v1 (10);
  for (int loc = 0; loc < v1.size (); loc++)
    v1[loc] = loc;
  vector <int> v2;
  // When templates are better supported, below will read:
  //insert_iterator <IVec> iter (v2, v2.begin ());
  insert_iterator<IVec, int, IVec::iterator> i(v2, v2.begin ());
  copy (v1.begin (), v1.end (), i);
  ostream_iterator<int> outIter (cout, " ");
  copy (v2.begin (), v2.end (), outIter);
  return 0;
}
```

```
0 1 2 3 4 5 6 7 8 9
```

copy_backward

Synopsis

Copy a range of items backwards to another area.

Signature

```
#include <algorithm.h>
template<class BidirectionalIterator1, class
BidirectionalIterator2>
BidirectionalIterator2 copy_backward
(
  BidirectionalIterator1 first_,
  BidirectionalIterator1 last_,
  BidirectionalIterator2 result_
)
```

Description

Copy the elements from the range [first_..last_) into a range of the same size ending immediately before result_, using operator= to replace the existing elements. Return an iterator of the same type as result_, positioned at the start of the newly created sequence. The elements in result_ will be in the same order as the elements in [first_, last_).

Complexity

Time complexity is linear, as (last_ - first_) assignments are performed. Space complexity is constant.

Example <copyb0.cpp>

```cpp
#include <algorithm.h>
#include <iostream.h>

int numbers[5] = { 1, 2, 3, 4, 5 };

int main ()
{
  int result[5];
  copy_backward (numbers, numbers + 5, result + 5);
  for (int i = 0; i < 5; i++)
    cout << numbers[i] << ' ';
  cout << endl;
  for (i = 0; i < 5; i++)
    cout << result[i] << ' ';
  cout << endl;
  return 0;
}
```

```
1 2 3 4 5
1 2 3 4 5
```

Example <copyb1.cpp>

```cpp
#include <algorithm.h>
#include <vector.h>
#include <iterator.h>
#include <iostream.h>

int main ()
{
  vector <int> v1 (10);
  for (int i = 0; i < v1.size (); i++)
    v1[i] = i;
  vector <int> v2(v1.size ());
  copy_backward (v1.begin (), v1.end (), v2.end ());
  ostream_iterator<int> iter (cout, " ");
  copy (v2.begin (), v2.end (), iter);
  return 0;
}
```

```
0 1 2 3 4 5 6 7 8 9
```

count

Synopsis
Count items in a range that match a value.

Signature
```
#include <algorithm.h>
template<class InputIterator, class T, class Size>
void count
(
    InputIterator first_,
    InputIterator last_,
    const T& value_,
    Size& n_
)
```

Description
Count the number of elements in the range [first_, last_) that match value_
using operator== and add this count to n_. Note that n_ is not automatically
initialized to zero prior to the counting procedure.

Complexity
Time complexity is linear, as (last_ - first_) comparisons are performed. Space
complexity is constant.

Helper
```
int os_count (const Container& c_, const T& value_)
```

Example <count0.cpp>

```
#include <algorithm.h>
#include <iostream.h>

int main ()
{
    int numbers[10] = { 1, 2, 4, 1, 2, 4, 1, 2, 4, 1 };
    int result = 0;
    count (numbers, numbers + 10, 1, result);
    cout << "Found " << result << " 1's." << endl;
    return 0;
}
```

```
Found 4 1's.
```

Example <count1.cpp>

```
#include <algorithm.h>
#include <vector.h>
#include <iostream.h>

int main ()
```

```
{
  vector <int> numbers(100);
  for (int i = 0; i < 100; i++)
    numbers[i] = i % 3;
  int elements = 0;
  count (numbers.begin (), numbers.end (), 2, elements);
  cout << "Found " << elements << " 2's." << endl;
  return 0;
}
```

Found 33 2's.

count_if

Synopsis
Count items in a range that satisfy a predicate.

Signature
```
#include <algorithm.h>
template<class InputIterator, class Predicate, class Size>
void count_if
(
  InputIterator first_,
  InputIterator last_,
  Predicate pred_,
  Size& n_
)
```

Description
Count the number of elements in the range [first_, last_) that cause predicate_ to return true and add this count to n_. Note that n_ is not automatically initialized to zero prior to the counting procedure.

Complexity
Time complexity is linear, as (last_ - first_) comparisons are performed. Space complexity is constant.

Helper
```
int os_count_if (const Container& c_, Predicate pred_)
```

Example <countif1.cpp>

```
#include <algorithm.h>
#include <iostream.h>

int odd (int a_)
{
  return a_ % 2;
}

int main ()
```

```
{
  vector <int> numbers(100);
  for (int i = 0; i < 100; i++)
    numbers[i] = i % 3;
  int elements = 0;
  count_if (numbers.begin (), numbers.end (), odd, elements);
  cout << "Found " << elements << " odd elements." << endl;
  return 0;
}
```

Found 33 odd elements.

equal

Synopsis
Check that two sequences match.

Signatures
```
#include <algorithm.h>
template<class InputIterator1, class InputIterator2>
bool equal
(
  InputIterator1 first1_,
  InputIterator1 last1_,
  InputIterator2 first2_
)

template
<
  class InputIterator1,
  class InputIterator2,
  class BinaryPredicate
>
bool equal
(
  InputIterator1 first1_,
  InputIterator1 last1_,
  InputIterator2 first2_,
  BinaryPredicate binary_pred_
)
```

Description
Compare the sequence [first1_..last1_) with a sequence of the same size starting at first2_. Return true if every corresponding pair of elements match. The first version uses operator== to perform the matching, whereas the second version uses the binary function binary_pred_.

Complexity
Time complexity is linear as N comparisons are performed. Space complexity is constant.

Example <equal0.cpp>

```
#include <algorithm.h>
#include <iostream.h>

int numbers1[5] = { 1, 2, 3, 4, 5 };
int numbers2[5] = { 1, 2, 4, 8, 16 };
int numbers3[2] = { 1, 2 };

int main ()
{
  if (equal (numbers1, numbers1 + 5, numbers2))
    cout << "numbers1 is equal to numbers2" << endl;
  else
    cout << "numbers1 is not equal to numbers2" << endl;
  if (equal (numbers3, numbers3 + 2, numbers1))
    cout << "numbers3 is equal to numbers1" << endl;
  else
    cout << "numbers3 is not equal to numbers1" << endl;
  return 0;
}
```

numbers1 is not equal to numbers2
numbers3 is equal to numbers1

Example <equal1.cpp>

```
#include <algorithm.h>
#include <vector.h>
#include <iostream.h>

int main ()
{
  vector <int> v1 (10);
  for (int i = 0; i < v1.size (); i++)
    v1[i] = i;
  vector <int> v2 (10);
  if (equal (v1.begin (), v1.end (), v2.begin ()))
    cout << "v1 is equal to v2" << endl;
  else
    cout << "v1 is not equal to v2" << endl;
  copy (v1.begin (), v1.end (), v2.begin ());
  if (equal (v1.begin (), v1.end (), v2.begin ()))
    cout << "v1 is equal to v2" << endl;
  else
    cout << "v1 is not equal to v2" << endl;
  return 0;
}
```

v1 is not equal to v2
v1 is equal to v2

Example <equal2.cpp>

```cpp
#include <algorithm.h>
#include <vector.h>
#include <iostream.h>

bool values_squared (int a_, int b_)
{
   return a_*a_ == b_ ? 1 : 0;
}

int main ()
{
   vector <int> v1 (10);
   vector <int> v2 (10);
   for (int i = 0; i < v1.size (); i++)
   {
     v1[i] = i;
     v2[i] = i * i;
   }
   if (equal (v1.begin (), v1.end (), v2.begin (),
   values_squared))
     cout << "v2[i] == v1[i]*v1[i]" << endl;
   else
     cout << "v2[i] != v1[i]*v1[i]" << endl;
   return 0;
}
```

v2[i] == v1[i]*v1[i]

equal_range

Synopsis
Return the lower and upper bounds within a range.

Signatures
```cpp
#include <algorithm.h>
template<class ForwardIterator, class T>
pair<ForwardIterator, ForwardIterator> equal_range
(
   ForwardIterator first_,
   ForwardIterator last_,
   const T& value_
)

template<class ForwardIterator, class T, class Compare>
pair<ForwardIterator, ForwardIterator> equal_range
(
   ForwardIterator first_,
   ForwardIterator last_,
   const T& value_,
   Compare compare_
)
```

Description

Search a pair of iterators equal to the lower bound and upper bound for value_.
The first version assumes that the elements in the range are already sorted
using operator<. The second version assumes that the elements in the range
are already sorted using compare_. For information about lower and upper
bounds, consult the algorithm catalog entries for lower_bound() and
upper_bound().

Complexity

Time complexity is O(Log N) for RandomAccessIterators, O(N) for all other
iterators. Space complexity is constant.

Example <eqlrnge0.cpp>

```
#include <algorithm.h>
#include <iostream.h>

int numbers[10] = { 0, 0, 1, 1, 2, 2, 2, 2, 3, 3 };

int main ()
{
  pair <int*, int*> range;
  range = equal_range (numbers, numbers + 10, 2);
  cout
    << "2 can be inserted from before index "
    << range.first - numbers
    << " to before index "
    << range.second - numbers
    << endl;
  return 0;
}
```

2 can be inserted from before index 4 to before index 8

Example <eqlrng1.cpp>

```
#include <algorithm.h>
#include <vector.h>
#include <iterator.h>
#include <iostream.h>

int main ()
{
  typedef vector <int> IntVec;
  IntVec v (10);
  for (int i = 0; i < v.size (); i++)
    v[i] = i / 3;
  ostream_iterator<int> iter (cout, " ");
  cout << "Within the collection:\n\t";
  copy (v.begin (), v.end (), iter);
  pair <IntVec::iterator, IntVec::iterator> range;
  range = equal_range (v.begin (), v.end (), 2);
```

```
        cout
          << "\n2 can be inserted from before index "
          << range.first - v.begin ()
          << " to before index "
          << range.second - v.begin ()
          << endl;
        return 0;
      }
```

Within the collection:
       0 0 0 1 1 1 2 2 2 3
2 can be inserted from before index 6 to before index 9

Example <eqlrng2.cpp>

```
    #include <algorithm.h>
    #include <iterator.h>
    #include <iostream.h>
    #include <string.h>

    char chars[] = "aabbccddggghhklllmqqqqssyyzz";

    int main ()
    {
      const unsigned count = sizeof (chars) - 1;
      ostream_iterator<char> iter (cout);
      cout << "Within the collection:\n\t";
      copy (chars, chars + count, iter);
      pair <char*, char*> range;
      range = equal_range (chars, chars + count, 'q', less<char>());
      cout
         << "\nq can be inserted from before index "
         << range.first - chars
         << " to before index "
         << range.second - chars
         << endl;
      return 0;
    }
```

Within the collection
       aabbccddggghhklllmqqqqssyyzz
q can be inserted from before index 18 to before index 22

fill

Synopsis
Set every item in a range to a particular value.

Signatures
```
    #include <algorithm.h>
    template<class ForwardIterator, class T>
    void fill
```

```
(
  ForwardIterator first_,
  ForwardIterator last_,
  const T& value_
)
```

Description

Assign value_ to each element in the range [first_..last_). Return an iterator equal to result_ + n where n = last_ - first_.

Complexity

Time complexity is linear as (last_ - first_) assignments are performed. Space complexity is constant.

Example <fill1.cpp>

```
#include <algorithm.h>
#include <vector.h>
#include <iostream.h>

int main ()
{
  vector <int> v (10);
  fill (v.begin (), v.end (), 42);
  for (int i = 0; i < 10; i++)
    cout << v[i] << ' ';
  cout << endl;
  return 0;
}
```

42 42 42 42 42 42 42 42 42 42

fill_n

Synopsis

Set n items to a particular value.

Signature

```
#include <algorithm.h>
template<class OutputIterator, class Size, class T>
void fill_n (OutputIterator first_, Size n_, const T& value_)
```

Description

Assign value_ to the n_ elements starting at position first_. Return an iterator equal to result_ + n_.

Complexity

Time complexity is linear as exactly n_ assignments are performed. Space complexity is constant.

Example <filln1.cpp>

```cpp
#include <algorithm.h>
#include <vector.h>
#include <iostream.h>

int main ()
{
  vector <int> v (10);
  fill_n (v.begin (), v.size (), 42);
  for (int i = 0; i < 10; i++)
    cout << v[i] << ' ';
  cout << endl;
  return 0;
}
```

42 42 42 42 42 42 42 42 42 42

find

Synopsis
Locate an item in a sequence.

Signature
```cpp
#include <algorithm.h>
template<class InputIterator, class T>
InputIterator find
(
  InputIterator first_,
  InputIterator last_,
  const T& value_
)
```

Description
Search for an element within [first_..last_) that matches value_ using operator==. Return an iterator to the first matching value, or last_ if no such element exists.

Complexity
Time complexity is linear, as a maximum of (last_ - first_) comparisons are performed. Space complexity is constant.

Helper
```cpp
void os_find (Container& c_, const T& value_, T*& result_)
```

Example <find0.cpp>

```cpp
#include <algorithm.h>
#include <iostream.h>

int numbers[10] = { 0, 1, 4, 9, 16, 25, 36, 49, 64 };
```

```
int main ()
{
  int* location;
  location = find (numbers, numbers + 10, 25);
  cout
     << "Found 25 at offset "
     << location - numbers
     << endl;
  return 0;
}
```

Found 25 at offset 5

Example <find1.cpp>

```
#include <algorithm.h>
#include <iostream.h>

int years[] = { 1942, 1952, 1962, 1972, 1982, 1992 };

int main ()
{
  const unsigned yearCount = sizeof (years) / sizeof (years[0]);
  int* location = find (years, years + yearCount, 1972);
  cout << "Found 1972 at offset " << location - years << endl;
  return 0;
}
```

Found 1972 at offset 3

find_if

Synopsis
Locate an item that satisfies a predicate in a range.

Signature
```
#include <algorithm.h>
template<class InputIterator, class Predicate>
InputIterator find_if
(
  InputIterator first_,
  InputIterator last_,
  Predicate pred_
)
```

Description
Return an input iterator positioned at the first element in the range [first_, last_) that causes predicate_ to return true. If no such element exists, return last_.

Complexity

Time complexity is linear, as a maximum of (last_ - first_) comparisons are performed. Space complexity is constant.

Helper

```
void os_find_if (Container& c_, Predicate pred_, T*& result_)
```

Example <findif0.cpp>

```cpp
#include <algorithm.h>
#include <iostream.h>

bool odd (int a_)
{
   return a_ % 2;
}

int numbers[6] = { 2, 4, 8, 15, 32, 64 };

int main ()
{
   int* location = find_if (numbers, numbers + 6, odd);
   if (location != numbers + 6)
     cout
        << "Value "
        << *location
        << " at offset "
        << location - numbers
        << " is odd"
        << endl;
   return 0;
}
```

Value 15 at offset 3 is odd

Example <findif1.cpp>

```cpp
#include <algorithm.h>
#include <vector.h>
#include <iostream.h>

bool div_3 (int a_)
{
   return a_ % 3 ? 0 : 1;
}

int main ()
{
   typedef vector <int> IntVec;
   IntVec v (10);
   for (int i = 0; i < v.size (); i++)
     v[i] = (i + 1) * (i + 1);
   IntVec::iterator iter;
```

```
    iter = find_if (v.begin (), v.end (), div_3);
    if (iter != v.end ())
       cout
          << "Value "
          << *iter
          << " at offset "
          << iter - v.begin ()
          << " is divisible by 3"
          << endl;
    return 0;
}
```

Value 9 at offset 2 is divisible by 3

for_each

Synopsis
Apply a function to every item in a range.

Signature
```
#include <algorithm.h>
template<class InputIterator, class Function>
Function for_each
(
   InputIterator first_,
   InputIterator last_,
   Function f_
)
```

Description
Apply f_ to every element in the range [first_, last_) and return the input parameter f_.

Complexity
Time complexity is linear, as function_ is called (last_ - first_) times. Space complexity is constant.

Helper
```
Function os_for_each (Container& c_, Function f_)
```

Example <foreach0.cpp>
```
#include <algorithm.h>
#include <iostream.h>

void print (int a_)
{
   cout << a_ << ' ';
}

int numbers[10] = { 1, 1, 2, 3, 5, 8, 13, 21, 34, 55 };
```

```
int main ()
{
   for_each (numbers, numbers + 10, print);
   cout << endl;
   return 0;
}
```

1 1 2 3 5 8 13 21 34 55

Example <foreach1.cpp>

```
#include <algorithm.h>
#include <vector.h>
#include <iostream.h>

void print_sqr (int a_)
{
   cout << a_ * a_ << " ";
}

int main ()
{
   vector <int> v1 (10);
   for (int i = 0; i < v1.size (); i++)
      v1[i] = i;
   for_each (v1.begin (), v1.end (), print_sqr);
   return 0;
}
```

0 1 4 9 16 25 36 49 64 81

generate

Synopsis
Fill a sequence using a generator function.

Signature
```
#include <algorithm.h>
template<class ForwardIterator, class Generator>
void generate
(
   ForwardIterator first_,
   ForwardIterator last_,
   Generator gen_
)
```

Description
Traverse the sequence [first_..last_), assigning to each element the result of executing gen_().

Complexity

Time complexity is linear, as gen_ is executed (last_ - first_) times. Space complexity is constant.

Example <gener1.cpp>

```cpp
#include <algorithm.h>
#include <iostream.h>
#include <stdlib.h>

int main ()
{
  int numbers[10];
  generate (numbers, numbers + 10, rand);
  for (int i = 0; i < 10; i++)
    cout << numbers[i] << ' ';
  cout << endl;
  return 0;
}
```

346 130 10982 1090 11656 7117 17595 6415 22948 31126

Example <gener2.cpp>

```cpp
#include <algorithm.h>
#include <vector.h>
#include <iterator.h>
#include <iostream.h>
#include <stdlib.h>

class Fibonacci
{
  public:
    Fibonacci () : v1 (0), v2 (1) {}
    int operator () ();
  private:
    int v1;
    int v2;
};

int
Fibonacci::operator () ()
{
  int r = v1 + v2;
  v1 = v2;
  v2 = r;
  return v1;
}

int main ()
{
  vector <int> v1 (10);
  Fibonacci generator;
```

```
    generate (v1.begin (), v1.end (), generator);
    ostream_iterator<int> iter (cout, " ");
    copy (v1.begin (), v1.end (), iter);
    return 0;
}
```

1 1 2 3 5 8 13 21 34 55

generate_n

Synopsis
Generate a specified number of items.

Signature
```
#include <algorithm.h>
template <class OutputIterator, class Size, class Generator>
void generate_n (OutputIterator first_, Size n_, Generator gen_)
```

Description
Traverse the sequence [first_..first_ + n_), assigning to each element the result
of executing gen_().

Complexity
Time complexity is linear, as gen_ is executed n_ times. Space complexity is
constant.

Example <genern1.cpp>

```
#include <algorithm.h>
#include <vector.h>
#include <iostream.h>
#include <stdlib.h>

int main ()
{
  vector <int> v1 (10);
  generate_n (v1.begin (), v1.size (), rand);
  for (int i = 0; i < 10; i++)
    cout << v1[i] << ' ';
  return 0;
}
```

346 130 10982 1090 11656 7117 17595 6415 22948 31126

Example <genern2.cpp>

```
#include <algorithm.h>
#include <vector.h>
#include <iterator.h>
#include <iostream.h>
```

```
#include <stdlib.h>

class Fibonacci
{
  public:
    Fibonacci () : v1 (0), v2 (1) {}
    int operator () ();
  private:
    int v1;
    int v2;
};

int
Fibonacci::operator () ()
{
  int r = v1 + v2;
  v1 = v2;
  v2 = r;
  return v1;
}

int main ()
{
  vector <int> v1 (10);
  Fibonacci generator;
  generate_n (v1.begin (), v1.size (), generator);
  ostream_iterator<int> iter (cout, " ");
  copy (v1.begin (), v1.end (), iter);
  return 0;
}
```

1 1 2 3 5 8 13 21 34 55

includes

Synopsis
Search for one sequence in another sequence.

Signatures
```
#include <algorithm.h>
template <class InputIterator1, class InputIterator2>
bool includes
(
   InputIterator1 first1_,
   InputIterator1 last1_,
   InputIterator2 first2_,
   InputIterator2 last2_
)

template<class InputIterator1, class InputIterator2, class
Compare>
bool includes
(
   InputIterator1 first1_,
```

```
      InputIterator1 last1_,
      InputIterator2 first2_,
      InputIterator2 last2_,
      Compare compare_
   )
```

Description

Search for one sequence of values in another sequence of values. Return true
if every element in [first2_..last2_) is in the sequence [first1_..last1_). The first
version assumes that both sequences are already sorted using operator<. The
second version assumes that both sequences are already sorted using com-
pare_.

Complexity

Time complexity is linear. Space complexity is constant.

Helper

```
   bool os_includes (const Container& c1_, const Container& c2_)
   bool os_includes
   (
      const Container& c1_,
      const Container& c2_,
      Compare compare_
   )
```

Example <incl0.cpp>

```cpp
   #include <algorithm.h>
   #include <iostream.h>

   int numbers1[5] = { 1, 2, 3, 4, 5 };
   int numbers2[5] = { 1, 2, 4, 8, 16 };
   int numbers3[2] = { 4, 8 };

   int main ()
   {
      if (includes (numbers1, numbers1 + 5, numbers3, numbers3 + 2))
         cout << "numbers1 includes numbers3" << endl;
      else
         cout << "numbers1 does not include numbers3" << endl;
      if (includes (numbers2, numbers2 + 5, numbers3, numbers3 + 2))
         cout << "numbers2 includes numbers3" << endl;
      else
         cout << "numbers2 does not include numbers3" << endl;
      return 0;
   }

   numbers1 does not include numbers3
   numbers2 includes numbers3
```

Example <incl1.cpp>

```
#include <algorithm.h>
#include <vector.h>
#include <iostream.h>

int main ()
{
  vector<int> v1(10);
  vector<int> v2(3);
  for (int i = 0; i < v1.size (); i++)
    v1[i] = i;
  if (includes (v1.begin (), v1.end (), v2.begin (), v2.end ()))
    cout << "v1 includes v2" << endl;
  else
    cout << "v1 does not include v2" << endl;
  for (i = 0; i < v2.size (); i++)
    v2[i] = i + 3;
  if (includes (v1.begin (), v1.end (), v2.begin (), v2.end ()))
    cout << "v1 includes v2" << endl;
  else
    cout << "v1 does not include v2" << endl;
  return 0;
}
```

v1 does not include v2
v1 includes v2

Example <incl2.cpp>

```
#include <algorithm.h>
#include <vector.h>
#include <iostream.h>
#include <string.h>

bool compare_strings (const char* s1_, const char* s2_)
{
  return ::strcmp (s1_, s2_) < 0 ? 1 : 0;
}

char* names[] = { "Todd", "Mike", "Graham", "Jack", "Brett"};

int main ()
{
  const unsigned nameSize = sizeof (names)/sizeof (names[0]);
  vector <char*> v1(nameSize);
  for (int i = 0; i < v1.size (); i++)
    v1[i] = names[i];
  vector <char*> v2 (2);
  v2[0] = "foo";
  v2[1] = "bar";
  sort (v1.begin (), v1.end (), compare_strings);
  sort (v2.begin (), v2.end (), compare_strings);
  bool inc = includes (v1.begin (), v1.end (),
```

```
                        v2.begin (), v2.end (),
                        compare_strings);
    if (inc)
      cout << "v1 includes v2" << endl;
    else
      cout << "v1 does not include v2" << endl;
    v2[0] = "Brett";
    v2[1] = "Todd";
    inc = includes (v1.begin (), v1.end (),
                        v2.begin (), v2.end (),
                        compare_strings);
    if (inc)
      cout << "v1 includes v2" << endl;
    else
      cout << "v1 does not include v2" << endl;
    return 0;
}
```

v1 does not include v2
v1 includes v2

inner_product

Synopsis
Calculate the inner product of two sequences.

Signatures
```
#include <algorithm.h>
template<class InputIterator1, class InputIterator2, class T>
T inner_product
(
    InputIterator1 first1_,
    InputIterator1 last1_,
    InputIterator2 first2_,
    T init_
)

template
<
    class InputIterator1,
    class InputIterator2,
    class T,
    class BinaryOperation1,
    class BinaryOperation2
>
T inner_product
(
    InputIterator1 first1_,
    InputIterator1 last1_,
    InputIterator2 first2_,
    T init_,
    BinaryOperation1 binary_op1_,
    BinaryOperation2 binary_op2_
)
```

Description

Use a pair of iterators i_ and j_ to traverse the two sequences [first1_..last1_) and [first2_..first2_+(last1_-first1_)). Apply the formula init_ = init_ op1_ (*i_ op2_ *j) and return the final value of init_. Note that init_ is not automatically initialized to zero prior to this operation. The first version automatically sets op1_ to operator+ and op2_ to operator*.

Complexity

Time complexity is linear. Space complexity is constant.

Example <inrprod0.cpp>

```
#include <algorithm.h>
#include <iostream.h>
#include <string.h>

int vector1[5] = { 1, 2, 3, 4, 5 };
int vector2[5] = { 1, 2, 3, 4, 5 };

int main ()
{
  int result;
  result = inner_product (vector1, vector1 + 5, vector2, 0);
  cout << "Inner product = " << result << endl;
  return 0;
}
```

Inner product = 55

Example <inrprod1.cpp>

```
#include <algorithm.h>
#include <vector.h>
#include <iterator.h>
#include <iostream.h>
#include <string.h>

int main ()
{
  vector <int> v1 (3);
  vector <int> v2 (v1.size ());
  for (int i = 0; i < v1.size (); i++)
  {
    v1[i] = i + 1;
    v2[i] = v1.size () - i;
  }
  ostream_iterator<int> iter (cout, " ");
  cout << "Inner product (sum of products) of:\n\t";
  copy (v1.begin (), v1.end (), iter);
  cout << "\n\t";
  copy (v2.begin (), v2.end (), iter);
  int result
```

```
      = inner_product (v1.begin (), v1.end (), v2.begin (), 0);
   cout << "\nis: " << result << endl;
   return 0;
}
```

Inner product (sum of products) of:
      1 2 3
      3 2 1
is: 10

Example <inrprod2.cpp>

```
#include <algorithm.h>
#include <vector.h>
#include <iterator.h>
#include <iostream.h>
#include <string.h>

int add (int a_, int b_)
{
   return a_ + b_;
}

int mult (int a_, int b_)
{
   return a_ * b_;
}

int main ()
{
   vector <int> v1 (3);
   vector <int> v2 (v1.size ());
   for (int i = 0; i < v1.size (); i++)
   {
     v1[i] = i + 1;
     v2[i] = v1.size () - i;
   }
   ostream_iterator<int> iter (cout, " ");
   cout << "Inner product (product of sums):\n\t";
   copy (v1.begin (), v1.end (), iter);
   cout << "\n\t";
   copy (v2.begin (), v2.end (), iter);
   int result =
     inner_product(v1.begin (), v1.end (),
                   v2.begin (),
                   1,
                   mult, add);
   cout << "\nis: " << result << endl;
   return 0;
}
```

Inner product (product of sums) of:
      1 2 3
      3 2 1
is: 64

inplace_merge

Synopsis
Merge two sorted lists in place into a single sorted list.

Signature
```
#include <algorithm.h>
template<class BidirectionalIterator>
void inplace_merge
(
  BidirectionalIterator first_,
  BidirectionalIterator middle_,
  BidirectionalIterator last_
)

template<class BidirectionalIterator, class Compare>
void inplace_merge
(
  BidirectionalIterator first_,
  BidirectionalIterator middle_,
  BidirectionalIterator last_,
  Compare compare_
)
```

Description
Given two sorted sub-sequences [first_..middle_) and [middle_..last_) within
the range [first_..last_), merge the two sub-sequence into one sorted sequence
from [first_..last_). This merge is stable in the sense that if both ranges
contain equal values, the value from the first range will be stored first. The
first version assumes that the ranges [first_..middle_) and [middle_..last_) are
sorted using operator<.

Complexity
Given enough memory, this algorithm's time complexity is linear and its space
complexity is last_ - first_. If enough memory is not available, the time complexity becomes N long N and the space complexity becomes constant.

Example <inplmrg1.cpp>
```
#include <algorithm.h>
#include <iostream.h>

int numbers[6] = { 1, 10, 42, 3, 16, 32 };

int main ()
{
  for (int i = 0; i < 6; i++)
    cout << numbers[i] << ' ';
  cout << endl;
  inplace_merge (numbers, numbers + 3, numbers + 6);
  for (i = 0; i < 6; i++)
    cout << numbers[i] << ' ';
```

```
      cout << endl;
      return 0;
}

1  10  42  3  16  32
1  3  10  16  32  42
```

Example <inplmrg2.cpp>

```
#include <algorithm.h>
#incldue <vector.h>
#include <iterator.h>
#include <iostream.h>

int main ()
{
    vector <int> v1(10);
    for (int i = 0; i < v1.size (); i++)
        v1[i] = (v1.size () - i - 1) % 5;
    ostream_iterator <int> iter (cout, " ");
    copy (v1.begin (), v1.end (), iter);
    cout << endl;
    inplace_merge (v1.begin (), v1.begin () + 5,
                   v1.end (),
                   greater<int>());
    copy (v1.begin (), v1.end (), iter);
    cout << endl;
    return 0;
}

4  3  2  1  0  4  3  2  1  0
4  4  3  3  2  2  1  1  0  0
```

iota

Synopsis

Fill a range with ascending values.

Signature

```
#include <algorithm.h>
template<class ForwardIterator, class T>
void iota (ForwardIterator first_, ForwardIterator last_, T
value_)
```

Description

Assign value_ to each element in the range [first_..last_), incrementing value_
using operator++ after each assignment.

Complexity

Time complexity is linear, as (last_ - first_) assignments are performed. Space complexity is constant.

Example <iota1.cpp>

```
#include <algorithm.h>
#include <iostream.h>

int main ()
{
  int numbers[10];
  iota (numbers, numbers + 10, 42);
  for (int i = 0; i < 10; i++)
    cout << numbers[i] << ' ';
  cout << endl;
  return 0;
}
```

42 43 44 45 46 47 48 49 50 51

iter_swap

Synopsis

Swap the two elements indicated by two iterators.

Signature

```
#include <algorithm.h>
template <class ForwardIterator1, class ForwardIterator2>
void iter_swap(ForwardIterator1 a_, ForwardIterator2 b_)
```

Description

Swap the two elements reference by a_ and b_.

Complexity

Time and space complexity are both constant.

Example <iterswp0.cpp>

```
#include <algorithm.h>
#include <iostream.h>

int numbers[6] = { 0, 1, 2, 3, 4, 5 };

int main ()
{
  iter_swap (numbers, numbers + 3);
  for (int i = 0; i < 6; i++)
    cout << numbers[i] << ' ';
  cout << endl;
  return 0;
```

```
}
```

```
3  1  2  0  4  5
```

Example <iterswp1.cpp>

```
#include <algorithm.h>
#include <vector.h>
#include <iterator.h>
#include <iostream.h>

int main ()
{
  vector <int> v1 (6);
  iota (v1.begin (), v1.end (), 0);
  iter_swap (v1.begin (), v1.begin () + 3);
  ostream_iterator <int> iter (cout, " ");
  copy (v1.begin (), v1.end (), iter);
  cout << endl;
  return 0;
}
```

```
3  1  2  0  4  5
```

lexicographical_compare

Synopsis
Lexicographically compare two sequences.

Signatures
```
#include <algorithm.h>
template<class InputIterator1, class InputIterator2>
bool lexicographical_compare
(
  InputIterator1 first1_,
  InputIterator1 last1_,
  InputIterator2 first2_,
  InputIterator2 last2_
)

template<class InputIterator1, class InputIterator2, class
Compare>
bool lexicographical_compare
(
  InputIterator1 first1_,
  InputIterator1 last1_,
  InputIterator2 first2_,
  InputIterator2 last2_,
  Compare compare_
)
```

Description

Use a pair of iterators i_ and j_ to traverse two sequences, starting at first1_
and first2_, respectively. While traversing the sequences, if *i_ is less than *j_,
immediately return true. Similarly, if *j_ < *i_, immediately return false. If the
end of the first sequence is reached before the end of the second sequence,
return true, otherwise return false. The first version uses operator< to perform
the comparison, whereas the second version uses compare_.

Complexity

Time complexity is linear, as at most (last1_ - first1_) comparisons are performed. Space complexity is constant.

Example <lexcmp1.cpp>

```
#include <algorithm.h>
#include <iostream.h>

int main ()
{
  const unsigned size = 6;
  char n1[size] = "shoe";
  char n2[size] = "shine";
  bool before
     = lexicographical_compare (n1, n1 + size, n2, n2 + size);
  if (before)
    cout << n1 << " is before " << n2 << endl;
  else
    cout << n2 << " is before " << n1 << endl;
  return 0;
}
```

shine is before shoe

Example <lexcmp2.cpp>

```
#include <algorithm.h>
#include <iostream.h>

int main ()
{
  const unsigned size = 6;
  char n1[size] = "shoe";
  char n2[size] = "shine";
  bool before =
    lexicographical_compare (n1, n1 + size,
                             n2, n2 + size,
                             greater<char>());
  if (before)
    cout << n1 << " is after " << n2 << endl;
  else
    cout << n2 << " is after " << n1 << endl;
  return 0;
```

```
    }
```

shoe is after shine

lower_bound

Synopsis
Return the lower bound within a range.

Signatures
```
#include <algorithm.h>
template<class ForwardIterator, class T>
ForwardIterator lower_bound
(
   ForwardIterator first_,
   ForwardIterator last_,
   const T& value_
)

template<class ForwardIterator, class T, class Compare>
ForwardIterator lower_bound
(
   ForwardIterator first_,
   ForwardIterator last_,
   const T& value_,
   Compare compare_
)
```

Description
Return an iterator positioned at the first position in the range [first_..last_)
that value_ can be inserted without violating the order of the collection. If no
such position exists, return last_. The first version assumes that the elements
are already sorted using operator<, whereas the second version assumes that
the elements are already sorted using the binary function compare_.

Complexity
Time complexity is O(Log N) for random access iterators, and O(N) for all
other iterators. Space complexity is constant.

Example <lwrbnd1.cpp>

```
#include <algorithm.h>
#include <vector.h>
#include <iostream.h>

int main ()
{
  vector <int> v1 (20);
  for (int i = 0; i < v1.size (); i++)
  {
    v1[i] = i/4;
```

```cpp
      cout << v1[i] << ' ';
    }
    int* location = lower_bound (v1.begin (), v1.end (), 3);
    cout
      << "\n3 can be inserted at index: "
      << location - v1.begin ()
      << endl;
    return 0;
}
```

```
0  0  0  0  1  1  1  1  2  2  2  2  3  3  3  3  4  4  4  4
3 can be inserted at index: 12
```

Example <lwrbnd2.cpp>

```cpp
#include <algorithm.h>
#include <iostream.h>
#include <string.h>

bool char_str_less (const char* a_, const char* b_)
{
  return ::strcmp (a_, b_) < 0 ? 1 : 0;
}

char* str [] = { "a", "a", "b", "b", "q", "w", "z" };

int main ()
{
  const unsigned count = sizeof (str) /sizeof (str[0]);
  cout
    << "d can be inserted at index: "
    << lower_bound (str, str + count, "d", char_str_less) - str
    << endl;
  return 0;
}
```

```
d can be inserted at index: 4
```

make_heap

Synopsis
Make a sequence into a heap

Signatures
```cpp
#include <algorithm.h>
template<class RandomAccessIterator>
void make_heap
(
  RandomAccessIterator first_,
  RandomAccessIterator last_
)
```

```
template<class RandomAccessIterator, class Compare>
void make_heap
(
   RandomAccessIterator first_,
   RandomAccessIterator last_,
   Compare compare_
)
```

Description

Arrange the elements in the range [first_..last_) into a heap. The first version uses operator< to perform the comparisons, whereas the second version uses the binary function compare_.

Complexity

Time complexity is linear. Space complexity is constant.

Example <mkheap0.cpp>

```cpp
#include <algorithm.h>
#include <iostream.h>

int numbers[6] = { 5, 10, 4, 13, 11, 19 };

int main ()
{
   make_heap (numbers, numbers + 6);
   for (int i = 6; i >= 1; i--)
   {
      cout << numbers[0] << endl;
      pop_heap (numbers, numbers + i);
   }
   return 0;
}
```

```
19
13
11
10
5
4
```

Example <mkheap1.cpp>

```cpp
#include <algorithm.h>
#include <iostream.h>

int numbers[6] = { 5, 10, 4, 13, 11, 19 };

int main ()
{
   make_heap (numbers, numbers + 6, greater<int> ());
   for (int i = 6; i >= 1; i--)
```

```
    {
      cout << numbers[0] << endl;
      pop_heap (numbers, numbers + i, greater<int> ());
    }
    return 0;
}
```

4
5
10
11
13
19

max

Synopsis
Return the maximum of two items.

Signatures
```
#include <algorithm.h>
template <class T>
const T& max (const T& a_, const T& b_)

template <class T, class Compare>
const T& max (const T& a_, const T& b_, Compare compare_)
```

Description
Return a reference to the larger of a_ and b_, or a_ if a_ and b_ are equal. The
first version uses operator< to perform the comparison, whereas the second version uses the binary function compare_. using either operator < or
compare_.

Complexity
Time and space complexity are constant.

Example <max1.cpp>

```
#include <algorithm.h>
#include <iostream.h>

int main ()
{
  cout << max (42, 100) << endl;
  return 0;
}
```

100

Example <max2.cpp>

```cpp
#include <algorithm.h>
#include <iostream.h>
#include <string.h>

bool str_compare (const char* a_, const char* b_)
{
   return ::strcmp (a_, b_) < 0 ? 1 : 0;
}

int main ()
{
   cout << max ("shoe", "shine", str_compare) << endl;
   return 0;
}
```

shoe

max_element

Synopsis
Return the maximum element within a range.

Signatures
```cpp
#include <algorithm.h>
template<class InputIterator>
InputIterator max_element (InputIterator first_, InputIterator
last_)

template<class InputIterator, class Compare>
InputIterator max_element
(
   InputIterator first_,
   InputIterator last_,
   Compare compare_
)
```

Description
Return an iterator positioned at the maximum element in the range [first_, last_). The first version uses operator< to perform the comparisons, whereas the second version uses the binary function compare_.

Complexity
Time complexity is linear, as (last_ - first_) comparisons are performed. Space complexity is constant.

Helper
```cpp
void os_max_element (const Container& c_, T*& t_)
bool os_max_element_value (const Container& c_, T& t_)
```

Example <maxelem1.cpp>

```cpp
#include <algorithm.h>
#include <iostream.h>

int numbers[6] = { 4, 10, 56, 11, -42, 19 };

int main ()
{
  cout
    << *max_element (numbers, numbers + 6)
    << endl;
  return 0;
}
```

56

Example <maxelem2.cpp>

```cpp
#include <algorithm.h>
#include <iostream.h>
#include <string.h>

bool str_compare (const char* a_, const char* b_)
{
  return ::strcmp (a_, b_) < 0 ? 1 : 0;
}

char* names[] = { "Brett", "Graham", "Jack", "Mike", "Todd" };

int main ()
{
  const unsigned namesCt = sizeof (names)/sizeof (names[0]);
  cout
    << *max_element (names, names + namesCt, str_compare)
    << endl;
  return 0;
}
```

Todd

merge

Synopsis
Merge two sorted lists into a single sorted list.

Signatures
```cpp
#include <algorithm.h>
template
<
  class InputIterator1,
  class InputIterator2,
```

```
    class OutputIterator
>
OutputIterator merge
(
   InputIterator1 first1_,
   InputIterator1 last1_,
   InputIterator2 first2_,
   InputIterator2 last2_,
   OutputIterator result_
)

template
<
   class InputIterator1,
   class InputIterator2,
   class OutputIterator,
   class Compare
>
OutputIterator merge
(
   InputIterator1 first1_,
   InputIterator1 last1_,
   InputIterator2 first2_,
   InputIterator2 last2_,
   OutputIterator result_,
   Compare compare_
)
```

Description

Merge two sorted ranges into one sorted range, result_. Return an iterator equal to result_ + n where n = (last1_ - first1_) + (last2_ - first2_). The merge is stable in the sense that if both ranges contain equivalent values, the first ranges' value will be put in result_ before the values in the second range. The result of merging overlapping ranges is undefined. The first version assumes that both ranges are already sorted using operator<, whereas the second version assumes that both ranges are already sorted using the binary function compare_.

Complexity

Time complexity is O (N) where N = (last1_ - first1_) + (last2_ - first2_). Space complexity is constant.

Example <merge0.cpp>

```
#include <algorithm.h>
#include <iostream.h>

int numbers1[5] = { 1, 6, 13, 25, 101 };
int numbers2[5] = {-5, 26, 36, 46, 99 };

int main ()
{
   int result[10];
   merge (numbers1, numbers1 + 5,
```

```
          numbers2, numbers2 + 5,
          result);
  for (int i = 0; i < 10; i++)
    cout << result[i] << ' ';
  cout << endl;
  return 0;
}
```

```
-5  1  6  13  25  26  36  46  99  101
```

Example <merge1.cpp>

```cpp
#include <algorithm.h>
#include <vector.h>
#include <iterator.h>
#include <iostream.h>

int main ()
{
  vector <int> v1 (5);
  vector <int> v2 (v1.size ());
  iota (v1.begin (), v1.end (), 0);
  iota (v2.begin (), v2.end (), 3);
  vector <int> result (v1.size () + v2.size ());
  merge (v1.begin (), v1.end (),
         v2.begin (), v2.end (),
         result.begin ());
  ostream_iterator <int> iter (cout, " ");
  copy (v1.begin (), v1.end (), iter);
  cout << endl;
  copy (v2.begin (), v2.end (), iter);
  cout << endl;
  copy (result.begin (), result.end (), iter);
  cout << endl;
  return 0;
}
```

```
0  1  2  3  4
3  4  5  6  7
0  1  2  3  3  4  4  5  6  7
```

Example <merge2.cpp>

```cpp
#include <algorithm.h>
#include <vector.h>
#include <iterator.h>
#include <iostream.h>

int main ()
{
  vector <int> v1 (5);
  vector <int> v2 (v1.size ());
  for (int i = 0; i < v1.size (); i++)
  {
```

```
      v1[i] = 10 - i;
      v2[i] = 7 - i;
   }
   vector <int> result (v1.size () + v2.size ());
   merge (v1.begin (), v1.end (),
          v2.begin (), v2.end (),
          result.begin (),
          greater<int>() );
   ostream_iterator <int> iter (cout, " ");
   copy (v1.begin (), v1.end (), iter);
   cout << endl;
   copy (v2.begin (), v2.end (), iter);
   cout << endl;
   copy (result.begin (), result.end (), iter);
   cout << endl;
   return 0;
}
```

```
10 9 8 7 6
7 6 5 4 3
10 9 8 7 7 6 6 5 4 3
```

min

Synopsis
Return the minimum of two items.

Signature
```
#include <algorithm.h>
template <class T>
const T& min (const T& a_, const T& b_)

template <class T, class Compare>
const T& min (const T& a_, const T& b_, Compare compare_)
```

Description
Return the smaller of a_ and b_, or a_ if a_ and b_ are equal. The first version uses operator< to perform the comparison, whereas the second version uses the binary function compare_.

Complexity
Space and time complexity are constant.

Example <min1.cpp>
```
#include <algorithm.h>
#include <iostream.h>

int main ()
{
   cout << min (42, 100) << endl;
```

```
    return 0;
}
```

42

Example <min2.cpp>

```cpp
#include <algorithm.h>
#include <iostream.h>
#include <string.h>

bool str_compare (const char* a_, const char* b_)
{
    return ::strcmp (a_, b_) < 0 ? 1 : 0;
}

int main ()
{
    cout << min ("shoe", "shine", str_compare) << endl;
    return 0;
}
```

shine

min_element

Synopsis
Return the minimum item within a range.

Signature
```cpp
#include <algorithm.h>
template <class InputIterator>
InputIterator min_element (InputIterator first_, InputIterator
last_)

template <class InputIterator, class Compare>
InputIterator min_element
(
    InputIterator first_,
    InputIterator last_,
    Compare compare_
)
```

Description
Return an iterator positioned at the minimum element in the range [first_,
last_). The first version uses operator< to perform the comparisons, whereas
the second version uses the binary function compare_ .

Complexity
Time complexity is linear, as (last_ - first_) comparisons are performed. Space
complexity is constant.

Helper

```
void os_min_element (const Container& c_, T*& t_)
bool os_min_element_value (const Container& c_, T& t_)
```

Example <minelem1.cpp>

```cpp
#include <algorithm.h>
#include <iostream.h>

int numbers[6] = { -10, 15, -100, 36, -242, 42 };

int main ()
{
  cout
    << *min_element (numbers, numbers + 6)
    << endl;
  return 0;
}
```

-242

Example <minelem2.cpp>

```cpp
#include <algorithm.h>
#include <iostream.h>
#include <string.h>

bool str_compare (const char* a_, const char* b_)
{
  return ::strcmp (a_, b_) < 0 ? 1 : 0;
}

char* names[] = { "Brett", "Graham", "Jack", "Mike", "Todd" };

int main ()
{
  const unsigned namesCt = sizeof (names)/sizeof (names[0]);
  cout
    << *min_element (names, names + namesCt, str_compare)
    << endl;
  return 0;
}
```

Brett

mismatch

Synopsis

Search two sequences for a mismatched item.

Signatures

```
#include <algorithm.h>
template<class InputIterator1, class InputIterator2>
pair<InputIterator1, InputIterator2> mismatch
(
   InputIterator1 first1_,
   InputIterator1 last1_,
   InputIterator2 first2_
)

template
<
   class InputIterator1,
   class InputIterator2,
   class BinaryPredicate
>
pair<InputIterator1, InputIterator2> mismatch
(
   InputIterator1 first1_,
   InputIterator1 last1_,
   InputIterator2 first2_,
   BinaryPredicate binary_pred_
)
```

Description

Use a pair of iterators i_ and j_ to traverse two sequences, starting at first1_ and first2_, respectively. Return the iterator pair <i_, j_> when either their respective elements mismatch or when i_ reaches last1_. The first version uses operator == to perform the comparisons, whereas the second version uses binary_pred_.

Complexity

Time complexity is linear, as at most (last1_ - first1_) comparisons are performed. Space complexity is constant.

Example <mismtch0.cpp>

```
#include <algorithm.h>
#include <iostream.h>

int n1[5] = { 1, 2, 3, 4, 5 };
int n2[5] = { 1, 2, 3, 4, 5 };
int n3[5] = { 1, 2, 3, 2, 1 };

int main ()
{
   pair <int*, int*> result;
   result = mismatch (n1, n1 + 5, n2);
   if (result.first == (n1 + 5) && result.second == (n2 + 5))
      cout << "n1 and n2 are the same" << endl;
   else
      cout << "Mismatch at offset: " << result.first - n1 << endl;
   result = mismatch (n1, n1 + 5, n3);
```

```
      if (result.first == (n1 + 5) && result.second == (n3 + 5))
        cout << "n1 and n3 are the same" << endl;
      else
        cout << "Mismatch at offset: " << result.first - n1 << endl;
      return 0;
    }
```

n1 and n2 are the same
Mismatch at offset: 3

Example <mismtch1.cpp>

```
    #include <algorithm.h>
    #include <vector.h>
    #include <iostream.h>

    int main ()
    {
      typedef vector <int> IntVec;
      IntVec v1 (10);
      IntVec v2 (v1.size ());
      iota (v1.begin (), v1.end (), 0);
      iota (v2.begin (), v2.end (), 0);
      pair <IntVec::iterator, IntVec::iterator> result;
      result = mismatch (v1.begin (), v1.end (), v2.begin ());
      if (result.first == v1.end () && result.second == v2.end ())
        cout << "v1 and v2 are the same" << endl;
      else
        cout << "mismatch at index: " << result.first - v1.begin ()
             << endl;
      v2[v2.size()/2] = 42;
      result = mismatch (v1.begin (), v1.end (), v2.begin ());
      if (result.first == v1.end () && result.second == v2.end ())
        cout << "v1 and v2 are the same" << endl;
      else
        cout << "mismatch at index: " << result.first - v1.begin ()
             << endl;
      return 0;
    }
```

v1 and v2 are the same
mismatch at index: 5

Example <mismtch2.cpp>

```
    #include <algorithm.h>
    #include <iostream.h>
    #include <string.h>

    bool str_equal (const char* a_, const char* b_)
    {
      return ::strcmp (a_, b_) == 0 ? 1 : 0;
    }
```

```
char* n1[size] = { "Brett", "Graham", "Jack", "Mike", "Todd" };

int main ()
{
  const unsigned size = 5;
  char* n2[size];
  copy (n1, n1 + 5, n2);
  pair <char**, char**> result;
  result = mismatch (n1, n1+ size, n2, str_equal);
  if (result.first == n1 + size && result.second == n2 + size)
    cout << "n1 and n2 are the same" << endl;
  else
    cout << "mismatch at index: " << result.first - n1 << endl;
  n2[2] = "QED";
  result = mismatch (n1, n1 + size, n2, str_equal);
  if (result.first == n2 + size && result.second == n2 + size)
    cout << "n1 and n2 are the same" << endl;
  else
    cout << "mismatch at index: " << result.first - n1 << endl;
  return 0;
}
```

n1 and n2 are the same
mismatch at index: 2

next_permutation

Synopsis
Change sequence to next lexicographic permutation.

Signatures
```
#include <algorithm.h>
template<class BidirectionalIterator>
bool next_permutation
(
  BidirectionalIterator first_,
  BidirectionalIterator last_
)

template<class BidirectionalIterator, class Compare>
bool next_permutation
(
  BidirectionalIterator first_,
  BidirectionalIterator last_,
  Compare compare_
)
```

Description
Arrange the sequence [first_..last_) to be its next permutation and return true.
If there is no next permutation, arrange the sequence to be the first permutation and return false. The first version orders the permutations using opera-
tor<, whereas the second version uses the binary function compare_.

Complexity

Time complexity is linear. Space complexity is constant.

Example \<nextprm0.cpp\>

```cpp
#include <algorithm.h>
#include <iostream.h>

int v1[3] = { 0, 1, 2 };

int main ()
{
  next_permutation (v1, v1 + 3);
  for (int i = 0; i < 3; i++)
    cout << v1[i] << ' ';
  cout << endl;
  return 0;
}
```

0 2 1

Example \<nextprm1.cpp\>

```cpp
#include <algorithm.h>
#include <vector.h>
#include <iterator.h>
#include <iostream.h>

int main ()
{
  vector <int> v1 (3);
  iota (v1.begin (), v1.end (), 0);
  ostream_iterator<int> iter (cout, " ");
  copy (v1.begin (), v1.end (), iter);
  cout << endl;
  for (int i = 0; i < 9; i++)
  {
    next_permutation (v1.begin (), v1.end ());
    copy (v1.begin (), v1.end (), iter);
    cout << endl;
  }
  return 0;
}
```

```
0 1 2
0 2 1
1 0 2
1 2 0
2 0 1
2 1 0
0 1 2
0 2 1
1 0 2
1 2 0
```

Example <nextprm2.cpp>

```cpp
#include <algorithm.h>
#include <vector.h>
#include <iterator.h>
#include <iostream.h>

int main ()
{
  vector <char> v1 (3);
  iota (v1.begin (), v1.end (), 'A');
  ostream_iterator<char> iter (cout);
  copy (v1.begin (), v1.end (), iter);
  cout << endl;
  for (int i = 0; i < 9; i++)
  {
    next_permutation (v1.begin (), v1.end (), less<char>());
    copy (v1.begin (), v1.end (), iter);
    cout << endl;
  }
  return 0;
}
```

ABC
ACB
BAC
BCA
CAB
CBA
ABC
ACB
BAC
BCA

nth_element

Synopsis
Partition a range by its nth element.

Signatures
```cpp
#include <algorithm.h>
template<class RandomAccessIterator>
void nth_element
(
  RandomAccessIterator first_,
  RandomAccessIterator nth_,
  RandomAccessIterator last_
)

template<class RandomAccessIterator, class Compare>
void nth_element
(
  RandomAccessIterator first_,
```

```
    RandomAccessIterator nth_,
    RandomAccessIterator last_,
    Compare compare_
)
```

Description

If the value referenced by nth_ is value_, partition the sequence [first_..last_)
so that all elements to the left of value_ are less than or equal to value_, and
all elements to the right of value_ are greater than or equal to value_. The first
version uses operator< to perform the comparisons, whereas the second version uses the binary function compare_.

Complexity

Time complexity is O(N), where N is (last_ - first_). Space complexity is
constant.

Example <nthelem0.cpp>

```cpp
#include <algorithm.h>
#include <iostream.h>

int numbers[6] = { 5, 2, 4, 1, 0, 3 };

int main ()
{
  nth_element (numbers, numbers + 3, numbers + 6);
  for (int i = 0; i < 6; i++)
    cout << numbers[i] << ' ';
  cout << endl;
  return 0;
}
1 0 2 3 4 5
```

Example <nthelem1.cpp>

```cpp
#include <algorithm.h>
#include <vector.h>
#include <iterator.h>
#include <iostream.h>

int main ()
{
  vector <int> v1 (10);
  for (int i = 0; i < v1.size (); i++)
    v1[i] = rand () % 10;
  ostream_iterator<int> iter (cout, " ");
  copy (v1.begin (), v1.end (), iter);
  cout << endl;
  nth_element (v1.begin (),
               v1.begin () + v1.size () / 2,
               v1.end ());
  copy (v1.begin (), v1.end (), iter);
```

```
      cout << endl;
      return 0;
    }

    6 0 2 0 6 7 5 5 8 6
    5 0 2 0 5 6 7 6 8 6
```

Example <nthelem2.cpp>

```
    #include <algorithm.h>
    #include <vector.h>
    #include <iterator.h>
    #include <iostream.h>

    int main ()
    {
      vector <int> v1 (10);
      for (int i = 0; i < v1.size (); i++)
        v1[i] = rand () % 10;
      ostream_iterator<int> iter (cout, " ");
      copy (v1.begin (), v1.end (), iter);
      cout << endl;
      nth_element (v1.begin (),
                   v1.begin () + v1.size () / 2,
                   v1.end (),
                   greater<int>());
      copy (v1.begin (), v1.end (), iter);
      cout << endl;
      return 0;
    }

    6 0 2 0 6 7 5 5 8 6
    6 8 7 6 6 5 5 2 0 0
```

os_binary_search

Synopsis
Locate an item in a sorted container.

Signatures
```
    #include <helper.h>
    template< class Container, class T >
    bool os_binary_search (const Container& c_, const T& value_)
```

Description
A helper algorithm for binary_search(). Return true if 'value' is in the container c_. This algorithm assumes that the elements in the container are already sorted using operator <.

Complexity
See binary_search.

Example <obinsch0.cpp>

```
#include <helper.h>
#include <vector.h>
#include <iostream.h>

int main ()
{
  vector<int> v;
  for (int i = 0; i < 100; i++)
    v.push_back (i);
  if (os_binary_search (v, 42))
    cout << "found 42" << endl;
  else
    cout << "did not find 42" << endl;
  return 0;
}
```

found 42

os_count

Synopsis
Count items in a container that match a value.

Signature
```
#include <helper.h>
template< class Container, class T >
int os_count (const Container& c_, const T& value_)
```

Description
A helper algorithm for count(). Return the number of elements in the container c_ that match value_ using operator==.

Complexity
See count().

Example <ocount0.cpp>

```
#include <helper.h>
#include <vector.h>
#include <iostream.h>

int numbers[10] = { 1, 2, 4, 1, 2, 4, 1, 2, 4, 1 };

int main ()
{
  vector<int> v (numbers, numbers + 10 );
  int result = os_count (v, 1);
  cout << "Found " << result << " 1's." << endl;
  return 0;
```

```
}
```

Found 4 1's.

os_count_if

Synopsis
Count items in a container that satisfy a predicate.

Signature
```
#include <helper.h>
template< class Container, class Predicate >
int os_count_if (const Container& c_, Predicate pred_)
```

Description
A helper algorithm for count_if(). Return the number of elements in container c_ that cause predicate pred_ to return true.

Complexity
See count_if().

Example <ocntif0.cpp>

```
#include <helper.h>
#include <vector.h>
#include <iostream.h>

int odd (int a_)
{
   return a_ % 2;
}

int main ()
{
   vector <int> numbers(100);
   for (int i = 0; i < 100; i++)
     numbers[i] = i % 3;
   int elements = os_count_if (numbers, odd);
   cout << "Found " << elements << " odd elements." << endl;
   return 0;
}
```

Found 33 odd elements.

os_erase

Synopsis
Erases all matching items from a container.

Signature
```
#include <helper.h>
template< class Container, class T >
void os_erase (Container& c_, const T& value_)
```

Description
A helper algorithm for remove(). Erase all occurrences of value_ from the container c_. Unlike remove(), the size of the container decreases by the number of items that are erased.

Complexity
See remove().

Example <remove1.cpp>
```
#include <helper.h>
#include <vector.h>
#include <iostream.h>

int numbers[6] = { 1, 2, 3, 1, 2, 3 };

int main ()
{
  vector<int> v (numbers, numbers + 6);
  os_erase (v, 1);
  vector<int>::iterator i;
  for (i = v.begin(); i != v.end(); i++)
    cout << *i << ' ';
  cout << endl;
  return 0;
}
```
```
2 3 2 3 2 3
```

os_erase_if

Synopsis
Erases items from a container that satisfy a predicate.

Signature
```
#include <helper.h>
template< class Container, class Predicate >
void os_erase_if (Container& c_, Predicate pred_)
```

Description
A helper algorithm for remove_if(). Erase all elements that satisfy pred_ from the container c_. Unlike remove_if(), the size of the container decreases by the number of elements that are erased.

Complexity
See remove_if().

Example <remif1.cpp>

```
#include <helper.h>
#include <vector.h>
#include <iostream.h>

bool odd (int a_)
{
   return a_ % 2;
}

int numbers[6] = { 0, 0, 1, 1, 2, 2 };

int main ()
{
   vector<int> v (numbers, numbers + 6);
   os_erase_if (v, odd);
   vector<int>::iterator i;
   for (i = v.begin(); i != v.end(); i++)
     cout << *i << ' ';
   cout << endl;
   return 0;
}
```

```
0  0  2  2  2  2
```

os_find

Synopsis
Locate an item in a container.

Signature
```
#include <helper.h>
template <class Container, class T>
void os_find (Container& c_, const T& value_, T*& result_)
```

Description
A helper algorithm for find(). Searches for an element in c_ that matches
value_ using operator==. Sets result_ to point to the first matching element,
or 0 if no match is found.

Complexity
See find().

Example <ofind0.cpp>

```
#include <helper.h>
#include <vector.h>
#include <iostream.h>

int numbers[10] = { 0, 1, 4, 9, 16, 25, 36, 49, 64 };
```

```
int main ()
{
  vector<int> v (numbers, numbers + 10);
  int* location = 0;
  os_find (v, 25, location);
  if (location)
    cout << "Found " << *location << endl;
  return 0;
}
```

Found 25

os_find_if

Synopsis
Locate an item that satisfies a predicate in a container.

Signature
```
#include <helper.h>
template <class Container, class Predicate, class T>
void os_find_if (Container& c_, Predicate pred_, T*& result_)
```

Description
A helper algorithm for find_if(). Set result_ to point to the first element in c_ that causes pred_ to return true, or 0 if no such element exists.

Complexity
See find_if().

Example <ofindif0.cpp>
```
#include <helper.h>
#include <vector.h>
#include <iostream.h>

bool odd (int a_)
{
  return a_ % 2;
}

int numbers[6] = { 2, 4, 8, 15, 32, 64 };

int main ()
{
  vector<int> v (numbers, numbers + 6);
  int* location = 0;
  os_find_if (v, odd, location);
  if (location)
    cout << "Found " << *location << endl;
  return 0;
}
```

Found 15

os_for_each

Synopsis
Apply a function to every item in a container.

Signature
```
#include <helper.h>
template<class Container, class Function>
Function os_for_each (Container& c_, Function f_)
```

Description
A helper algorithm for for_each(). Apply f_ to every element in c_ and return the input parameter f_.

Complexity
See for_each().

Example <oforech0.cpp>
```cpp
#include <helper.h>
#include <vector.h>
#include <iostream.h>

void print (int a_)
{
   cout << a_ << ' ';
}

int numbers[10] = { 1, 1, 2, 3, 5, 8, 13, 21, 34, 55 };

int main ()
{
   vector<int> v (numbers, numbers + 10);
   os_for_each (v, print);
   cout << endl;
   return 0;
}
```
```
1 1 2 3 5 8 13 21 34 55
```

os_includes

Synopsis
Search for one container in another container.

Signatures
```
#include <helper.h>
template <class Container>
bool os_includes (const Container& c1_, const Container& c2_)
```

```
template<class Container, class Compare>
bool os_includes
  (
  const Container& c1_,
  const Container& c2_,
  Compare compare_
  )
```

Description

A helper algorithm for includes(). Search for one container in another container. Return true if the container c1_ is embedded in container c2_. The first version assumes that both sequences are already sorted using operator<. The second version assumes that both sequences are already sorted using compare_.

Complexity

See includes().

Example <oincl0.cpp>

```
#include <helper.h>
#include <vector.h>
#include <iostream.h>

int numbers1[5] = { 1, 2, 3, 4, 5 };
int numbers2[5] = { 1, 2, 4, 8, 16 };
int numbers3[2] = { 4, 8 };

int main ()
{
  vector<int> v1 (numbers1, numbers1 + 5 );
  vector<int> v2 (numbers2, numbers2 + 5 );
  vector<int> v3 (numbers3, numbers3 + 2 );
  if (os_includes (v1, v3))
    cout << "numbers1 includes numbers3" << endl;
  else
    cout << "numbers1 does not include numbers3" << endl;
  if (os_includes (v2, v3))
    cout << "numbers2 includes numbers3" << endl;
  else
    cout << "numbers2 does not include numbers3" << endl;
  return 0;
}
```

```
numbers1 does not include numbers3
numbers2 includes numbers3
```

os_max_element, os_max_element_value

Synopsis

Find the maximum element in a container.

Signatures
```
#include <helper.h>
template<class Container, class T>
void os_max_element (const Container& c_, T*& t_)

template<class Container, class T>
bool os_max_element_value (const Container& c_, T& t_)
```

Description
Helper algorithms for max_element(). The first version sets t_ to point to the maximum element of c_, or 0 if c_ is empty. If c_ is not empty, the second version sets t_ to the maximum element of c_ and returns true, otherwise it returns false.

Complexity
See max_element().

Example <omaxelm0.cpp>
```
#include <helper.h>
#include <vector.h>
#include <iostream.h>

int numbers[6] = { -10, 15, -100, 36, -242, 42 };

int main ()
{
  vector<int> v (numbers, numbers + 6);
  int* ptr;
  os_max_element (v, ptr);
  if (ptr)
    cout << "maximum = " << *ptr << endl;;
  int value;
  bool result = os_max_element_value (v, value);
  if (result)
    cout << "maximum = " << value << endl;
  return 0;
}
```
```
maximum 42
maximum 42
```

os_min_element, os_min_element_value

Synopsis
Find the minimum item in a container.

Signature
```
#include <helper.h>
template<class Container, class T>
void os_min_element (const Container& c_, T*& t_)
```

```
template<class Container, class T>
bool os_min_element_value (const Container& c_, T& t_)
```

Description

Helper algorithms for min_element(). The first version sets t_ to point to the minimum element of c_, or 0 if c_ is empty. If c_ is not empty, the second version sets t_ to the minimum element of c_ and returns true, otherwise it returns false.

Complexity

See min_element().

Example <ominelm0.cpp>

```
#include <helper.h>
#include <vector.h>
#include <iostream.h>

int numbers[6] = { -10, 15, -100, 36, -242, 42 };

int main ()
{
  vector<int> v (numbers, numbers + 6);
  int* ptr;
  os_min_element (v, ptr);
  if (ptr)
    cout << "minimum = " << *ptr << endl;;
  int value;
  bool result = os_min_element_value (v, value);
  if (result)
    cout << "minimum = " << value << endl;
  return 0;
}
```

```
minimum = -242
minimum = -242
```

os_random_shuffle

Synopsis

Randomize a container using random shuffles.

Signatures

```
#include <helper.h>
template<class Container>
void os_random_shuffle (Container& c_)
```

Description

A helper algorithm for random_shuffle(). Shuffle all elements in the container c_ using uniformly selected random swaps. Use operator= to perform the swaps.

Complexity

See random_shuffle().

Example <orndshf0.cpp>

```
#include <helper.h>
#include <vector.h>
#include <iostream.h>

int numbers[6] = { 1, 2, 3, 4, 5, 6 };

int main ()
{
  vector<int> v (numbers, numbers + 6);
  os_random_shuffle (v);
  for (int i = 0; i < v.size(); i++)
    cout << v[i] << ' ';
  cout << endl;
  return 0;
}
```

    3 1 6 2 4 5

os_release

Synopsis

Deletes a container of heap-based objects.

Signature

```
#include <helper.h>
template <class Container>
void os_release (Container& c_)
```

Description

Calls operator `delete` on every item in the container. Assume that each item is a pointer to a heap-based object. If more than one item points to the same heap-based object, an error will most probably occur.

Complexity

Time complexity is linear. Space complexity is constant.

Example <oreleas0.cpp>

```
#include <helper.h>
#include <vector.h>
#include <iostream.h>

class X
{
  public:
```

```
        X (int i_) : i (i_) {}
        ~X () { cout << "Delete X(" << i << ")" << endl; }
        int i;
};

ostream& operator << (ostream& stream_, const X& x_)
{
    return stream_ << "X(" << x_.i << ")";
}

int main ()
{
    vector<X*> v;
    v.push_back (new X (2));
    v.push_back (new X (1));
    v.push_back (new X (4));
    vector<X*>::iterator i;
    for (i = v.begin (); i != v.end (); i++)
        cout << *(*i) << endl;
    os_release (v); // Delete all heap-based objects in container.
    return 0;
}
```

X(2)
X(1)
X(4)
Delete X(2)
Delete X(1)
Delete X(4)

os_replace

Synopsis
Replace a specified value in a sequence with another value.

Signature
```
#include <helper.h>
template<class Container, class T>
void os_replace (Container& c_, const T& old_, const T& new_)
```

Description
A helper algorithm for replace(). Replaces every occurrence of old_ in the container c_ with new_.

Complexity
See replace().

Example <oreplac0.cpp>

```
#include <helper.h>
#include <vector.h>
#include <iostream.h>
```

```
int numbers[6] = { 0, 1, 2, 0, 1, 2 };

int main ()
{
  vector<int> v (numbers, numbers + 6);
  os_replace (v, 2, 42);
  vector<int>::iterator i;
  for (i = v.begin(); i != v.end(); i++)
    cout << *i << ' ';
  cout << endl;
  return 0;
}
```

0 1 42 0 1 42

os_replace_if

Synopsis
Replace specified values that satisfy a predicate.

Signature
```
#include <helper.h>
template<class Container, class Predicate, class T>
void os_replace_if (Container& c_, Predicate pred_, const T&
value_)
```

Description
A helper algorithm for replace_if(). Replaces every element in the container c_
that satisfies pred_ with new_value_.

Complexity
See replace_if().

Example <oreplif1.cpp>

```
#include <helper.h>
#include <vector.h>
#include <iostream.h>

bool odd (int a_)
{
  return a_ % 2;
}

int main ()
{
  vector<int> v1 (10);
  for (int i = 0; i < v1.size (); i++)
  {
    v1[i] = i % 5;
    cout << v1[i] << ' ';
```

```
    }
    cout << endl;
    os_replace_if (v1, odd, 42);
    for (i = 0; i < v1.size (); i++)
      cout << v1[i] << ' ';
    cout << endl;
    return 0;
}
```

```
0  1  2  3  4  0  1  2  3  4
0 42  2 42  4  0 42  2 42  4
```

os_rotate

Synopsis
Rotate a sequence by n positions.

Signature
```
#include <helper.h>
template<class Container>
void os_rotate (Container& c_, int n_)
```

Description
A helper algorithm for rotate(). If n_ is positive, rotate the container to the right by n_ positions, otherwise rotate the container to the left by n_ positions.

Complexity
See rotate().

Example <orotate0.cpp>

```
#include <helper.h>
#include <vector.h>
#include <iostream.h>

int numbers[6] = { 0, 1, 2, 3, 4, 5 };

int main ()
{
  vector<int> v (numbers, numbers + 6);
  os_rotate (v, 3);
  vector<int>::iterator i;
  for (i = v.begin(); i != v.end(); i++)
    cout << *i << ' ';
  cout << endl;
  return 0;
}
```

```
3  4  5  0  1  2
```

os_sort

Synopsis
Sort a sequence

Signature
```
#include <helper.h>
template<class Container>
void os_sort (Container& c_)

template<class Container, class Compare>
void os_sort (Container& c_, Compare compare_)
```

Description
Helper algorithms for sort(). Sort all elements in the container c_ into ascending order. The first version uses operator< to compare elements, whereas the second version uses the binary function compare_.

Complexity
See sort().

Example <osort0.cpp>

```
#include <helper.h>
#include <vector.h>
#include <iostream.h>

int array[6] = { 1, 50, -10, 11, 42, 19 };

int main ()
{
  vector<int> v (array, array + 6);
  os_sort (v);
  for (int i = 0; i < v.size(); i++)
    cout << v[i] << ' ';
  cout << endl;
  return 0;
}
```

```
-10 1 11 19 42 50
```

Example <osort1.cpp>

```
#include <helper.h>
#include <vector.h>
#include <iostream.h>

int array[] = { 1, 50, -10, 11, 42, 19 };

int main ()
{
```

```
      vector<int> v (array, array + 6);
      os_sort (v, greater<int> ());
      for (int i = 0; i < v.size(); i++)
        cout << v[i] << ' ';
      cout << endl;
      return 0;
}
```

50 42 19 11 1 -10

partial_sort

Synopsis
Sort the smallest n elements of a sequence.

Signatures
```
#include <algorithm.h>
template<class RandomAccessIterator>
void partial_sort
(
   RandomAccessIterator first_,
   RandomAccessIterator middle_,
   RandomAccessIterator last_
)

template<class RandomAccessIterator, class Compare>
void partial_sort
(
   RandomAccessIterator first_,
   RandomAccessIterator middle_,
   RandomAccessIterator last_,
   Compare compare_
)
```

Description
Sort the first N elements in the range [first_..last_) where N = middle_ - first_. The remaining elements in the range [first_..last_) end up in an undefined order in the range [middle_..last_). The first version performs the sort using operator<, whereas the second version uses the binary function compare_.

Complexity
Time complexity is (last_ - first_) * log N. Space complexity is constant.

Example <parsrt0.cpp>

```
#include <algorithm.h>
#include <iostream.h>

int numbers[6] = { 5, 2, 4, 3, 1, 6 };

int main ()
```

```
{
  partial_sort (numbers, numbers + 3, numbers + 6);
  for (int i = 0; i < 6; i++)
    cout << numbers[i] << ' ';
  cout << endl;
  return 0;
}
```

1 2 3 5 4 6

Example <parsrt1.cpp>

```
#include <algorithm.h>
#include <vector.h>
#include <iterator.h>
#include <iostream.h>

int main ()
{
  vector <int> v1 (10);
  for (int i = 0; i < v1.size (); i++)
    v1[i] = rand () % 10;
  ostream_iterator<int> iter (cout, " ");
  copy (v1.begin (), v1.end (), iter);
  cout << endl;
  partial_sort (v1.begin (),
                v1.begin () + v1.size () / 2,
                v1.end ());
  copy (v1.begin (), v1.end (), iter);
  cout << endl;
  return 0;
}
```

6 0 2 0 6 7 5 5 8 6
0 0 2 5 5 7 6 6 8 6

Example <parsrt2.cpp>

```
#include <algorithm.h>
#include <vector.h>
#include <iterator.h>
#include <iostream.h>
#include <string.h>

bool str_compare (const char* a_, const char* b_)
{
  return ::strcmp (a_, b_) < 0 ? 1 : 0;
}

char* names[] = { "aa", "ff", "dd", "ee", "cc", "bb" };

int main ()
{
```

```
      const unsigned nameSize = sizeof (names) / sizeof (names[0]);
      vector <char*> v1 (nameSize);
      for (int i = 0; i < v1.size (); i++)
        v1[i] = names[i];
      ostream_iterator<char*> iter (cout, " ");
      copy (v1.begin (), v1.end (), iter);
      cout << endl;
      partial_sort (v1.begin (),
                    v1.begin () + nameSize / 2,
                    v1.end (),
                    str_compare);
      copy (v1.begin (), v1.end (), iter);
      cout << endl;
      return 0;
}
```

aa ff dd ee cc bb
aa dd ff ee cc bb

partial_sort_copy

Synopsis
Sort the smallest N elements of a sequence and copy the result.

Signatures
```
#include <algorithm.h>
template<class InputIterator, class RandomAccessIterator>
RandomAccessIterator partial_sort_copy
(
  InputIterator first_,
  InputIterator last_,
  RandomAccessIterator result_first_,
  RandomAccessIterator result_last_
)

template
<
  class InputIterator,
  class RandomAccessIterator,
  class Compare
>
RandomAccessIterator partial_sort_copy
(
  InputIterator first_,
  InputIterator last_,
  RandomAccessIterator result_first_,
  RandomAccessIterator result_last_,
  Compare compare_
)
```

Description
Sort the first N elements of [first_..last_) where N = min ((last_ - first_),
(result_last_ - result_first_)) and place the result into [result_first_..result_

first_ + N). Return the smaller of result_last_ or result_first + n where n = last_ - first_. The first version sorts the elements using operator<, whereas the second version uses the binary function compare_.

Complexity

Time complexity is (last_ - first_) * log N. Space complexity is constant.

Example <parsrtc0.cpp>

```cpp
#include <algorithm.h>
#include <iostream.h>

int numbers[6] = { 5, 2, 4, 3, 1, 6 };

int main ()
{
  int result[3];
  partial_sort_copy (numbers, numbers + 6, result, result + 3);
  for (int i = 0; i < 3; i++)
    cout << result[i] << ' ';
  cout << endl;
  return 0;
}
```

1 2 3

Example <parsrtc1.cpp>

```cpp
#include <algorithm.h>
#include <vector.h>
#include <iterator.h>
#include <iostream.h>

int main ()
{
  vector <int> v1 (10);
  for (int i = 0; i < v1.size (); i++)
    v1[i] = rand () % 10;
  vector <int> result (5);
  ostream_iterator<int> iter (cout, " ");
  copy (v1.begin (), v1.end (), iter);
  cout << endl;
  partial_sort_copy (v1.begin (),
                     v1.end (),
                     result.begin (),
                     result.end ());
  copy (result.begin (), result.end (), iter);
  cout << endl;
  return 0;
}
```

6 0 2 0 6 7 5 5 8 6
0 0 2 5 5

Example <parsrtc2.cpp>

```cpp
#include <algorithm.h>
#include <vector.h>
#include <iterator.h>
#include <iostream.h>
#include <string.h>

bool str_compare (const char* a_, const char* b_)
{
  return ::strcmp (a_, b_) < 0 ? 1 : 0;
}

char* names[] = { "aa", "ff", "dd", "ee", "cc", "bb" };

int main ()
{
  const unsigned nameSize = sizeof (names) / sizeof (names[0]);
  vector <char*> v1 (nameSize);
  for (int i = 0; i < v1.size (); i++)
    v1[i] = names[i];
  ostream_iterator<char*> iter (cout, " ");
  copy (v1.begin (), v1.end (), iter);
  cout << endl;
  vector <char*> result (5);
  partial_sort_copy (v1.begin (),
                     v1.end (),
                     result.begin (),
                     result.end (),
                     str_compare);
  copy (v1.begin (), v1.end (), iter);
  cout << endl;
  return 0;
}
```

```
aa ff dd ee cc bb
aa ff dd ee cc bb
```

partial_sum

Synopsis
Fill a range with a running total.

Signatures
```cpp
#include <algorithm.h>
template<class InputIterator, class OutputIterator>
OutputIterator partial_sum
(
  InputIterator first_,
  InputIterator last_,
  OutputIterator result_
)
```

```
template
<
   class InputIterator,
   class OutputIterator,
   class BinaryOperation
>
OutputIterator partial_sum
(
   InputIterator first_,
   InputIterator last_,
   OutputIterator result_,
   BinaryOperation binary_op_
)
```

Description

Assign to (result_ + N) the running total first_..(first_ + N) and return an iterator positioned immediately after the last element in result_. The first version uses operator+ to perform the summation, whereas the second version uses the binary function binary_op_.

Complexity

Space complexity is constant. Time complexity is linear as (last - first) applications of either operator + or binary_op_ are performed. result_ is can hold at least n elements where n = last_ - first).

Example <partsum0.cpp>

```
#include <algorithm.h>
#include <iostream.h>

int numbers[6] = { 1, 2, 3, 4, 5, 6 };

int main ()
{
   int result[6];
   partial_sum (numbers, numbers + 6, result);
   for (int i = 0; i < 6; i ++)
      cout << result[i] << ' ';
   cout << endl;
   return 0;
}
```

1 3 6 10 15 21

Example <partsum1.cpp>

```
#include <algorithm.h>
#include <vector.h>
#include <iterator.h>
#include <iostream.h>
```

```
int main ()
{
  vector <int> v1 (10);
  iota (v1.begin (), v1.end (), 0);
  vector <int> v2 (v1.size());
  partial_sum (v1.begin (), v1.end (), v2.begin ());
  ostream_iterator <int> iter (cout, " ");
  copy (v1.begin (), v1.end (), iter);
  cout << endl;
  copy (v2.begin (), v2.end (), iter);
  cout << endl;
  return 0;
}
```

```
0 1 2 3 4 5 6 7 8 9
0 1 3 6 10 15 21 28 36 45
```

Example <partsum2.cpp>

```
#include <algorithm.h>
#include <vector.h>
#include <iterator.h>
#include <iostream.h>

int main ()
{
  vector <int> v1 (5);
  iota (v1.begin (), v1.end (), 1);
  vector <int> v2 (v1.size());
  partial_sum (v1.begin (), v1.end (), v2.begin (),
times<int>());
  ostream_iterator <int> iter (cout, " ");
  copy (v1.begin (), v1.end (), iter);
  cout << endl;
  copy (v2.begin (), v2.end (), iter);
  cout << endl;
  return 0;
}
```

```
1 2 3 4 5
1 2 6 24 120
```

partition

Synopsis
Partition a range using a predicate.

Signatures
```
#include <algorithm.h>
template<class BidirectionalIterator, class Predicate>
BidirectionalIterator partition
(
```

```
    BidirectionalIterator first_,
    BidirectionalIterator last_,
    Predicate pred_
)
```

Description

Place all elements in the range [first_..last_) that make pred_ evaluate to true before all elements in the range that make pred_ evaluate to false. Return an iterator positioned at the first element of the second sequence.

Complexity

Time complexity is O(N), where N = (last_ - first_), as pred_ will be evaluated N times and at most N / 2 swaps will be performed.

Example <ptition0.cpp>

```cpp
#include <algorithm.h>
#include <iostream.h>

int less_10 (int a_)
{
   return a_ < 10 ? 1 : 0;
}

int numbers[6] = { 6, 12, 3, 10, 1, 20 };

int main ()
{
   partition (numbers, numbers + 6, less_10);
   for (int i = 0; i < 6; i++)
      cout << numbers[i] << ' ';
   cout << endl;
   return 0;
}
```

6 1 3 10 12 20

Example <ptition1.cpp>

```cpp
#include <algorithm.h>
#include <vector.h>
#include <iterator.h>
#include <iostream.h>

int main ()
{
   vector <int> v1 (10);
   for (int i = 0; i < v1.size (); i++)
      v1[i] = rand () % 20;
   ostream_iterator <int> iter (cout, " ");
   copy (v1.begin (), v1.end (), iter);
   cout << endl;
```

```
    partition (v1.begin (), v1.end (), bind2nd(less<int>(), 11));
    copy (v1.begin (), v1.end (), iter);
    cout << endl;
    return 0;
}
```

```
6  10  2  10  16  17  15  15  8  6
6  10  2  10  6  8  15  15  17  16
```

pop_heap

Synopsis
Pop the top element from a heap.

Signature
```
#include <algorithm.h>
template<class RandomAccessIterator>
void pop_heap
(
  RandomAccessIterator first_,
  RandomAccessIterator last_
)

template<class RandomAccessIterator, class Compare>
void pop_heap
(
  RandomAccessIterator first_,
  RandomAccessIterator last_,
  Compare compare_
)
```

Description
Starting with [first_..last_) as a heap, swap the first and last elements on the heap [first_..last_) and then make [first_..(last_ - 1)) a heap. The first version uses operator< to perform the comparisons, whereas the second version uses the binary function compare_.

Complexity
Time complexity is 2 * log (last - first). Space complexity is constant.

Examples
See make_heap.

prev_permutation

Synopsis
Change a sequence to its previous lexicographical permutation.

Signatures

```
#include <algorithm.h>
template<class BidirectionalIterator>
bool prev_permutation
(
   BidirectionalIterator first_,
   BidirectionalIterator last_
)

template<class BidirectionalIterator, class Compare>
bool prev_permutation
(
   BidirectionalIterator first_,
   BidirectionalIterator last_,
   Compare compare_
)
```

Description

Arrange the sequence [first_..last_) to be its previous permutation and return true. If there is no previous permutation, arrange the sequence to be the last permutation and return false. The first version orders the permutations using operator<, whereas the second version uses the binary function compare_.

Complexity

Time complexity is linear. Space complexity is constant.

Example <prevprm0.cpp>

```
#include <algorithm.h>
#include <iostream.h>

int v1[3] = { 0, 1, 2 };

int main ()
{
   prev_permutation (v1, v1 + 3);
   for (int i = 0; i < 3; i++)
      cout << v1[i] << ' ';
   cout << endl;
   return 0;
}
```

```
2 1 0
```

Example <prevprm1.cpp>

```
#include <algorithm.h>
#include <vector.h>
#include <iterator.h>
#include <iostream.h>

int main ()
```

```
  {
    vector <int> v1 (3);
    iota (v1.begin (), v1.end (), 0);
    ostream_iterator<int> iter (cout, " ");
    copy (v1.begin (), v1.end (), iter);
    cout << endl;
    for (int i = 0; i < 9; i++)
    {
      prev_permutation (v1.begin (), v1.end ());
      copy (v1.begin (), v1.end (), iter);
      cout << endl;
    }
    return 0;
  }
```

```
0 1 2
2 1 0
2 0 1
1 2 0
1 0 2
0 2 1
0 1 2
2 1 0
2 0 1
1 2 0
```

Example <prevprm2.cpp>

```
#include <algorithm.h>
#include <vector.h>
#include <iterator.h>
#include <iostream.h>

int main ()
{
  vector <int> v1 (3);
  iota (v1.begin (), v1.end (), 0);
  ostream_iterator<int> iter (cout, " ");
  copy (v1.begin (), v1.end (), iter);
  cout << endl;
  for (int i = 0; i < 9; i++)
  {
    prev_permutation (v1.begin (), v1.end (), greater<int>());
    copy (v1.begin (), v1.end (), iter);
    cout << endl;
  }
  return 0;
}
```

```
0 1 2
0 2 1
1 0 2
1 2 0
2 0 1
```

```
2  1  0
0  1  2
0  2  1
1  0  2
1  2  0
```

push_heap

Synopsis
Place the last element into a heap.

Signatures
```
#include <algorithm.h>
template<class RandomAccessIterator>
void push_heap
(
   RandomAccessIterator first_,
   RandomAccessIterator last_
)

template<class RandomAccessIterator, class Compare>
void push_heap
(
   RandomAccessIterator first_,
   RandomAccessIterator last_,
   Compare compare_
)
```

Description
Starting with the heap [first_..(last_-1)), insert the element referenced by last_ into the heap [first_..(last_ - 1)] so that [first_..last_) is a heap. The first version uses operator< to perform comparisons, whereas the second version uses the binary function compare_.

Complexity
Time complexity is O(logN), where N is the size of the heap. Space complexity is constant.

Example <pheap1.cpp>
```
#include <algorithm.h>
#include <vector.h>
#include <iterator.h>
#include <iostream.h>

int main ()
{
   vector<int> v;
   v.push_back (1);
   v.push_back (20);
   v.push_back (4);
```

```
    make_heap (v.begin (), v.end ());
    v.push_back (7);
    push_heap (v.begin (), v.end ());
    sort_heap (v.begin (), v.end ());
    ostream_iterator<int> iter (cout, " ");
    copy (v.begin (), v.end (), iter);
    cout << endl;
    return 0;
}
```

1 4 20
1 4 7 20

Examples <pheap2.cpp>

```
#include <algorithm.h>
#include <vector.h>
#include <iterator.h>
#include <iostream.h>

int main ()
{
  vector<int> v;
  v.push_back (1);
  v.push_back (20);
  v.push_back (4);
  make_heap (v.begin (), v.end (), greater<int> ());
  v.push_back (7);
  push_heap (v.begin (), v.end (), greater<int> ());
  sort_heap (v.begin (), v.end (), greater<int> ());
  ostream_iterator<int> iter (cout, " ");
  copy (v.begin (), v.end (), iter);
  cout << endl;

  return 0;
}
```

20 7 4 1

random_shuffle

Synopsis
Randomize a sequence using random shuffles.

Signatures
```
#include <algorithm.h>
template<class RandomAccessIterator>
void random_shuffle
(
  RandomAccessIterator first_,
  RandomAccessIterator last_
)
```

```
template<class RandomAccessIterator, class RandomNumberGenerator>
void random_shuffle
(
   RandomAccessIterator first_,
   RandomAccessIterator last_,
   RandomNumberGenerator& rand_
)
```

Description

Shuffle all elements in the sequence [first_..last_) using uniformly selected random swaps. Use operator= to perform the swaps. The first version uses an internal random number generator to generate the indices of the elements to swap, whereas the second version uses the random number generator rand_. rand_ must be a random number generator that takes a parameter n_ and returns a integral random number between 0 and (n_ - 1).

Complexity

Time complexity is linear as (last_ - first_) swaps are performed. Space complexity is constant.

Helper

```
void os_random_shuffle (Container& c_)
```

Example <rndshuf0.cpp>

```
#include <algorithm.h>
#include <iostream.h>

int numbers[6] = { 1, 2, 3, 4, 5, 6 };

int main ()
{
   random_shuffle (numbers, numbers + 6);
   for (int i = 0; i < 6; i++)
      cout << numbers[i] << ' ';
   cout << endl;
   return 0;
}

3 1 6 2 4 5
```

Example <rndshuf1.cpp>

```
#include <algorithm.h>
#include <vector.h>
#include <iterator.h>
#include <iostream.h>

int main ()
{
   vector <int> v1(10);
```

```
   iota (v1.begin (), v1.end (), 0);
   ostream_iterator <int> iter (cout, " ");
   copy (v1.begin (), v1.end (), iter);
   cout << endl;
   for (int i = 0; i < 3; i++)
   {
     random_shuffle (v1.begin (), v1.end ());
     copy (v1.begin (), v1.end (), iter);
     cout << endl;
   }
   return 0;
}
```

```
0 1 2 3 4 5 6 7 8 9
2 8 9 1 3 4 0 7 6 5
2 5 3 1 4 8 7 6 0 9
8 1 3 6 7 9 2 5 0 4
```

Example <rndshuf2.cpp>

```cpp
#include <algorithm.h>
#include <vector.h>
#include <iterator.h>
#include <iostream.h>

class MyRandomGenerator
{
  public:
    unsigned long operator () (unsigned long n_);
};

unsigned long
MyRandomGenerator::operator () (unsigned long n_)
{
   return time(0) % n_;
}

int main ()
{
   vector <int> v1(10);
   iota (v1.begin (), v1.end (), 0);
   ostream_iterator <int> iter (cout, " ");
   copy (v1.begin (), v1.end (), iter);
   cout << endl;
   for (int i = 0; i < 3; i++)
   {
     random_shuffle (v1.begin (), v1.end (), MyRandomGenerator());
     copy (v1.begin (), v1.end (), iter);
     cout << endl;
   }
   return 0;
}
```

```
0  1  2  3  4  5  6  7  8  9
5  0  7  1  9  2  8  3  4  6
2  5  3  0  6  7  4  1  9  8
7  2  1  5  8  3  9  0  6  4
```

remove

Synopsis

Remove all matching items from a sequence.

Signature

```
#include <algorithm.h>
template<class ForwardIterator, class T>
ForwardIterator remove
(
    ForwardIterator first_,
    ForwardIterator last_,
    const T& value_
)
```

Description

Remove all occurrences of value_ from the sequence [first_..last_). Return an iterator equal to last_ - n where n = number of elements removed. The size of the container is not altered; if n_ elements are removed, the last n_ elements of the sequence [first_..last_) will have undefined values.

Complexity

Time complexity is linear, as (last_ - first_) comparisons are performed. Space complexity is constant.

Helper

```
void os_erase (Container& c_, const T& t_)
```

Example <remove1.cpp>

```
#include <algorithm.h>
#include <iostream.h>

int numbers[6] = { 1, 2, 3, 1, 2, 3 };

int main ()
{
    remove (numbers, numbers + 6, 1);
    for (int i = 0; i < 6; i++)
        cout << numbers[i] << ' ';
    cout << endl;
    return 0;
}
```

```
2  3  2  3  2  3
```

remove_copy

Synopsis
Copy a sequence, removing all matching items.

Signature
```
#include <algorithm.h>
template<class InputIterator, class OutputIterator, class T>
OutputIterator remove_copy
(
    InputIterator first_,
    InputIterator last_,
    OutputIterator result_,
    const T& value_
)
```

Description
Copy the sequence [first_..last_) to a sequence starting at result_, skipping any occurrences of value_. Return an iterator positioned immediately after the last new element.

Complexity
Time complexity is linear, as (last_ - first_) comparisons are performed. Space complexity is constant.

Example <remcopy1.cpp>

```
#include <algorithm.h>
#include <iostream.h>

int numbers[6] = { 1, 2, 3, 1, 2, 3 };
int result[6] = { 0, 0, 0, 0, 0, 0 };

int main ()
{
    remove_copy (numbers, numbers + 6, result, 2);
    for (int i = 0; i < 6; i++)
        cout << result[i] << ' ';
    cout << endl;
    return 0;
}
```

```
1 3 1 3 0 0
```

remove_copy_if

Synopsis
Copy a sequence, removing all items that satisfy a predicate.

Signature

```
#include <algorithm.h>
template<class InputIterator, class OutputIterator, class
Predicate>
OutputIterator remove_copy_if
(
   InputIterator first_,
   InputIterator last_,
   OutputIterator result_,
   Predicate pred_
)
```

Description

Copy the sequence [first_..last_) to a sequence starting at result_, skipping any elements that satisfy pred_. Return an iterator positioned immediately after the last new element.

Complexity

Time complexity is linear, as (last_ - first_) comparisons are performed. Space complexity is constant.

Example <remcpif1.cpp>

```
#include <algorithm.h>
#include <iostream.h>

bool odd (int a_)
{
   return a_ % 2;
}

int numbers[6] = { 1, 2, 3, 1, 2, 3 };
int result[6] = { 0, 0, 0, 0, 0, 0 };

int main ()
{
   remove_copy_if (numbers, numbers + 6, result, odd);
   for (int i = 0; i < 6; i++)
     cout << result[i] << ' ';
   cout << endl;
   return 0;
}

2 2 0 0 0 0
```

remove_if

Synopsis

Remove items from a sequence that satisfy a predicate.

Signature

```
#include <algorithm.h>
template<class ForwardIterator, class Predicate>
ForwardIterator remove_if
(
    ForwardIterator first_,
    ForwardIterator last_,
    Predicate pred_
)
```

Description

Remove all elements that satisfy pred_ from the sequence [first_..last_).
Return an iterator equal to first_ + n where n = number of elements removed.
The size of the container is not altered; if n_ elements are removed, the last n_
elements of the sequence [first_..last_) will have undefined values.

Complexity

Time complexity is linear, as (last_ - first_) comparisons are performed. Space
complexity is constant.

Helper

```
void os_erase_if (Container& c_, Predicate p_)
```

Example <remif1.cpp>

```
#include <algorithm.h>
#include <iostream.h>

bool odd (int a_)
{
    return a_ % 2;
}

int numbers[6] = { 0, 0, 1, 1, 2, 2 };

int main ()
{
    remove_if (numbers, numbers + 6, odd);
    for (int i = 0; i < 6; i++)
        cout << numbers[i] << ' ';
    cout << endl;
    return 0;
}

0  0  2  2  2  2
```

replace

Synopsis

Replace a specified value in a sequence with another value.

Signature

```
#include <algorithm.h>
template<class ForwardIterator, class T>
void replace
(
  ForwardIterator first_,
  ForwardIterator last_,
  const T& old_value_,
  const T& new_value_
)
```

Description

Replace every occurrence of old_value_ in the range [first_..last_) with new_value_.

Complexity

Time complexity is linear, as (last_ - first_) comparisons are performed. Space complexity is constant.

Helper

```
void os_replace (Container& c_, const T& old_, const T& new_)
```

Example <replace0.cpp>

```
#include <algorithm.h>
#include <iostream.h>

int numbers[6] = { 0, 1, 2, 0, 1, 2 };

int main ()
{
  replace (numbers, numbers + 6, 2, 42);
  for (int i = 0; i < 6; i++)
    cout << numbers[i] << ' ';
  cout << endl;
  return 0;
}
```

```
0  1  42  0  1  42
```

replace_copy

Synopsis

Copy a sequence, replacing matching values.

Signature

```
#include <algorithm.h>
template<class InputIterator, class OutputIterator, class T>
OutputIterator replace_copy
(
  InputIterator first_,
```

```
    InputIterator last_,
    OutputIterator result_,
    const T& old_value_,
    const T& new_value_
)
```

Description

Copy the sequence [first_..last_) to a sequence of the same size starting at result_, replacing all occurrences of old_value_ with new_value_. Return an iterator positioned immediately after the last new element.

Complexity

Time complexity is linear, as (last_ - first_) comparisons are performed. Space complexity is constant.

Example <replcpy1.cpp>

```cpp
#include <algorithm.h>
#include <iostream.h>

int numbers [6] = { 0, 1, 2, 0, 1, 2 };
int result [6] = { 0, 0, 0, 0, 0, 0 };

int main ()
{
    replace_copy (numbers, numbers + 6, result, 2, 42);
    for (int i = 0; i < 6; i++)
        cout << result[i] << ' ';
    cout << endl;
    return 0;
}
```

```
0 1 42 0 1 42
```

replace_copy_if

Synopsis

Copy a sequence, replacing values that satisfy a predicate.

Signature

```cpp
#include <algorithm.h>
template
<
    class InputIterator,
    class OutputIterator,
    class Predicate,
    class T
>
OutputIterator replace_copy_if
(
    InputIterator first_,
    InputIterator last_,
```

```
    OutputIterator result_,
    Predicate pred_,
    const T& new_value_
)
```

Description

Copy the sequence [first_..last_) to a sequence of the same size starting at result_, replacing all elements that satisfy pred_ with new_value_. Return an iterator positioned immediately after the last new element.

Complexity

Time complexity is linear, as (last_ - first_) comparisons are performed. Space complexity is constant.

Example <repcpif1.cpp>

```cpp
#include <algorithm.h>
#include <vector.h>
#include <iterator.h>
#include <iostream.h>

bool odd (int a_)
{
   return a_ % 2;
}

int main ()
{
   vector <int> v1 (10);
   for (int i = 0; i < v1.size (); i++)
     v1[i] = i % 5;
   ostream_iterator <int> iter (cout, " ");
   copy (v1.begin (), v1.end (), iter);
   cout << endl;
   vector <int> v2 (v1.size ());
   replace_copy_if (v1.begin (), v1.end (), v2.begin (), odd, 42);
   copy (v1.begin (), v1.end (), iter);
   cout << endl;
   copy (v2.begin (), v2.end (), iter);
   cout << endl;
   return 0;
}
```

```
0  1  2  3  4  0  1  2  3  4
0  1  2  3  4  0  1  2  3  4
0  42 2  42 4  0  42 2  42 4
```

replace_if

Synopsis

Replace specified values that satisfy a predicate.

Signature
```
#include <algorithm.h>
template<class ForwardIterator, class Predicate, class T>
void replace_if
(
  ForwardIterator first_,
  ForwardIterator last_,
  Predicate pred_,
  const T& new_value_
)
```

Description
Replace every element in the range [first_..last_) that satisfy pred_ with new_value_.

Complexity
Time complexity is linear, as (last_ - first_) comparisons are performed. Space complexity is constant.

Helper
```
void os_replace_if (Container& c_, Predicate pred_, const T&
value_)
```

Example <replif1.cpp>
```
#include <algorithm.h>
#include <vector.h>
#include <iostream.h>

bool odd (int a_)
{
  return a_ % 2;
}

int main ()
{
  vector <int> v1 (10);
  for (int i = 0; i < v1.size (); i++)
  {
    v1[i] = i % 5;
    cout << v1[i] << ' ';
  }
  cout << endl;
  replace_if (v1.begin (), v1.end (), odd, 42);
  for (i = 0; i < v1.size (); i++)
    cout << v1[i] << ' ';
  cout << endl;
  return 0;
}

0 1 2 3 4 0 1 2 3 4
0 42 2 42 4 0 42 2 42 4
```

reverse

Synopsis
Reverse the items in a sequence.

Signature
```
#include <algorithm.h>
template<class BidirectionalIterator>
void reverse
(
   BidirectionalIterator first_,
   BidirectionalIterator last_
)
```

Description
Reverse the order of the elements in the range [first_, last_).

Complexity
Time complexity is linear, as (last_ - first_) swaps are performed. Space complexity is constant.

Example <reverse1.cpp>
```
#include <algorithm.h>
#include <iostream.h>

int numbers[6] = { 0, 1, 2, 3, 4, 5 };

int main ()
{
   reverse (numbers, numbers + 6);
   for (int i = 0; i < 6; i++)
      cout << numbers[i] << ' ';
   cout << endl;
   return 0;
}

5 4 3 2 1 0
```

reverse_copy

Synopsis
Create a reversed copy of a sequence.

Signature
```
#include <algorithm.h>
template <class BidirectionalIterator, class OutputIterator>
OutputIterator reverse_copy
(
   BidirectionalIterator first_,
```

```
    BidirectionalIterator last_,
    OutputIterator result_
)
```

Description

Copy a reverse of the sequence [first_..last_) into a sequence of the same size, starting at result_. Return an iterator positioned immediately after the last new element.

Complexity

Time complexity is linear, as (last_ - first_) assignments are performed. Space complexity is constant.

Example <revcopy1.cpp>

```
#include <algorithm.h>
#include <iostream.h>

int numbers[6] = { 0, 1, 2, 3, 4, 5 };

int main ()
{
  int result[6];
  reverse_copy (numbers, numbers + 6, result);
  for (int i = 0; i < 6; i++)
    cout << numbers[i] << ' ';
  cout << endl;
  for (i = 0; i < 6; i++)
    cout << result[i] << ' ';
  cout << endl;
  return 0;
}
```

```
0 1 2 3 4 5
5 4 3 2 1 0
```

rotate

Synopsis

Rotate a sequence by n positions.

Signature

```
#include <algorithm.h>
template<class ForwardIterator>
void rotate
(
  ForwardIterator first_,
  ForwardIterator middle_,
  ForwardIterator last_
)
```

Description
Rotate the sequence [first_..last_) to the right by (middle_ - first_) positions.

Complexity
Time complexity is linear. Space complexity is constant.

Helper
```
void os_rotate (Container& c_, int n_)
```

Example <rotate0.cpp>

```cpp
#include <algorithm.h>
#include <iostream.h>

int numbers[6] = { 0, 1, 2, 3, 4, 5 };

int main ()
{
  rotate (numbers, numbers + 3, numbers + 6);
  for (int i = 0; i < 6; i++)
    cout << numbers[i] << ' ';
  cout << endl;
  return 0;
}
```

```
3 4 5 0 1 2
```

Example <rotate1.cpp>

```cpp
#include <algorithm.h>
#include <vector.h>
#include <iterator.h>
#include <iostream.h>

int main ()
{
  vector <int> v1 (10);
  iota (v1.begin (), v1.end (), 0);
  ostream_iterator <int> iter (cout, " ");
  copy (v1.begin (), v1.end (), iter);
  cout << endl;
  for (int i = 0; i < v1.size (); i++)
  {
    rotate (v1.begin (), v1.begin () + i, v1.end ());
    ostream_iterator <int> iter (cout, " ");
    copy (v1.begin (), v1.end (), iter);
    cout << endl;
  }
  cout << endl;
  return 0;
}
```

```
0 1 2 3 4 5 6 7 8 9
0 1 2 3 4 5 6 7 8 9
1 2 3 4 5 6 7 8 9 0
3 4 5 6 7 8 9 0 1 2
6 7 8 9 0 1 2 3 4 5
0 1 2 3 4 5 6 7 8 9
5 6 7 8 9 0 1 2 3 4
1 2 3 4 5 6 7 8 9 0
8 9 0 1 2 3 4 5 6 7
6 7 8 9 0 1 2 3 4 5
5 6 7 8 9 0 1 2 3 4
```

rotate_copy

Synopsis
Copy a sequence, rotating it by n positions.

Signature
```
#include <algorithm.h>
template<class ForwardIterator, class OutputIterator>
OutputIterator rotate_copy
(
   ForwardIterator first_,
   ForwardIterator middle_,
   ForwardIterator last_,
   OutputIterator result_
)
```

Description
Perform the same operations as rotate (first_, middle_, last_), except that the result is placed into a sequence of the same size starting at result_. Return an iterator positioned immediately after the last new element.

Complexity
Time complexity is linear. Space complexity is constant.

Example <rotcopy0.cpp>
```
#include <algorithm.h>
#include <iostream.h>

int numbers[6] = { 0, 1, 2, 3, 4, 5 };

int main ()
{
   int result[6];
   rotate_copy (numbers, numbers + 3, numbers + 6, result);
   for (int i = 0; i < 6; i++)
     cout << result[i] << ' ';
   cout << endl;
   return 0;
}
```

```
3 4 5 0 1 2
```

Example <rotcopy1.cpp>

```cpp
#include <algorithm.h>
#include <vector.h>
#include <iterator.h>
#include <iostream.h>

int main ()
{
  vector <int> v1 (10);
  iota (v1.begin (), v1.end (), 0);
  ostream_iterator <int> iter (cout, " ");
  copy (v1.begin (), v1.end (), iter);
  cout << endl;
  vector <int> v2 (v1.size ());
  for (int i = 0; i < v1.size (); i++)
  {
    rotate_copy (v1.begin (),
                 v1.begin () + i,
                 v1.end (),
                 v2.begin ());
    ostream_iterator <int> iter (cout, " ");
    copy (v2.begin (), v2.end (), iter);
    cout << endl;
  }
  cout << endl;
  return 0;
}
```

```
0 1 2 3 4 5 6 7 8 9
0 1 2 3 4 5 6 7 8 9
1 2 3 4 5 6 7 8 9 0
2 3 4 5 6 7 8 9 0 1
3 4 5 6 7 8 9 0 1 2
4 5 6 7 8 9 0 1 2 3
5 6 7 8 9 0 1 2 3 4
6 7 8 9 0 1 2 3 4 5
7 8 9 0 1 2 3 4 5 6
8 9 0 1 2 3 4 5 6 7
9 0 1 2 3 4 5 6 7 8
```

search

Synopsis

Locate one sequence within another.

Signature

```cpp
#include <algorithm.h>
template<class ForwardIterator1, class ForwardIterator2>
ForwardIterator1 search
```

```
(
  ForwardIterator1 first1_,
  ForwardIterator1 last1_,
  ForwardIterator2 first2_,
  ForwardIterator2 last2_
)

template
<
  class ForwardIterator1,
  class ForwardIterator2,
  class BinaryPredicate
>
ForwardIterator1 search
(
  ForwardIterator1 first1_,
  ForwardIterator1 last1_,
  ForwardIterator2 first2_,
  ForwardIterator2 last2_,
  BinaryPredicate binary_pred_
)
```

Description

Search for the sequence [first2_..last2_) within the sequence [first1_, last1).
Return an iterator into first1_..last1 where the second sequence was found, or
last1_ if the sequence was not found. The first version uses operator== to compare elements, whereas the second version uses the binary function
binary_pred_.

Complexity

Time complexity is quadratic. Space complexity is constant.

Example <search0.cpp>

```
#include <algorithm.h>
#include <iostream.h>

int v1[6] = { 1, 1, 2, 3, 5, 8 };
int v2[6] = { 0, 1, 2, 3, 4, 5 };
int v3[2] = { 3, 4 };

int main ()
{
  int* location;
  location = search (v1, v1 + 6, v3, v3 + 2);
  if (location == v1 + 6)
    cout << "v3 not contained in v1" << endl;
  else
    cout
      << "Found v3 in v1 at offset: "
      << location - v1
      << endl;
  location = search (v2, v2 + 6, v3, v3 + 2);
```

```
    if (location == v2 + 6)
      cout << "v3 not contained in v2" << endl;
    else
      cout
        << "Found v3 in v2 at offset: "
        << location - v2
        << endl;
    return 0;
}
```

v3 not contained in v1
Found v2 in v2 at offset: 3

Example <search1.cpp>

```
#include <algorithm.h>
#include <vector.h>
#include <iterator.h>
#include <iostream.h>

int main ()
{
  typedef vector <int> IntVec;
  IntVec v1 (10);
  iota (v1.begin (), v1.end (), 0);
  IntVec v2 (3);
  iota (v2.begin (), v2.end (), 50);
  ostream_iterator <int> iter (cout, " ");
  cout << "v1: ";
  copy (v1.begin (), v1.end (), iter);
  cout << endl;
  cout << "v2: ";
  copy (v2.begin (), v2.end (), iter);
  cout << endl;
  IntVec::iterator location;
  location = search (v1.begin (), v1.end (), v2.begin (), v2.end
());
  if (location == v1.end ())
    cout << "v2 not contained in v1" << endl;
  else
    cout
      << "Found v2 in v1 at offset: "
      << location - v1.begin ()
      << endl;
  iota (v2.begin (), v2.end (), 4);
  cout << "v1: ";
  copy (v1.begin (), v1.end (), iter);
  cout << endl;
  cout << "v2: ";
  copy (v2.begin (), v2.end (), iter);
  cout << endl;
  location = search (v1.begin (), v1.end (), v2.begin (), v2.end
());
  if (location == v1.end ())
```

```
      cout << "v2 not contained in v1" << endl;
   else
      cout
        << "Found v2 in v1 at offset: "
        << location - v1.begin ()
        << endl;
   return 0;
}
```

v1: 0 1 2 3 4 5 6 7 8 9
v2: 50 51 52
v2 not contained in v1
v1: 0 1 2 3 4 5 6 7 8 9
v2: 4 5 6
Found v2 in v1 at offset: 4

Example <search2.cpp>

```
#include <algorithm.h>
#include <iterator.h>
#include <iostream.h>
#include <string.h>

bool str_equal (const char* a_, const char* b_)
{
   return ::strcmp (a_, b_) == 0 ? 1 : 0;
}

char* grades[] = { "A", "B", "C", "D", "F" };
char* letters[] = { "Q", "E", "D" };

int main ()
{
   const unsigned gradeCount = sizeof (grades) / sizeof
   (grades[0]);
   const unsigned letterCount = sizeof (letters) / sizeof(let-
   ters[0]);
   ostream_iterator <char*> iter (cout, " ");
   cout << "grades: ";
   copy (grades, grades + gradeCount, iter);
   cout << "\nletters:";
   copy (letters, letters + letterCount, iter);
   cout << endl;
   char** location =
      search (grades, grades + gradeCount,
              letters, letters + letterCount,
              str_equal);
   if (location == grades + gradeCount)
      cout << "letters not found in grades" << endl;
   else
      cout
        << "letters found in grades at offset: "
        << location - grades << endl;
   copy (grades + 1, grades + 1 + letterCount, letters);
```

```
    cout << "grades: ";
    copy (grades, grades + gradeCount, iter);
    cout << "\nletters:";
    copy (letters, letters + letterCount, iter);
    cout << endl;
    location = search (grades, grades + gradeCount,
                       letters, letters + letterCount,
                       str_equal);
    if (location == grades + gradeCount)
      cout << "letters not found in grades" << endl;
    else
      cout
        << "letters found in grades at offset: "
        << location - grades
        << endl;
    return 0;
}
```

grades: A B C D F
letters:Q E D
letters not found in grades
grades: A B C D F
letters:B C D
letters found in grades at offset: 1

set_difference

Synopsis
Create set of elements in 1st sequence that are not in 2nd.

Signature
```
#include <algorithm.h>
template
<
   class InputIterator1,
   class InputIterator2,
   class OutputIterator
>
OutputIterator set_difference
(
   InputIterator1 first1_,
   InputIterator1 last1_,
   InputIterator2 first2_,
   InputIterator2 last2_,
   OutputIterator result_
)

template
<
   class InputIterator1,
   class InputIterator2,
   class OutputIterator,
   class Compare
>
```

```
OutputIterator set_difference
(
   InputIterator1 first1_,
   InputIterator1 last1_,
   InputIterator2 first2_,
   InputIterator2 last2_,
   OutputIterator result_,
   Compare compare_
)
```

Description

Place the sorted difference of all the elements in the sequences [first1_..last_) and [first2_..last2_) into a sequence starting at result_. The output sequence will contain all elements that are in the first sequence but not in the second. Return an iterator positioned immediately after the end of the new sequence. The result is undefined if the two input sequences overlap. The first version assumes that the elements were sorted using operator<, whereas the second version assumes that the elements were sorted using the binary function compare_.

Complexity

Time complexity is linear. Space complexity is constant.

Example <setdiff0.cpp>

```cpp
#include <algorithm.h>
#include <iostream.h>

int v1[3] = { 13, 18, 23 };
int v2[4] = { 10, 13, 17, 23 };
int result[4] = { 0, 0, 0, 0 };

int main ()
{
   set_difference (v1, v1 + 3, v2, v2 + 4, result);
   for (int i = 0; i < 4; i++)
      cout << result[i] << ' ';
   cout << endl;
   set_difference (v2, v2 + 4, v1, v1 + 2, result);
   for (i = 0; i < 4; i++)
      cout << result[i] << ' ';
   cout << endl;
   return 0;
}
```

18 0 0 0
10 17 23 0

Example <setdiff1.cpp>

```cpp
#include <algorithm.h>
#include <vector.h>
#include <iterator.h>
#include <iostream.h>

int main ()
{
  vector <int> v1 (10);
  iota (v1.begin (), v1.end (), 0);
  vector <int> v2 (10);
  iota (v2.begin(), v2.end (), 7);
  ostream_iterator <int> iter (cout, " ");
  cout << "v1: ";
  copy (v1.begin (), v1.end (), iter);
  cout << "\nv2: ";
  copy (v2.begin (), v2.end (), iter);
  cout << endl;
  set_difference (v1.begin (), v1.end (),
                  v2.begin (), v2.end (),
                  iter);
  return 0;
}
```

```
v1: 0 1 2 3 4 5 6 7 8 9
v2: 7 8 9 10 11 12 13 14 15 16
0 1 2 3 4 5 6
```

Example <setdiff2.cpp>

```cpp
#include <algorithm.h>
#include <iterator.h>
#include <iostream.h>
#include <string.h>

char* word1 = "ABCDEFGHIJKLMNO";
char* word2 = "LMNOPQRSTUVWXYZ";

int main ()
{
  ostream_iterator <char> iter (cout, " ");
  cout << "word1: ";
  copy (word1, word1 + ::strlen (word1), iter);
  cout << "\nword2: ";
  copy (word2, word2 + ::strlen (word2), iter);
  cout << endl;
  set_difference (word1, word1 + ::strlen (word1),
                  word2, word2 + ::strlen (word2),
                  iter,
                  less<char>());
  return 0;
}
```

```
word1: A B C D E F G H I J K L M N O
word2: L M N O P Q R S T U V W X Y Z
A B C D E F G H I J K
```

set_intersection

Synopsis
Create set of elements that are in both sequences.

Signature
```
#include <algorithm.h>
template
<
    class InputIterator1,
    class InputIterator2,
    class OutputIterator
>
OutputIterator set_intersection
(
    InputIterator1 first1_,
    InputIterator1 last1_,
    InputIterator2 first2_,
    InputIterator2 last2_,
    OutputIterator result_
)

template
<
    class InputIterator1,
    class InputIterator2,
    class OutputIterator,
    class Compare
>
OutputIterator set_intersection
(
    InputIterator1 first1_,
    InputIterator1 last1_,
    InputIterator2 first2_,
    InputIterator2 last2_,
    OutputIterator result_,
    Compare compare_
)
```

Description
Place the sorted intersection of all the elements in the sequences [first1_..last_) and [first2_..last2_) into a sequence starting at result_. Return an iterator positioned immediately after the end of the new sequence. The result is undefined if the two input sequences overlap. The first version assumes that both sequences are already sorted using operator<, whereas the second version assumes that both sequences are already sorted using the binary function compare_.

Complexity
Time complexity is linear. Space complexity is constant.

Example <setintr0.cpp>

```
#include <algorithm.h>
#include <iostream.h>

int v1[3] = { 13, 18, 23 };
int v2[4] = { 10, 13, 17, 23 };
int result[4] = { 0, 0, 0, 0 };

int main ()
{
  set_intersection (v1, v1 + 3, v2, v2 + 4, result);
  for (int i = 0; i < 4; i++)
    cout << result[i] << ' ';
  cout << endl;
  return 0;
}
```

13 23 0 0

Example <setintr1.cpp>

```
#include <algorithm.h>
#include <vector.h>
#include <iterator.h>
#include <iostream.h>

int main ()
{
  vector <int> v1 (10);
  iota (v1.begin (), v1.end (), 0);
  vector <int> v2 (10);
  iota (v2.begin(), v2.end (), 7);
  ostream_iterator <int> iter (cout, " ");
  cout << "v1: ";
  copy (v1.begin (), v1.end (), iter);
  cout << "\nv2: ";
  copy (v2.begin (), v2.end (), iter);
  cout << endl;
  set_intersection (v1.begin (), v1.end (),
                    v2.begin (), v2.end (),
                    iter);
  return 0;
}
```

v1: 0 1 2 3 4 5 6 7 8 9
v2: 7 8 9 10 11 12 13 14 15 16
7 8 9

Example <setintr2.cpp>

```cpp
#include <algorithm.h>
#include <iterator.h>
#include <iostream.h>
#include <string.h>

char* word1 = "ABCDEFGHIJKLMNO";
char* word2 = "LMNOPQRSTUVWXYZ";

int main ()
{
  ostream_iterator <char> iter (cout, " ");
  cout << "word1: ";
  copy (word1, word1 + ::strlen (word1), iter);
  cout << "\nword2: ";
  copy (word2, word2 + ::strlen (word2), iter);
  cout << endl;
  set_intersection (word1, word1 + ::strlen (word1),
                    word2, word2 + ::strlen (word2),
                    iter,
                    less<char>());
  return 0;
}
```

```
word1: A B C D E F G H I J K L M N O
word2: L M N O P Q R S T U V W X Y Z
L M N O
```

set_symmetric_difference

Synopsis
Create set of elements that are not in both sequences.

Signature
```cpp
#include <algorithm.h>
template
<
  class InputIterator1,
  class InputIterator2,
  class OutputIterator
>
OutputIterator set_symmetric_difference
(
  InputIterator1 first1_,
  InputIterator1 last1_,
  InputIterator2 first2_,
  InputIterator2 last2_,
  OutputIterator result_
)

template
<
```

```
      class InputIterator1_,
      class InputIterator2_,
      class OutputIterator_,
      class Compare_
  >
  OutputIterator set_symmetric_difference
  (
      InputIterator1 first1_,
      InputIterator1 last1_,
      InputIterator2 first2_,
      InputIterator2 last2_,
      OutputIterator result_,
      Compare compare_
  )
```

Description

Place all elements that are not in both sequences into result_, in their sorted order. Return an iterator positioned immediately after the end of the new sequence. The result is undefined if the two input sequences overlap. The first version assumes that both sequences are already sorted using operator<, whereas the second version assumes that both sequences are already sorted using the binary function compare_.

Complexity

Time complexity is linear. Space complexity is constant.

Example <setsymd0.cpp>

```cpp
#include <algorithm.h>
#include <iostream.h>

int v1[3] = { 13, 18, 23 };
int v2[4] = { 10, 13, 17, 23 };
int result[4] = { 0, 0, 0, 0 };

int main ()
{
  set_symmetric_difference (v1, v1 + 3, v2, v2 + 4, result);
  for (int i = 0; i < 4; i++)
    cout << result[i] << ' ';
  cout << endl;
  return 0;
}
```

10 17 18 0

Example <setsymd1.cpp>

```cpp
#include <algorithm.h>
#include <vector.h>
#include <iterator.h>
#include <iostream.h>
```

```
int main ()
{
  vector <int> v1 (10);
  iota (v1.begin (), v1.end (), 0);
  vector <int> v2 (10);
  iota (v2.begin(), v2.end (), 7);
  ostream_iterator <int> iter (cout, " ");
  cout << "v1: ";
  copy (v1.begin (), v1.end (), iter);
  cout << "\nv2: ";
  copy (v2.begin (), v2.end (), iter);
  cout << endl;
  set_symmetric_difference (v1.begin (), v1.end (),
                            v2.begin (), v2.end (),
                            iter);
  return 0;
}
```

v1: 0 1 2 3 4 5 6 7 8 9
v2: 7 8 9 10 11 12 13 14 15 16
 0 1 2 3 4 5 6 10 11 12 13 14 15 16

Example <setsymd2.cpp>

```
#include <algorithm.h>
#include <iterator.h>
#include <iostream.h>
#include <string.h>

char* word1 = "ABCDEFGHIJKLMNO";
char* word2 = "LMNOPQRSTUVWXYZ";

int main ()
{
  ostream_iterator <char> iter (cout, " ");
  cout << "word1: ";
  copy (word1, word1 + ::strlen (word1), iter);
  cout << "\nword2: ";
  copy (word2, word2 + ::strlen (word2), iter);
  cout << endl;
  set_symmetric_difference (word1, word1 + ::strlen (word1),
                            word2, word2 + ::strlen (word2),
                            iter,
                            less<char>());
  return 0;
}
```

word1: A B C D E F G H I J K L M N O
word2: L M N O P Q R S T U V W X Y Z
 A B C D E F G H I J K P Q R S T U V W X Y Z

set_union

Synopsis
Create set of elements that are in either sequence.

Signature
```
#include <algorithm.h>
template
<
    class InputIterator1,
    class InputIterator2,
    class OutputIterator
>
OutputIterator set_union
(
    InputIterator1 first1_,
    InputIterator1 last1_,
    InputIterator2 first2_,
    InputIterator2 last2_,
    OutputIterator result_
)
template
<
    class InputIterator1,
    class InputIterator2,
    class OutputIterator,
    class Compare
>
OutputIterator set_union
(
    InputIterator1 first1_,
    InputIterator1 last1_,
    InputIterator2 first2_,
    InputIterator2 last2_,
    OutputIterator result_,
    Compare compare_
)
```

Description
Place the sorted union of all the elements in the sequences [first1_..last_) and [first2_..last2_) into a sequence starting at result_. Return an iterator positioned immediately after the end of the new sequence. The result is undefined if the two input sequences overlap. If an element occurs in both sequences, the element from the first sequence is copied into the result sequence. The first version assumes that both sequences were already sorted using operator<, whereas the second version assumes that both sequences were already sorted using the binary function compare_.

Example <setunon0.cpp>

```
#include <algorithm.h>
#include <iostream.h>
```

```
int v1[3] = { 13, 18, 23 };
int v2[4] = { 10, 13, 17, 23 };
int result[7] = { 0, 0, 0, 0, 0, 0, 0 };

int main ()
{
  set_union (v1, v1 + 3, v2, v2 + 4, result);
  for (int i = 0; i < 7; i++)
    cout << result[i] << ' ';
  cout << endl;
  return 0;
}
```

10 13 17 18 23 0 0

Example \<setunon1.cpp\>

```
#include <algorithm.h>
#include <vector.h>
#include <iterator.h>
#include <iostream.h>

int main ()
{
  vector <int> v1 (10);
  iota (v1.begin (), v1.end (), 0);
  vector <int> v2 (10);
  iota (v2.begin(), v2.end (), 7);
  ostream_iterator <int> iter (cout, " ");
  cout << "v1: ";
  copy (v1.begin (), v1.end (), iter);
  cout << "\nv2: ";
  copy (v2.begin (), v2.end (), iter);
  cout << endl;
  set_union (v1.begin (), v1.end (),
             v2.begin (), v2.end (),
             iter);
  return 0;
}
```

v1: 0 1 2 3 4 5 6 7 8
v2: 7 8 9 10 11 12 13 14 15 16
0 1 2 3 4 5 6 7 8 9 10 11 12 13 14 15 16

Example \<setunon2.cpp\>

```
#include <algorithm.h>
#include <iterator.h>
#include <iostream.h>
#include <string.h>

char* word1 = "ABCDEFGHIJKLMNO";
char* word2 = "LMNOPQRSTUVWXYZ";
```

```cpp
int main ()
{
    ostream_iterator <char> iter (cout, " ");
    cout << "word1: ";
    copy (word1, word1 + ::strlen (word1), iter);
    cout << "\nword2: ";
    copy (word2, word2 + ::strlen (word2), iter);
    cout << endl;
    set_union (word1, word1 + ::strlen (word1),
               word2, word2 + ::strlen (word2),
               iter,
               less<char>());
    return 0;
}
```

word1: A B C D E F G H I J K L M N O
word2: L M N O P Q R S T U V W X Y Z
A B C D E F G H I J K L M N O P Q R S T U V W X Y Z

sort

Synopsis
Sort a sequence

Signature
```cpp
#include <algorithm.h>
template<class RandomAccessIterator>
void sort (RandomAccessIterator first_, RandomAccessIterator
last_)

template<class RandomAccessIterator, class Compare>
void sort
(
    RandomAccessIterator first_,
    RandomAccessIterator last_,
    Compare compare_
)
```

Description
Sort all elements in the range [first_..last_) into ascending order. The first version uses operator< to compare elements, whereas the second version uses the binary function compare_.

Complexity
Time complexity is O(NlogN). Space complexity is constant.

Helper
```cpp
void os_sort (Container& c_)
void os_sort (Container& c_, Compare compare_)
```

Example <sort1.cpp>

```cpp
#include <algorithm.h>
#include <iostream.h>

int vector[6] = { 1, 50, -10, 11, 42, 19 };

int main ()
{
  sort (vector, vector + 6);
  for (int i = 0; i < 6; i++)
    cout << vector[i] << ' ';
  cout << endl;
  return 0;
}
```

-10 1 11 19 42 50

Example <sort2.cpp>

```cpp
#include <algorithm.h>
#include <iterator.h>
#include <iostream.h>

int vector[] = { 1, 50, -10, 11, 42, 19 };

int main ()
{
  int count = sizeof (vector) / sizeof (vector[0]);
  ostream_iterator <int> iter (cout, " ");
  cout << "before: ";
  copy (vector, vector + count, iter);
  cout << "\nafter: ";
  sort (vector, vector + count, greater<int>());
  copy (vector, vector + count, iter);
  return 0;
}
```

before: 1 50 -10 11 42 19
after: 50 42 19 11 1 -10

sort_heap

Synopsis
Sort a heap.

Signature
```cpp
#include <algorithm.h>
template<class RandomAccessIterator>
void sort_heap
(
  RandomAccessIterator first_,
```

```
    RandomAccessIterator last_
)

template<class RandomAccessIterator, class Compare>
void sort_heap
(
    RandomAccessIterator first_,
    RandomAccessIterator last_,
    Compare compare_
)
```

Description
Starting with a heap as an input sequence, produce a sorted collection. The first version uses operator< to compare elements, whereas the second version uses the binary function compare_. *Note that a heap ceases to be a heap when it is sorted.*

Complexity
Time complexity is NlogN. Space complexity is constant.

Examples
See push_heap.

stable_partition

Synopsis
Partition a range using a predicate.

Signature
```
#include <algorithm.h>
template<class BidirectionalIterator, class Predicate>
BidirectionalIterator stable_partition
(
    BidirectionalIterator first_,
    BidirectionalIterator last_,
    Predicate pred_
)
```

Description
Place all elements in the range [first_..last_) that make pred_ evaluate to true before all elements in the range that make pred_ evaluate to false. Return an iterator i such that all elements in the range [first_..i) make pred_ evaluate to true and all elements in the range [i..last_) make pred_ evaluate to false. This algorithm is stable in the sense that elements which satisfy pred_ that were before other elements which also satisfied pred_ before the partition will remain in the same relative order after the partition.

Complexity

Time complexity is O(NlogN), where N = (last_ - first_), as pred_ will be evaluated N times and at most NlogN swaps are performed. If there is enough available memory, O(N) swaps be performed instead

Example <stblptn0.cpp>

```
#include <algorithm.h>
#include <iostream.h>

bool less_10 (int a_)
{
   return a_ < 10 ? 1 : 0;
}

int numbers[6] = { 10, 5, 11, 20, 6, -2 };

int main ()
{
   stable_partition (numbers, numbers + 6, less_10);
   for (int i = 0; i < 6; i++)
     cout << numbers[i] << ' ';
   cout << endl;
   return 0;
}
```

5 6 -2 10 11 20

Example <stblptn1.cpp>

```
#include <algorithm.h>
#include <vector.h>
#include <iterator.h>
#include <iostream.h>

int main ()
{
   vector <int> v1 (10);
   for (int i = 0; i < v1.size (); i++)
     v1[i] = rand () % 20;
   ostream_iterator <int> iter (cout, " ");
   copy (v1.begin (), v1.end (), iter);
   cout << endl;
   stable_partition (v1.begin (), v1.end (),
   bind2nd(less<int>(), 11));
   copy (v1.begin (), v1.end (), iter);
   cout << endl;
   return 0;
}
```

6 10 2 10 16 17 15 15 8 6
6 10 2 10 8 6 16 17 15 15

stable_sort

Synopsis
Sort a sequence in ascending order.

Signature
```
#include <algorithm.h>
template<class RandomAccessIterator>
void stable_sort
(
  RandomAccessIterator first_,
  RandomAccessIterator last_
)
template<class RandomAccessIterator, class Compare>
void stable_sort
(
  RandomAccessIterator first_,
  RandomAccessIterator last_,
  Compare compare_
)
```

Description
Sort all of elements in the range [first_..last_). The relative order of equal objects is preserved. The first version uses operator< to compare elements, whereas the second version uses the binary function compare_.

Complexity
Time complexity is $O(N(\log N)^2)$ where N = (last_ - first_). If enough memory is available, time complexity becomes $O(N \log N)$. Space complexity is N if enough memory is available, otherwise it is constant.

Example <stblsrt1.cpp>
```cpp
#include <algorithm.h>
#include <vector.h>
#include <iostream.h>

int vector[6] = { 1, 50, -10, 11, 42, 19 };

int main ()
{
  stable_sort (vector, vector + 6);
  for (int i = 0; i < 6; i++)
    cout << vector[i] << ' ';
  cout << endl;
  return 0;
}

-10 1 11 19 42 50
```

Example <stblsrt2.cpp>

```
#include <algorithm.h>
#include <iostream.h>
#include <string.h>

bool string_less (const char* a_, const char* b_)
{
  return ::strcmp (a_, b_) < 0 ? 1 : 0;
}

char* letters[6] = {"bb", "aa", "ll", "dd", "qq", "cc" };

int main ()
{
  stable_sort (letters, letters + 6, string_less);
  for (int i = 0; i < 6; i++)
    cout << letters[i] << ' ';
  cout << endl;
  return 0;
}
```

aa bb cc dd ll qq

swap

Synopsis
Swap two values.

Signature
```
#include <algorithm.h>
template <class T>
void swap(T& a_, T& b_)
```

Description
Swap the elements a_ and b_.

Complexity
Time and space complexity are constant.

Example <swap1.cpp>

```
#include <algorithm.h>
#include <iostream.h>

int main ()
{
  int a = 42;
  int b = 19;
  cout << "a = " << a << " b = " << b << endl;
  swap (a, b);
  cout << "a = " << a << " b = " << b << endl;
```

```
    return 0;
  }

a = 41  b = 19
a = 19  b = 42
```

swap_ranges

Synopsis
Swap two ranges of items.

Signature
```
#include <algorithm.h>
template <class ForwardIterator1, class ForwardIterator2>
ForwardIterator2 swap_ranges
(
   ForwardIterator1 first1_,
   ForwardIterator1 last1_,
   ForwardIterator2 first2_
)
```

Description
Swap the elements in the range [first1_, last1_) with the elements in the range of the same size starting at first2_. Return an iterator positioned immediately after the last element in the second range.

Complexity
Time complexity is linear. Space complexity is constant.

Example <swprnge1.cpp>
```
#include <algorithm.h>
#include <iostream.h>
#include <string.h>

int main ()
{
   char* word1 = "World";
   char* word2 = "Hello";
   cout << word1 << " " << word2 << endl;
   swap_ranges (word1, word1 + ::strlen (word1), word2);
   cout << word1 << " " << word2 << endl;
   return 0;
}

World Hello
Hello World
```

transform

Synopsis

Transform one sequence into another.

Signature

```
#include <algorithm.h>
template
<
   class InputIterator,
   class OutputIterator,
   class UnaryOperation
>
OutputIterator transform
(
   InputIterator first_,
   InputIterator last_,
   OutputIterator result_,
   UnaryOperation op_
)

template
<
   class InputIterator1,
   class InputIterator2,
   class OutputIterator,
   class BinaryOperation
>
OutputIterator transform
(
   InputIterator1 first1_,
   InputIterator1 last1_,
   InputIterator2 first2_,
   OutputIterator result_,
   BinaryOperation binary_op_
)
```

Description

The first version traverses the sequence [first_..last_) and store the results of invoking op_ on each element into a sequence of the same size starting at result_. The second version uses a pair of iterators i_ and j_ to traverse two sequences, starting at first1_ and first2_, respectively, until i_ reaches last1_. The second version stores the results of invoking binary_op_ on the elements referenced by the iterator pair into a sequence of the same size starting at result_. Both versions return an iterator positioned immediately after the last new element.

Complexity

Time complexity is linear, as (last1_ - first1_) operations are performed. Space complexity is constant.

Example <trnsfrm1.cpp>

```cpp
#include <algorithm.h>
#include <iostream.h>

int negate_int (int a_)
{
   return -a_;
}

int numbers[6] = { -5, -1, 0, 1, 6, 11 };

int main ()
{
   int result[6];
   transform (numbers, numbers + 6, result, negate_int);
   for (int i = 0; i < 6; i++)
     cout << result[i] << ' ';
   cout << endl;
   return 0;
}
```

5 1 0 -1 -6 -11

Example <trnsfrm2.cpp>

```cpp
#include <algorithm.h>
#include <iteratot.h>
#include <iostream.h>
#include <string.h>

char map_char (char a_, int b_)
{
   return char (a_ + b_);
}

int trans[] = {-4, 4, -6, -6, -10, 0, 10, -6, 6, 0, -1, -77};

int main ()
{
   char n[] = "Larry Mullen";
   const unsigned count = ::strlen (n);
   ostream_iterator <char> iter (cout);
   transform (n, n + count, trans, iter, map_char);
   return 0;
}
```

Hello World!

unique

Synopsis

Collapse all consecutive values in a sequence.

Signature

```
#include <algorithm.h>
template<class ForwardIterator>
ForwardIterator unique
(
  ForwardIterator first_,
  ForwardIterator last_
)

template<class ForwardIterator, class BinaryPredicate>
ForwardIterator unique
(
  ForwardIterator first_,
  ForwardIterator last_,
  BinaryPredicate binary_pred_
)
```

Description

Replace all consecutive matching occurrences of a value in the range [first_..last_) by a single instance of that value. Return an iterator positioned immediately after the last element of the new sequence. The size of the container is not altered; if n_ elements are removed, the last n_ elements of the sequence [first_..last_) will have undefined values. The first version uses operator== to match values, whereas the second version uses the binary function binary_pred_.

Complexity

Time complexity is linear, as (last_ - first_) comparisons are performed. Space complexity is constant.

Example <unique1.cpp>

```
#include <algorithm.h>
#include <iostream.h>

int numbers[8] = { 0, 1, 1, 2, 2, 2, 3, 4 };

int main ()
{
  unique (numbers, numbers + 8);
  for (int i = 0; i < 8; i ++)
    cout << numbers[i] << ' ';
  cout << endl;
  return 0;
}

0 1 2 3 4 2 3 4
```

Example <unique2.cpp>

```
#include <algorithm.h>
```

```
#include <iterator.h>
#include <iostream.h>
#include <string.h>

bool str_equal (const char* a_, const char* b_)
{
  return ::strcmp (a_, b_) == 0 ? 1 : 0;
}

char* labels[] = { "Q","Q","W","W","E","E","R","T","T","Y","Y" };

int main ()
{
  const unsigned count = sizeof (labels) / sizeof (labels[0]);
  ostream_iterator <char*> iter (cout);
  copy (labels, labels + count, iter);
  cout << endl;
  unique (labels, labels + count, str_equal);
  copy (labels, labels + count, iter);
  cout << endl;
  return 0;
}
```

QQWWERRTTYY
QWERTYRTTYY

unique_copy

Synopsis
Copy a sequence, collapsing consecutive values.

Signature
```
#include <algorithm.h>
template<class InputIterator, class OutputIterator>
OutputIterator unique_copy
(
  InputIterator first_,
  InputIterator last_,
  OutputIterator result_
)

template
<
  class InputIterator,
  class OutputIterator,
  class BinaryPredicate
>
OutputIterator unique_copy
(
  InputIterator first_,
  InputIterator last_,
  OutputIterator result_,
  BinaryPredicate binary_pred_
)
```

Description

Copy the sequence [first_..last_) to a sequence starting at result_, replacing all consecutive occurrences of a value by a single instance of that value. Return an iterator positioned immediately after the last element of new sequence. The first version uses operator== to determine equality, whereas the second version uses the binary function binary_pred_.

Complexity

Time complexity is linear, as (last_ - first_) comparisons are performed. Space complexity is linear.

Example <uniqcpy1.cpp>

```
#include <algorithm.h>
#include <iostream.h>

int numbers[8] = { 0, 1, 1, 2, 2, 2, 3, 4 };
int result[8] = { 0, 0, 0, 0, 0, 0, 0, 0 };

int main ()
{
  unique_copy (numbers, numbers + 8, result);
  for (int i = 0; i < 8; i++)
    cout << result[i] << ' ';
  cout << endl;
  return 0;
}
```

```
0 1 2 3 4 0 0 0
```

Example <uniqcpy2.cpp>

```
#include <algorithm.h>
#include <iterator.h>
#include <iostream.h>
#include <string.h>

bool str_equal (const char* a_, const char* b_)
{
  return ::strcmp (a_, b_) == 0 ? 1 : 0;
}

char* labels[] = { "Q","Q","W","W","E","E","R","T","T","Y","Y" };

int main ()
{
  const unsigned count = sizeof (labels) / sizeof (labels[0]);
  ostream_iterator <char*> iter (cout);
  copy (labels, labels + count, iter);
  cout << endl;
  char* uCopy[count];
  fill (uCopy, uCopy + count, "");
```

```
    unique_copy (labels, labels + count, uCopy, str_equal);
    copy (labels, labels + count, iter);
    cout << endl;
    copy (uCopy, uCopy + count, iter);
    cout << endl;
    return 0;
}
```

QQWWEERRTTYY
QQWWEERRTTYY
QWERTY

upper_bound

Synopsis
Return the upper bound within a range.

Signature
```
#include <algorithm.h>
template<class ForwardIterator, class T>
ForwardIterator upper_bound
(
    ForwardIterator first_,
    ForwardIterator last_,
    const T& value_
)

template<class ForwardIterator, class T, class Compare>
ForwardIterator upper_bound
(
    ForwardIterator first_,
    ForwardIterator last_,
    const T& value_,
    Compare compare_
)
```

Description
Return the last position in the range [first_..last_) that value_ can be inserted without violating the order of the collection. The first version uses operator< for comparison, whereas the second version uses the binary function compare_.

Complexity
Time complexity is O(Log N) for RandomAccessIterators, O(N) for all other iterators. Space complexity is constant.

Example <uprbnd1.cpp>

```
#include <algorithm.h>
#include <vector.h>
#include <iostream.h>
```

```
int main ()
{
  int vector[20];
  for (int i = 0; i < 20; i++)
  {
    vector[i] = i/4;
    cout << vector[i] << ' ';
  }
  cout
    << "\n3 can be inserted at index: "
    << upper_bound (vector, vector + 20, 3) - vector
    << endl;
  return 0;
}
```

0 0 0 0 1 1 1 1 2 2 2 2 3 3 3 3 4 4 4 4
3 can be inserted at index: 16

Example <uprbnd2.cpp>

```
#include <algorithm.h>
#include <iostream.h>
#include <string.h>

bool char_str_less (const char* a_, const char* b_)
{
  return ::strcmp (a_, b_) < 0 ? 1 : 0;
}

char* str [] = { "a", "a", "b", "b", "q", "w", "z" };

int main ()
{
  const unsigned strCt = sizeof (str)/sizeof (str[0]);
  cout
    << "d can be inserted at index: "
    << upper_bound (str,  str + strCt, "d", char_str_less) - str
    << endl;
  return 0;
}
```

d can be inserted at index: 4

Appendix

Appendix

Standard Header Files

Here is a list of all the standard header files that are referenced in this book:

Header File	Contents
algorithm[10]	template algorithms
deque	the deque container
functional[11]	template function objects.
iterator	iterators
list	the list container
map	the map and multimap containers
memory	the allocator classes and some simple algorithms
queue	the queue and priority_queue containers
set	the set and multiset containers
stack	the stack container
string	the templatized ANSI string and traits classes
utility	the templatized relational operators and the pair class
vector	the vector container

Additional STL Resources

Here is a list of the additional STL-related resources:

- "http://www.objectspace.com" is the ObjectSpace world wide web site that contains a great deal of information about STL and other object technology, including white papers about their C++ products. This site contains the examples and helper algorithms described in this book.

- Hewlett Packard's public domain version of STL is available from the FTP site "butler.hpl.hp.com" in the directory "stl". This site also contains several hundred STL examples.

---

[10]Called algorith.h in some 8.3 implementations
[11]Called function.h in some 8.3 implementations

- "http://www.cs.rpi.edu/~musser/stl.html" is a WWW site created by Dave Musser, one of the creators of the associative container implementations. It contains very handy information about STL, some implementations of portions of STL, and some examples.

Trouble Shooting

STL is a fairly complicated bit of software. However, what makes some STL-related problems hard to track down are the bugs within the compilers themselves. Here is a list of some common problems that are not compiler-related, together with their solutions.

Closing angled brackets are together
When nesting templates, you must take care not to place two closing angle brackets together, as this will cause a compiler error.

```
set<int, less<int>> s; // Wrong
set<int, less<int> > s; // Right
```

Const and Typedef problems
Many compilers do not process const and typedefs properly. In fact, every single compiler that we've tested has at least one problem in this area. Cfront users should probably avoid storing const items in template containers, including const char* declarations for strings. For example, we recommend that you define a vector of strings as vector<char*>.

Using a non-const iterator to iterate over a const collection
Most compilers give you a lot of seemingly unrelated error messages if you try to do this. Therefore, always check that the const-ness of your iterators match.

Missing == and/or < operators
STL associative containers require operator== and operator< to function correctly with the commonly-used comparitor function object less. You cannot store items into an associative container using less unless they understand these operations. Check that all of your classes support these functions.

Comparing non random-access iterators using <
You may only compare random access iterators using <. In general, it's good practice to use operator!= to check for past-the-end values.

Algorithms require the second parameter of a range to be a past-the-end value
It's very easy to pass a pointer to the first element and a pointer to the last element of a "C" array when applying an algorithm to it. Remember that the second pointer should point *immediately after* the last element.

remove() doesn't alter the size of a container

It's tempting to think that remove() actually removes an item from a container. It doesn't. Use the os_erase() helper algorithm to actually erase items from a container.

Heaps are not sorted

When a container is organized into a heap, it is arranged into a structure that has special characteristics. However, the elements are not sorted in the usual sense. To sort a heap, use sort_heap(). Realize, however, that sort_heap() destroys the container's heap characteristics, so you can't perform a push_heap() after a sort_heap().

Check insertion boundaries

To insert an element at the end of a container, insert using the container's past-the-end value.

The Implementation of STL

There are some algorithms whose implementation can be optimized for a particular kind of iterator. For example, it is slightly faster to reverse a sequence using a random access iterator than using a bidirectional iterator. In these cases, STL supplies both forms of the algorithm and uses a compile-time technique for automatically selecting the best version based on the types of the iterator arguments. The technique that STL uses for accomplishing this makes use of *iterator tags* and *auxiliary functions*.

Every category of iterator has a function called iterator_category that returns a structure whose type is unique for each category. For example, here's the definition of the abstract class bidirectional_iterator that all bidirectional iterators are derived from, the definition of its tag structure, and the definition of its iterator_category function:

```
template <class T, class Distance>
struct bidirectional_iterator // abstract base class.
{
};

struct bidirectional_iterator_tag // tag structure.
{
};

template <class T, class Distance>
inline // category function.
bidirectional_iterator_tag iterator_category
(
   const bidirectional_iterator<T, Distance>&
)
{
   return bidirectional_iterator_tag ();
}
```

Each other category of iterator has a similar set of structures and functions.

reverse() does not perform the algorithm directly. Instead, it's an inline function that calls an auxiliary function that is specialized for each category of iterator. Here's the code for reverse() and its two associated auxiliary functions:

```
template <class BidirectionalIterator>
void __reverse // aux function for strictly bidirectional itera-
tors.
(
  BidirectionalIterator first_,
  BidirectionalIterator last_,
  bidirectional_iterator_tag
)
{
  while (true)
  {
    if (first_ == last_ || first_ == --last_)
      return;
    else
      iter_swap (first_++, last_);
  }
}

template <class RandomAccessIterator>
void __reverse // aux function for random access iterators.
(
  RandomAccessIterator first_,
  RandomAccessIterator last_,
  random_access_iterator_tag
)
{
  while (first_ < last_)
    iter_swap (first_++, --last_);
}

template <class BidirectionalIterator>
inline void reverse
(
  BidirectionalIterator first_,
  BidirectionalIterator last_
)
{
  // Call auxiliary function to do the work.
  __reverse (first_, last_, iterator_category (first_));
}
```

This technique is used extensively throughout STL, and is a generally useful approach for compile-time selection of alternatives.

List of Examples

Index

Index